LARGE PRINT EDITION

Every Day
with the Savior

DAILY DEVOTIONS

Rudolph F. Norden

CONCORDIA PUBLISHING HOUSE • SAINT LOUIS

Copyright © 2004 Concordia Publishing House
3558 S. Jefferson Avenue, St. Louis, MO 63118-3968
Manufactured in the United States of America
First Large Print Edition 2004

Library of Congress Cataloging-in-Publication Data

Norden, Rudolph F.
    Every day with the Savior : daily devotions / Rudolph F. Norden.
        p. cm.
    ISBN 0-7586-0821-7
    1. Devotional calendars. I. Title.
    BV4811.N642 2003
    242'.2—dc21   2003009627

2   3   4   5   6   7   8   9   10   11   14   13   12   11   10   09   08   07   06   05

*T*O THE GRATEFUL AND JOYFUL MEMORY OF
RUDOLF F. NORDEN, MY FATHER,
WHO READ MORNING AND EVENING DEVOTIONS
EVERY DAY TO HIS SEVEN CHILDREN
GATHERED ABOUT THE FAMILY TABLE.

PREFACE

A favorite hymn, "Let Us Ever Walk with Jesus," compares our everyday living to our journey with Jesus. The way we "walk" is not always smooth and easy; we may encounter problems. This encourages us to seek the companionship of Jesus to guide and guard us with His Word. He enriches our understanding of the Gospel as He did in His "walking devotion" with two disciples on the Emmaus road. In His invisible—but very real—presence, Jesus walks with us in all of life. We hear Him speak His Word, and He hears the prayers we speak to Him.

In these devotional readings, the saving, sin-forgiving love of Jesus comes to the fore to give us strength to get on with our Christian vocations. The truths He speaks linger in our hearts. Day or night, we sense that the Lord who speaks to us in Holy Scripture is walking and working and watching over us. We know the song: "And He walks with me and He talks with me, And He tells me I am His own." This blessed assurance comes straight out of the Gospel of Jesus Christ, our risen Savior.

Consider this brief biography of an Old Testament saint: "Enoch walked with God." It is a tribute to all Christians who daily meditate on God's Word, as did Enoch. They are walking with Jesus.

This volume is a sequel to previous books: *Day by Day with Jesus, Each Day with Jesus*, and *With Jesus Every Day.* All follow the same pattern for any given day: Scripture reading, topic and text, meditation, and a prayer suggestion to encourage readers to pray from the heart. Additional devotions for occasions and festivals not falling on set dates are found at the back of the book.

May these devotions remind you to always walk with Jesus.

A Loud Thanksgiving

Shout for joy to the LORD, all the earth. Psalm 100:1

People observe New Year's Day in various ways. For example, the Chinese New Year includes firecrackers and other noise-makers to drive away evil spirits.

This is hardly what the psalmist had in mind when he urged his readers to "make a joyful noise unto the Lord" (KJV). He didn't mean we should make noise to drive away the devil. The devil is attracted to noise—the noise of battle that kills, the clamor that often accompanies sinful activities. The noise the psalmist encouraged is to be "to the Lord."

Psalm 65 states the reason for thankfulness and joy on New Year's Day: "You crown the year with Your bounty" (verse 11). This is what God has done in the past year and what He will do in the new year. He enriches us with blessings for the sustenance of body and soul. He guards us against danger. He guides us when we are confused and bewildered.

And God will crown the new year with *spiritual* gifts. As Paul wrote to the Ephesians: "Praise be to the God and Father of our Lord Jesus Christ, who has blessed us in the heavenly realms with every spiritual blessing in Christ. ... In love He predestined us to be adopted as His sons through Jesus Christ. ... In Him we have redemption through His blood, the forgiveness of sins, in accordance with the riches of God's grace that He lavished on us with all wisdom and understanding" (Ephesians 1:3–8).

God's grace in Christ is consistent. What He has given us in the past He will give in the future.

PRAYER SUGGESTION

Thank God for His many blessings. Ask Him to continue to enrich you in Christ, your Savior.

Now Is the Time

"As long as it is day, we must do the work of Him who sent Me. Night is coming, when no one can work." John 9:4

Displayed in a museum was a rather poignant picture of a funeral wreath hanging on a wooden door with this inscription: "That which I should have done I didn't do." It was too late for that person to make amends.

It is tempting to postpone the actions we should take. We often say, "I will do it tomorrow." But tomorrow never comes. Important deeds remain undone. Then something happens, death perhaps, and it is too late.

Jesus and His apostles were aware of this. We hear our Lord say that God's works are to be done while there is yet time. "Settle matters quickly with your adversary. ... Do it while you are still with him on the way" (Matthew 5:25). Similarly the apostle Paul said: "Do not let the sun go down while you are still angry" (Ephesians 4:26).

As for helping others, Paul taught, "As we have opportunity, let us do good to all people, especially to those who belong to the family of believers" (Galatians 6:10). There is no time like the present to serve others.

Christians are the "now generation." Now is the time to repent of our sins and to focus on Jesus Christ, who died for us to pay the penalty of our sin. Again St. Paul: "'In the time of My favor I heard you, and in the day of salvation I helped you.' I tell you, now is the time of God's favor, now is the day of salvation" (2 Corinthians 6:2).

Yes, the time is now—time to show love to those near and dear to us, time to act.

PRAYER SUGGESTION

Request God's help and guidance to do His will while there is yet time.

God Understands All Languages

"The tax collector ... beat his breast and said, 'God, have mercy on me, a sinner.'" Luke 18:13

In the movie *My Fair Lady*, Eliza has trouble pronouncing "a" and is told by her mentor to repeat a rhyme about the rain in Spain as her bedtime prayer. The instructor adds, "You will get much further with the Lord if you learn not to offend His ears with mispronunciation."

This is not true of course. The Lord understands all languages and dialects regardless of pronunciation. Jesus looks on the heart rather than on the words of our prayers. We learn this from Jesus' parable of two men who pray in the temple. The Pharisee spoke correctly and formally as far as language was concerned, but the content of his prayer was self-righteous. The publican, on the other hand, prayed briefly in the tone and words of a common man, yet he exhibited true repentance. His was the prayer God heard.

We have divine assistance when we pray. St. Paul told the Roman Christians, "The Spirit helps us in our weakness. We do not know what we ought to pray for, but the Spirit Himself intercedes for us with groans that words cannot express" (Romans 8:26).

When God looks on our heart, He looks for faith in the redeeming merit of Jesus Christ, His Son. Jesus is the conduit that makes our prayers acceptable to God. Jesus is also our prayer instructor. During His stay on earth He prayed both lengthily (see His high-priestly prayer in John 17) and briefly (His prayers on the cross were fragments, brief and to the point).

So let Eliza practice correct speech before she goes to sleep, but not as a substitute for prayer!

PRAYER SUGGESTION

If you have a special need, tell God about it in your own words, but always in Jesus' name.

Sin: Its Cause, Its Cost, Its Cure

Each one is tempted when, by his own evil desire, he is dragged away and enticed. Then, after desire has conceived, it gives birth to sin; and sin, when it is full-grown, gives birth to death. James 1:14–15

On an interstate in Kentucky an intoxicated driver collided with a church bus, killing 27. In the sight of God, drunkenness is a sin, a sin that grows until, if it reaches maturity, brings death to the individual and, sometimes, to the innocent.

Every sin—greed, pride, dishonesty, hatred—follows a pattern, according to St. James. Its root is in improper, impure desire. It was so with Adam and Eve, who brought sin into the world. What is said of Eve was true of Adam also: "When the woman saw that the fruit of the tree was good for food and pleasing to the eye, and also desirable for gaining wisdom, she took some and ate it" (Genesis 3:6). This sad story is repeated when all their offspring are tempted by their own desire, yield to it, and fall deeper into sin.

But the process doesn't stop there. Sin, like a cancer, grows and grows; it tightens its hold on the individual. The erstwhile guest becomes a permanent boarder, yes, the master. And what is the harvest? Death, sometimes physical death or worse—spiritual death leading to eternal death.

But God does not give sin the last word. He provides a cure— the Messiah, His own Son, to break the power of sin and Satan. That Son is Jesus Christ, whom God made "to be sin for us" (2 Corinthians 5:21). His blood, shed on Calvary's cross, cleanses and purifies us from all sin. By faith in Jesus, the Sin-Breaker, we are declared righteous in God's sight and are empowered by the Holy Spirit to grow in holiness.

PRAYER SUGGESTION

Thank the Savior for breaking the power of sin and for making you a child of God.

A Woman of Courageous Faith

Jesus answered, "Woman, you have great faith!" Matthew 15:28

Hannah Cole's husband was killed during the War of 1812 by Indians that had been supplied with firearms and "fire water" by enemy agents. No funds were available to the widow to provide for her nine dependent children. A person of great pluck, however, she made ends meet by running a ferry across the Missouri River.

The Bible speaks of courageous women, and what it says was written for our learning and emulation. Certainly the Canaanite woman, who was a Greek, is one example. Her courage stemmed from her faith in Jesus as the promised Christ, for she addressed Him as "Son of David," a Messianic title. She had to cross ethnic and cultural barriers to do this. It took courageous faith for her, a non-Israelite, to approach Jesus for help for her demon-possessed daughter. It took persevering faith for her to persist in her plea. It took daring to hold Jesus to His word, applying to herself His implied promise that even pagans were covered by His saving love.

During Epiphany we may sing, "Savior of the Nations, Come." We base such a prayer on our Lord's own declaration that He, the Good Shepherd, had "other sheep that are not of this sheep pen" (John 10:16) for whom He would lay down His life and bring into His church. To this end He charged His followers to "make disciples of all nations" (Matthew 28:19).

The woman of Canaan, who was one of these "other sheep," had courageous faith in Jesus. And Jesus proved His acceptance of her when He said, "Woman, you have great faith. Your request is granted." She is an example to all of us as we boldly show and share our faith in Jesus as Savior and Lord.

PRAYER SUGGESTION

Say to Jesus that you come to Him not only with all your problems but also with words of praise for your salvation through Him.

The Light of Epiphany

The people walking in darkness have seen a great light. Isaiah 9:2

Come winter, especially in northern climes, daylight is of short duration and the desire for "more light" is often expressed.

Our world is in a spiritual darkness, winter and summer. The gloom that is sin deepens into the total darkness of godlessness, greed, hatred. People speak of the "seven deadly sins." Truth is, sins are more numerous than seven, more than seventy times seven. And each one is as deadly as the next because every sin merits God's condemnation. This is darkness—fatal darkness—and what is all the more frightening is that people, in Christ's day and now, "loved darkness instead of light" (John 3:19). If given the choice, they choose the darkness of sin over the light of salvation.

The Epiphany festival celebrates God's outreach to the heathen world. The coming of the Magi to worship the Christ Child anticipated the worldwide mission command given by the same Christ thirty years later. At the end of His ministry on earth, Jesus told His followers to evangelize the world—"all nations" (Matthew 28:19). Salvation from sin is God's gift to all who believe in Christ as Savior and are baptized.

Jesus is the "Light of the world" (John 8:12), the "Sun of righteousness" (Malachi 4:2), the "Radiance of God's glory" (Hebrews 1:3), the total expression of "the grace of God that brings salvation ... to all men" (Titus 2:11). He enlightens the road leading to heaven; He is our guiding light for a purposeful life here and now.

PRAYER SUGGESTION

Pray that the same Christ the Wise Men worshiped is proclaimed throughout the world as the one and only Savior.

Light Has Pierced the Gloom

"Arise, shine, for your light has come." Isaiah 60:1

Winston Churchill said that Russia was "a riddle wrapped up in a mystery inside an enigma." That is what Christianity is to non-believers. St. Paul wrote, "The man without the Spirit does not accept the things that come from the Spirit of God for they are foolishness to him, and he cannot understand them, because they are spiritually discerned" (1 Corinthians 2:14).

As though that were not enough, Satan works to deepen to the mystery: "The god of this age has blinded the minds of unbelievers, so that they cannot see the light of the Gospel of the glory of Christ" (2 Corinthians 4:4). Satan turns out the lights and tries to lead people into the darkness of paganism: greed, pride, immorality.

But it doesn't have to be. We can lay emphasis on Epiphany, asking the Holy Spirit to enlighten darkened, confused minds and praying for our own continued illumination: "Holy Spirit, light divine, Dawn upon this soul of mine."

God is still in charge. He "made His light shine in our hearts" (2 Corinthians 4:6) so we would acknowledge Him as the only true God; catch a glimpse of His might, wisdom, glory, and majesty; and come to know Him as our loving Father in Jesus Christ.

As we look into the face of God's Son made flesh, the veil of the mystery of God is removed. With our finite eyes we still cannot see the infinite God, but with the eyes of faith we can behold His loving acts on our behalf. "No one has ever seen God, but God the One and Only, who is at the Father's side, has made Him known" (John 1:18).

PRAYER SUGGESTION

Pray that the beacon of the Gospel may guide many people to the knowledge of Jesus Christ, the world's Light.

A Surprising Faith

"I have not found such great faith even in Israel." Luke 7:9

The gold found in California in 1849 gave impetus to opening roads to the west for prospecting and other enterprises. Gold is where you find it. And it is because gold is sometimes found in unexpected places that we think of it as "hidden treasure." So it is with faith.

The Roman centurion stationed in Capernaum sought Jesus' help on behalf of his sick servant. In so doing, this Gentile expressed great faith in the healing power and unconditional love of the Son of God for all people.

The New Testament calls attention to four centurions: the one stationed in Capernaum, the one standing at the foot of Jesus' cross, Cornelius in Caesarea, and Julius, who led Paul to Rome where he was imprisoned. The first three were believers, and of Julius it is said that he treated the apostle kindly, gave him special privileges, and later saved his life. It is not much of a leap to think that Julius may have been a Christian as well.

Sometimes we are surprised by the people who express faith in the Lord Jesus: the thief on the cross, the jailer in Philippi, Saul the Pharisee. The gold of faith is where you find it.

That is why the Christian church proclaims the Gospel "to all creation" (Mark 16:15), to all mankind without distinction, leaving it to the Holy Spirit to perform the miracle of conversion. The Gospel of salvation through faith in our Savior, Jesus Christ, has been brought to us as well, and from us it is to go out into all the world.

PRAYER SUGGESTION

Pray that you, like the Wise Men of old, may serve Christ with the gold of faith, the frankincense of prayer, and the myrrh of repentance.

Reading the Scriptures Carefully

"Let the reader understand." Matthew 24:15

The Vietnam War Memorial in Washington, D.C. lists the names of those who were killed in that war. Despite great care in compiling this list, included are names of three men who were not killed in battle. To err is human.

It is possible to err when we read the Bible, which may give rise to false teachings. The problem is not with the Bible, of course, but with the imperfect human mind. To guard against misunderstanding, God adds explanatory sentences in many places.

Jesus' words above were a response to Daniel's prophecies about the end times. Many have misinterpreted them by putting their own meanings into the words, so it is necessary to read the Book of Daniel and the words of Jesus carefully and in the light of Scripture's own clear interpretation.

We find quite a few parenthetical statements in the Gospel of John, always for the purpose of aiding the reader. When reporting that Jesus asked Philip, "Where shall we buy bread for these people to eat?" John inserted, "He asked this only to test him, for He already had in mind what He was going to do" (John 6:5–6). Again, when John quoted Jesus as saying to the Twelve, "One of you is a devil," John explained parenthetically that Jesus meant Judas Iscariot (John 6:70–71).

Let us read God's written Word diligently and carefully, considering the text and the context.

This is always the main point in Scripture—that we find the promises of Jesus Christ, our Redeemer from sin and death.

PRAYER SUGGESTION

Ask the Lord Jesus to open our eyes and minds, through Word and Spirit, to the truths of the salvation He has provided for us.

When Good Comes out of Evil

"You intended to harm me, but God intended it for good."
Genesis 50:20

In 1985 terrorists commandeered a plane and for 17 days held its passengers hostage under unpleasant conditions and the constant threat of death. When freed, the hostages were each given a medical examination. During that examination, it was found out that one of the passengers had a potentially fatal skin cancer—something of which he was not aware. It could now be treated.

Sometimes good emerges from evil. Consider Joseph. His brothers wanted him out of the way, so they sold him into slavery in Egypt. In Egypt, Joseph eventually was promoted from slave to prime minister. Later he told his brothers, without rancor "You intended to harm me, but God intended it for good to accomplish what is now being done, the saving of many lives."

We realize that under God's authority good comes out of evil, a bane contains a blessing, the dark cloud has a silver lining. So we judge nothing before the time but await outcomes.

God can override evil with good, turn sickness into health, convert a loss into a gain. God is in control. William Cullen Bryant wrote in the poem, "To a Waterfowl," "He who for zone to zone, Guides through the boundless sky thy certain flight, In the long way that I must tread alone, Will lead my steps aright."

We have faith in God during difficult times because that is precisely how our salvation became a reality: the enemies hated Jesus; they falsely accused and convicted Him, and they executed Him. We know that the greatest good came from the most evil time. Just as our heavenly Father promised, Jesus rose from the dead and opened to us the door to eternal life.

PRAYER SUGGESTION

Thank God for turning bad times into good in your life.

From Trivia to Treasures

"While your servant was busy here and there, the man disappeared."
1 Kings 20:40

According to the account in 1 Kings, a prophet told King Ahab a fictitious story. He said he had been guarding a prisoner, but he had been negligent ("busy here and there") and the prisoner escaped. The lesson was meant to get Ahab's attention because he had let his enemy, King Ben-Hadad of Syria, escape.

Many people leave the important tasks of life undone because they are preoccupied with trivia; life's big picture escapes them. The result is what we might call "the terrible triumph of trivialities."

The pursuit of trifles has a long history. Tourists in Rome can visit the Fountain of Trevi. It derives its name from the Latin *trivium,* that is, a junction of three roads. You can well imagine how enterprising people would have set up shops to sell goods to travelers there. Because of the location, the goods (which often had little value) were called "trivia."

Jesus Christ came into our world and into our hearts on the bridge of faith built by the Holy Spirit, through the Gospel, for the purpose of saving us from sin and death. The Redeemer took our attention away from the trifles of this world, from man's gaudy lights that keep us from seeing God's sun, from the fragmentation of life through our pursuit of selfish interests—from being "busy here and there." Instead, He focused it on the treasures of His Word and the joy of serving Him in His kingdom. In a hymn we sing: "Many spend their lives in fretting, Over trifles and in getting Things that have no solid ground." For us Christians this is no longer true.

PRAYER SUGGESTION

Ask Jesus, your priceless Treasure, your truest Friend, to keep you always close to Him.

Good Health for Soul and Body

A cheerful look brings joy to the heart, and good news gives health to the bones. Proverbs 15:30

In his book *Bones of Contention*, Roger Lewin addressed some of the controversies that arise when human remains are unearthed. That prompted a reviewer to say that such remains "quickly become the bones of contention."

Contention is widespread, which serves to emphasize what a blessing it is when "brothers live together in unity" (Psalm 133:1) and when individual Christians have inner peace, unity, and harmony.

We all recognize that health of mind and health of body are closely linked. The Bible reinforces this. It was not a happy psalmist who declared (22:14), "I am poured out like water, and all my bones are out of joint." One might hear an anxious person say "I feel it in my bones." And when the body reacts to the mind's distress signals, the result can be called a contention of the bones.

On the other hand, a cheerful mind or spirit can improve physical health. The writer of Proverbs made several references to this fact: "A heart at peace gives life to the body, but envy rots the bones" (14:30). "Pleasant words are a honeycomb, sweet to the soul and healing to the bones" (16:24). "A cheerful heart is good medicine, but a crushed spirit dries up the bones" (17:22).

The best medicine is the Gospel of Jesus Christ. It is the good news that the Lamb of God has taken away our sin and has reconciled us to God. This says it all: "since we have been justified through faith, we have peace with God through our Lord Jesus Christ" (Romans 5:1). We can feel it in our bones!

PRAYER SUGGESTION

Give thanks to the Lord Jesus, the great Physician, for bringing joy into your life by taking away your sins.

The Key: Symbol of Christ's Authority

"I will place on His shoulder the key to the house of David;
what He opens no one can shut, and what He shuts no one can
open." Isaiah 22:22

When Randolph Churchill ended his term in office as Chancellor of the Exchequer, a representative of Parliament came to his house to pick up the official robes. But Mrs. Churchill refused to give up the tokens of authority, saying she was keeping the robes for her son—Winston.

There are other symbols of authority: scepter, crown, key. In particular, the key, the instrument that locks and unlocks doors, is, well, key to authority. Whoever has the key has control of the house. In the Bible, the key symbolizes the royal authority of the Messiah. God says that He has "the key to the house of David," that is, to the church as the kingdom of grace. Jesus, who fulfilled the office of the Messiah, has all authority over heaven and earth. Having been crucified for the world's sin and raised again from the dead, Jesus has the power to forgive, the key to open heaven to all who believe in Him.

John quoted Isaiah: "These are the words of Him who is holy and true, who holds the key of David. What He opens no one can shut, and what He shuts no one can open" (Revelation 3:7).

As the one who possesses all power in heaven and on earth, Jesus exercises His power to delegate authority by entrusting to His disciples the Office of the Keys: the authority to retain the sins of the impenitent and to remit the sins of those who repent and believe in Jesus as their Savior. This is the power the church exercises through the public ministry: It is the power to close and to open heaven.

PRAYER SUGGESTION

Thank the Lord Jesus, the Head of the church, for having given His followers the power to forgive.

How to Overcome Satan

"I have given you authority to … overcome all the power of the enemy. …However, do not rejoice that the spirits submit to you, but rejoice that your names are written in heaven." Luke 10:19–20

In England in the early 1800s, the Luddites opposed the Industrial Revolution. They thought they could stop it by smashing the machines in textile factories.

Very little is accomplished when externals are attacked and the inner powers are left intact. This principle certainly applies to Christ's work of destroying the power of the devil. Our Lord could not have done it by smashing a few fixtures in the dens of iniquity or by picketing the "synagogue of Satan" (Revelation 2:9). Satan's influence far exceeds local manifestations; it is a worldwide, God-defying power. Jesus knew that opposing "the prince of this world" (John 12:31) would be difficult. He knew that a power far greater than the Judas-led posse was at work in Gethsemane.

Great as Satan's power was, Jesus' was greater. By His death and resurrection, Christ utterly destroyed the devil's kingdom. Paul wrote, "Having disarmed the powers and authorities, He made a public spectacle of them, triumphing over them by the cross" (Colossians 2:15).

We still have the Evil One to deal with daily. Learning from Jesus, we know we cannot resist him by smashing a few terrorist rings, by making a few cosmetic changes in dangerous places, or by changing our own bad habits. That is why we faithfully turn to Jesus and His Word when Satan tempts us. Martin Luther's line, "One little word can fell him," holds because Jesus won the victory.

PRAYER SUGGESTION

Thank God for giving you the victory over Satan through Jesus Christ, our Lord.

Jesus, Wounded But a Winner

*"I will put enmity between you and the woman,
and between your offspring and hers; He will crush your head,
and you will strike His heel." Genesis 3:15*

The dik-dik, the smallest of the antelopes, is so little that lions on the plains of Africa don't even bother to chase them. But there is no person so small or insignificant that the devil doesn't bother with.

Peter testified: "Your enemy the devil prowls around like a roaring lion looking for someone to devour" (1 Peter 5:8). This takes us back to the Garden of Eden, where Adam and Eve yielded to the devil's temptation and fell into sin. That was the beginning of human sin; satanic sin began earlier when Satan and his angels disobeyed our heavenly Father. As God's avowed enemy, Satan seeks to destroy God's noblest work: human beings created in His image.

But God frustrated the devil's plan by faithfully keeping His promise to provide us with a Savior, who in the Gospel is called the woman's Seed or Offspring. A great battle was to take place between Satan and the Son of God, and in this deadly duel Satan's power would be crushed, but not without wounds suffered by Jesus. However, these were mere mortal wounds. After His human death, Jesus rose again to life and proclaimed His victory. Our Lord, "the Lion of the tribe of Judah" (Revelation 5:5), once and for all overcame him who like a roaring lion tried to devour Christians, large and small.

Since no one is too small for Satan to pursue, no one is too insignificant for the Savior to seek and to save. Jesus Christ died for all. Rest assured that Jesus loves you, for the Bible tells you so!

PRAYER SUGGESTION

Thank the Lord Jesus for thinking so highly of you that He gave His life for your salvation.

The Heavenly Bridegroom and Bride

I saw the Holy City, the new Jerusalem, coming down out of heaven from God, prepared as a bride beautifully dressed for her husband.
Revelation 21:2

In Charles Dickens's story *Great Expectations,* Miss Havisham was jilted on her wedding night. She never recovered from the experience, continuing to wear her wedding dress, lace veil, satin shoes, and bridal flowers for a long time.

The Bible often refers to marriage and family life as similes for the love that Jesus Christ, the heavenly Bridegroom, has for His bride, the church. For example, in Christ's parable of the ten virgins, the bridegroom was a long time in coming. What if he had not shown up at all? Imagine how the bride would have suffered!

But the bridegroom who is Christ did not treat His church like Miss Havisham's groom treated her. Because the Messiah came, as the prophets had foretold, God blessed His church, bestowing "a crown of beauty instead of ashes, the oil of gladness instead of mourning, and a garment of praise instead of a spirit of despair" (Isaiah 61:3). Later in this book, the prophet declared, "As a bridegroom rejoices over his bride, so will your God rejoice over you" (Isaiah 62:5). Christ loved His bride, the church, and died for her. Now we, the members of His church, are at peace with God.

But that isn't the end of the story. The heavenly Bridegroom will come again in glory. St. John had a highly symbolic vision of the forthcoming reunion of Christ with His church. We are pictured as coming to meet Him "prepared as a bride beautifully dressed for her husband." The dress is the righteousness of Christ in which we are clad through faith in the Savior.

PRAYER SUGGESTION

Pray that the Holy Spirit may sustain in you the great expectation of Jesus' return in glory.

Man's Greed, God's Grace

You know the grace of our Lord Jesus Christ, that though He was rich, yet for your sakes He became poor, so that you through His poverty might become rich. 2 Corinthians 8:9

In her play *The Little Foxes*, Lillian Hellmann tells of the greediness of a turn-of-the-century family. The title of the play came from the Old Testament, "Catch for us the foxes, the little foxes that ruin the vineyards" (Song of Songs 2:15), and refers to the craftiness of the greedy characters.

The Bible has much to say about greed as *morally* wrong. In the First Commandment, God declares: "You shall have no other gods before Me" (Deuteronomy 5:7). He tells us to fear, love, and trust in Him above all things. It is a transgression of God's Law to be greedy, to make an idol of wealth of any kind.

What is more, greed is not *practical*. When it controls people, it ruins their lives and brings only grief. Paul wrote: "People who want to get rich fall into temptation and a trap and into many foolish and harmful desires that plunge men into ruin and destruction" (1 Timothy 6:9).

How is greed to be overcome? We look to Jesus Christ. He, the Son of God, gave up everything when He became incarnate and was born into deep poverty. He came to atone for all our sins, greed included, and to bring us the incomparable riches of heaven. His poverty resulted in great spiritual wealth for us: peace with God, the full and free forgiveness of sins as His children and heirs of eternal life. The temporary things of this world lose their appeal; greed vanishes, for we have the riches of Christ's grace.

PRAYER SUGGESTION

Thank Jesus for His grace in sacrificing everything, even His very life, for your eternal welfare.

A Lie That Wouldn't Fly

The chief priests… gave the soldiers a large sum of money, telling them, "You are to say, 'His disciples came during the night and stole Him away while we were asleep.'" Matthew 28:12–13

When the Environmental Protection Agency found that 24 of 32 sites examined contained no dioxin, a newspaper headline screamed, "Dioxin at Eight New Sites." Nothing was said about the 24 clean sites. Truth can be presented in various ways.

On the first Easter, the enemies of Christ did not stay within any aspect of the truth when they told the guards to say the disciples had stolen Jesus' body. They had already taken extra measures to secure the tomb. A cord was stretched across the entrance and fastened at both ends with wax or clay on which the seal of the governor was stamped. Guards were stationed at the tomb. These precautions backfired. They were, in and of themselves, proof that the circulated story of the theft of Jesus' body was a lie.

One can think of further contradictions of this charge. If the soldiers slept, how would they know what had occurred? Further, when we consider how frightened the disciples were, we would infer that they were the least likely candidates for grave robbery. Nevertheless, some people believed the soldiers' lie. In the second century A.D., Justin Martyr, a Christian convert, referred to it in his *Dialog with Trypho.* To this day some would rather believe a preposterous lie than a simple, well-documented fact.

The truth is simply this: "Christ has indeed been raised from the dead" (1 Corinthians 15:20). And, "He was delivered over to death for our sins and was raised to life for our justification" (Romans 4:25). The truth prevails.

PRAYER SUGGESTION

Give thanks to the Lord Jesus Christ for atoning for your sins and for rising again in proof of the sufficiency of His sacrifice.

The Story of Two Cities

The Lord is good, a refuge in times of trouble. He cares for those who trust in Him, but … He will make an end of Nineveh. Nahum 1:7–8

"O Jerusalem, Jerusalem ..." Matthew 23:37

The story of Nineveh and Jerusalem could be called A Tale of Two Cities.

Jonah preached repentance to Nineveh, but later generations rejected God's Word. Nahum called it a bloody city "full of lies, full of plunder, never without victims" (Nahum 3:1). Around 606 B.C., the city was destroyed so thoroughly that very little remained.

Jesus wept over Jerusalem because He knew its people would kill God's messengers, including God's own Son. He predicted a siege after which no stone would be left atop another. The Romans destroyed the city in a.d. 70; only the Wailing Wall remains.

Jesus taught, "From everyone who has been given much, much will be demanded" (Luke 12:48). Applying this truth to these two cities, He declared, "The men of Nineveh will stand up at the judgment with this generation and will condemn it; for they repented at the preaching of Jonah, and now one greater than Jonah is here" (Matthew 12:41). The people of Jerusalem had so many opportunities to honor and serve the true God—they even had His Son in their midst. But they rejected God's Word.

Nahum spoke of judgment on Nineveh, but he testified also of God's forgiving grace. He foresaw the Good News, saying, "Look, there on the mountains, the feet of One who brings good news, who proclaims peace!" (Nahum 1:15). Jesus cared about Jerusalem—and for all the people of the world—so much that He died for their salvation. In Christ we have forgiveness and peace with God.

PRAYER SUGGESTION

Ask God to bless your city and community with the gift of faith in the redeeming merit of His Son, our Savior Jesus Christ.

Letting the Lord Settle It

Judge nothing before the appointed time; wait till the Lord comes.
1 Corinthians 4:5

A New England author wrote about impatient people who were not content to let tadpoles develop into frogs the natural way. They thought they could hasten the process by cutting off their tails. Of course, the tadpoles died.

How often does impatience prevent natural development! A fig tree, not yielding fruit when the owner wanted it, was in danger of being cut down prematurely. Some field workers wanted to separate the tares from the wheat before harvest time. In contemporary life, some judgments must be suspended until more information becomes available. And some questions must await answers until Christ returns.

In Corinth some people were too quick in judging the work of St. Paul, saying, "His speech is contemptible" (2 Corinthians 10:10KJV). Their judgments were not only premature but also totally wrong. St. Paul's work remains to this day because he preached Christ crucified and risen. As our Savior is the same yesterday, today, and forever, so also is His Gospel everlasting.

Impatience, premature judgment, loveless conclusions hastily drawn—these are still problems. It is helpful if we learn to distinguish between things to be decided here and now and things that must "wait till the Lord comes." (We cannot, for example, determine who is a hypocrite in the church because we cannot look into the heart to determine whether faith is there.)

Some things we will gladly leave to the Lord. When He comes again, He will take things in hand and settle them once and for all.

PRAYER SUGGESTION

Ask the Savior to grant you wisdom and love to make the right choices when it is the time to do so.

Jesus—a Member of Our Family

Jesus is not ashamed to call them brothers. Hebrews 2:11

Paul wrote to the Romans that he was "not ashamed of the Gospel" (Romans 1:16). The Latin translation of "not ashamed" has the apostle say that he doesn't blush, doesn't turn red, when testifying to Christ's Gospel. Blushing is a human reaction to something that causes discomfort.

How wonderful to know that Jesus is not embarrassed to call us His brothers and sisters! The writer of Hebrews explained that Jesus, the Son of God, "Suffered death so that by the grace of God He might taste death for everyone" (2:9). By suffering for all sinners, He became "the author of their salvation" (2:10). Although now exalted in heaven, Jesus maintains a close relationship with us. The Savior and those saved are close to one another, as the Hebrews writer stated, "Both the one who makes men holy and those who are made holy are of the same family" (2:11). We are adopted through Baptism into Christ as members of the heavenly Father's family. Jesus is our Brother and He acknowledges us as His brothers and sisters.

Jesus is truly God's Son but also of the same family with us, for He is human. How close is the bond we have with Him! Christ's acknowledgment of us as His family bespeaks a mutual relationship. It is a coin with another side, and that side is that we are not ashamed to call Jesus our Brother. We, in faith, confess Him unblushingly before the world.

PRAYER SUGGESTION

"Jesus! and it shall it ever be, A mortal man ashamed of Thee? Ashamed of Thee, who angels praise, Whose glories shine through endless days?"

Christ, a Conqueror on Our Behalf

You have shattered the yoke that burdens them, the bar across their shoulders, the rod of their oppressor. Isaiah 9:4

William the Conqueror ordered more than 50 hamlets destroyed so he could plant forests to satisfy his personal desire for deer hunting. In many other respects William proved to be a tyrant. We can imagine him treating people as though they were oxen.

All the people of the earth languished under the yoke and rod of spiritual oppressors—sin and Satan. Sin was their master, and Satan, through the fear of death, held them all in bondage.

God delivered us from these combined evil forces that bound us. Isaiah prophesied the coming Messiah, speaking of it as already fulfilled: "To us a Child is born, to us a Son is given" (9:6). Isaiah said that the Messiah's names are "Wonderful Counselor, Mighty God, Everlasting Father, Prince of Peace" (9:6).

This Child was born in Bethlehem of the virgin Mary. In Him, as in the heavenly Father, might and mercy dwell. In fact, so close is His relation to the Father that they share the name "Everlasting Father." He is also, in common with the Holy Spirit, our Counselor and Comforter.

Our benign Lord Jesus comes to us with all the tokens of royalty for our good, as the hymn states, "His kingly crown is holiness, His scepter, pity in distress." He does not come to obliterate homes to fulfill selfish desires, as King William did, but to help us build them so that in them we may serve Him with joy and security. We join all Christendom in the doxology: "O blest the land, the city blest, Where Christ the Ruler is confessed. O happy hearts and happy homes To whom this King in triumph comes."

PRAYER SUGGESTION

Express your gratitude to the Lord Jesus for conquering sin, death, and Satan in your behalf.

St. Paul's Second Birthday

As he [Saul] neared Damascus on his journey, suddenly a light from heaven flashed around him. Acts 9:3

A woman who survived a difficult surgery said, "I feel like I have two birthdays: my real one in January and the other the day of my surgery."

Saul also had two birthdays. The first was his natural one in Tarsus. We know that he was born into a well-known family and was a Roman citizen. Like his father, Saul became a Pharisee. As a zealous young man, he persecuted the Christians, witnessing and heartily approving the stoning of Stephen.

It was during a journey to Damascus, with the intent to persecute Christians there, that Saul was converted to Christianity and called into the apostleship. This encounter with the exalted Jesus is described in Acts 22:3–21. It was his second birthday.

Saul the Pharisee became St. Paul the apostle. His conversion was a major event in Christendom and his spiritual birthday is observed on this day. No person did as much as Paul to bring the Gospel to the world.

Paul exemplified the meaning of conversion, or regeneration. He wrote, "If anyone is in Christ, he is a new creation" (2 Corinthians 5:17). The Gospel, as St. Paul experienced and then proclaimed it, still brings about this spiritual birthday. The Holy Spirit has made us a new creation, a people committed to Christ, who for us and for the whole world died on a cross and rose again. As Saul the Pharisee was baptized and put on Christ, so also we came to faith, emerging from the water of Holy Baptism as new persons who follow Jesus from the cradle to the grave.

PRAYER SUGGESTION

Ask the Holy Spirit to keep you in the faith so the Savior Jesus Christ may be glorified in and through you.

Reconciliation with God Comes First

We implore you on Christ's behalf: Be reconciled to God.
2 Corinthians 5:20

In a Midwestern city, some people joined a neighborhood church "to effect racial reconciliation." It followed the action of a major church body that publicly asked forgiveness from present-day people whose ancestors were slaves.

The desire to live in peace is biblical, as the apostle Paul wrote to the Romans, "If it is possible, as far as it depends on you, live at peace with everyone" (Romans 12:18). The main reason for joining a church is, however, not social reconciliation but reconciliation with God. To place reconciliation with people first is to put the cart before the horse. It is to come with a basket to pick fruit when no fruit tree exists.

God's reconciliation of sinners is the topmost truth of the Gospel. While Christ gained it for all—for the whole world—only those who grasp it in faith as an outright gift of God have the benefit of it. In the holy Christian church, the Holy Spirit "daily and richly forgives all sins to me and all believers" (*The Small Catechism*). This is what it means to be reconciled to God and as a result to join and to be active in a local congregation.

Reconciliation with God precedes—not follows—reconciliation to one another in the community. The former prompts us to join a congregation. In the visible church, flesh-and-blood people rub elbows with one another as they hear God's Word and do God's work. The solid basis for peace in all human relationships is the peace we have with God through our Lord Jesus Christ.

PRAYER SUGGESTION

Thank God for declaring you righteous in His sight for the sake of Jesus. Ask His help for effecting greater reconciliation among people.

Jesus, the Go-Between

He Himself is our peace, who has made the two one. Ephesians 2:14

The Mississippi River separated the east bank from the west bank. That changed in the 1870s when James B. Eads designed and built a bridge across the river near St. Louis. The bridge helped to make the two sides one.

Sin was like the Mississippi in that it separated all of Adam's offspring from God. God was in His heaven and the whole human race was separated from Him by sin and its consequences: disobedience, defiance, death. On their own, people could not bridge the separation.

Only God could do it—and He did. He sent His one and only Son, Jesus Christ, into this sinful world to be the Reconciler (1 Timothy 2:5). In a spiritual sense, He was the Eads Bridge. By His active obedience to God's law and by His endurance of death as sin's penalty, He opened the way to God. The Christmas hymn says it simply: "God and sinners reconciled." Paul wrote that God was in Christ, reconciling the world to Himself, for "God made Him who had no sin to be sin for us, so that in Him we might become the righteousness of God" (2 Corinthians 5:21).

By faith in the redeeming work of Christ Jesus, we are at peace with God, who is our heavenly Father and we are His sons and daughters. As God's children, we are brothers and sisters to one another and strive to live in peace. The psalmist declares, "How good and pleasant it is when brothers live together in unity!" (133:1). Whenever we cross a bridge, we can be reminded that through our spiritual Bridge, we are one with God and with one another.

PRAYER SUGGESTION

Thank the Lord Jesus for enabling you to be at peace with God for you can now pray to Him boldly and confidently in Jesus' name.

Possessing All, Yet Poor

Christ Jesus ... being in very nature God ... made Himself nothing, taking the very nature of a servant. Philippians 2:5–7

As a result of the Battle of Hastings in A.D. 1066, William the Conqueror became the master of England. Yet when he was about to be interred after losing his life in battle, a knight stepped forward and protested: "You can't bury him here; this is my land that he took from my father." The knight demanded 60 shillings. Someone had to pay this sum (about $15.00 today) before the burial could proceed.

In a similar way, Jesus' resting places were not His own. At birth, He rested in a borrowed cradle. At the other end of His life, He rested in another man's tomb. Jesus had no home of his own. His "headquarters" in Capernaum belonged to another. The donkey He rode into Jerusalem was appropriated. The Upper Room where He celebrated His last Passover was also borrowed.

This extreme poverty emphasizes the extent to which the Son of God, King of kings, divested Himself of His divine majesty to be the Servant and Savior of all. By the act of assuming true human nature and becoming a servant, He "made Himself nothing" (Philippians 2:7). It was not His intent to earn merit for Himself by taking a vow of poverty, as some have done. His purpose was to earn wealth for us, to provide us with the spiritual assets Adam and Eve had cast aside: peace with God, an inheritance with the saints in light, standing as the members of God's family.

William the Conqueror enriched himself by collecting taxes from unwilling subjects. King Jesus exacts no taxes. He enriched us by His grace, giving us willing hearts to share His love with all.

PRAYER SUGGESTION

Give thanks to God for His unspeakable grace in sending His Son into the world as the all-sufficient Savior.

The Two Trees

Christ redeemed us from the curse of the law by becoming a curse for us, for it is written: "Cursed is everyone who is hung on a tree." Galatians 3:13

Trees have a purpose. They provide shade and shelter. They are the source of fruit to eat and wood for building.

Spiritually speaking, the story of salvation can be told around a tree motif. In the Garden of Eden, the "tree of the knowledge of good and evil" (Genesis 2:9) was significant in the lives of Adam and Eve. Aided and abetted by the devil, they ate its forbidden fruit and committed the sin of disobedience that brought on death.

Of Satan it is said in a familiar collect, "that He who by a tree once overcame, might likewise by a tree be overcome." That tree was the cross on which Jesus defeated the devil. In overcoming Satan, God's Son overcame sin and death. He bore the curse of sin in our place. Through faith in Him as our Savior we are redeemed and given eternal life.

The tree motif continues into Christian life. In the holy Christian church, the communion of saints—Christians—form whole forests of believers. Christians are like trees that stand tall for spiritual strength. The prophet Isaiah called us "oaks of righteousness" (61:3). We are like fruit trees planted by streams of water and yielding fruit in the proper time. The Holy Spirit, working through the Gospel, makes the Christian fruitful: "The fruit of the Spirit is love, joy, peace, patience, kindness, goodness, faithfulness, gentleness and self-control" (Galatians 5:22–23a). Only faith in the Savior, Jesus Christ, can produce such fruit, as it is written, "Without faith it is impossible to please God" (Hebrews 11:6).

PRAYER SUGGESTION

Ask the Holy Spirit to enrich your understanding of the Gospel so you may glorify Christ with your works, words, and thoughts.

Christ's Peace: Perfect, Permanent

He will be called ... Prince of Peace. Isaiah 9:6

The story is told of an embattled man who complied literally with the adage to "bury the hatchet." He said he was willing to stop the hostility, but he let the handle of the buried hatchet stick out of the ground so he could readily find it if needed.

Jeremiah knew of "prophets and priests alike" (Jeremiah 6:13) who failed to resolve people's conflicts, who "dress the wound of my people as though it were not serious. 'Peace, peace,' they say, when there is no peace" (Jeremiah 6:14). At best they settled for a truce or an armistice. They encouraged people to bury their hatchets, but allowed them to let the handles protrude.

In prophesying the coming of the Prince of Peace, Isaiah spoke of God's true peace with mankind through the mediating Messiah. He described the sinners' war with God in very graphic terms, referring to the "warrior's boot used in battle and every garment rolled in blood" (Isaiah 6:5). But these war items, wrote Isaiah, "will be destined for burning, and will be fuel for the fire" (9:5).

How can we be sure of the permanence of Christ's peace? The prophet continued with this proof: "For to us a Child is born, to us a Son is given" (Isaiah 9:6). This Child made a perfect and permanent peace with God through the reconciliation He effected as the Lamb of God sacrificed for our sins. Now the church's spokesmen can comfort God's people by proclaiming to them that their warfare is accomplished, their iniquity is pardoned.

As God in Christ forgives us, so we forgive others. We do more than bury the hatchet with the handle sticking out. We forgive really and truly—from the heart. We live in peace with all people.

PRAYER SUGGESTION

Thank the Savior, the Prince of Peace, for carrying out His ministry of reconciliation and for granting you peace.

Our Third Childhood

Now if we are children, then we are heirs—heirs of God and co-heirs with Christ. Romans 8:17

In Shakespeare's *Hamlet* these words occur: "They say an old man is twice a child." The first childhood is during the years following our birth. The second is when, over time, old age brings weaknesses.

As Christians we have yet a third childhood: our state of being God's sons and daughters. We are all the children of God, having been adopted through our Baptism into Christ, whose mantle of righteousness we now bear.

The third childhood has needs, as does one's natural childhood. There is a need to grow, as St. Peter stated, "Like newborn babies, crave pure spiritual milk, so that by it you may grow up in your salvation" (1 Peter 2:2). Notice the stress on "pure" spiritual food, the Word of God without any additions or subtractions of human teachings—a watered down Christianity will not produce spiritual growth. The writer of the book of Hebrews urged that, as adults, we advance beyond the ABCs of Christianity, that we turn from milk to the meat and potatoes as proper food for adults (Hebrews 5:11–14).

In our third childhood we are the recipients of many divine blessings. St. Paul drew this conclusion: "Now if we are children, then we are heirs—heirs of God and co-heirs with Christ." The gift of eternal life comes to all who are God's sons and daughters.

How wonderful is our third childhood!

PRAYER SUGGESTION

Ask the Holy Spirit to assure you, on the basis of God's promises in His Word, that you belong to Christ's family.

The Day of Hope Has Dawned

Someone calls to me from Seir, "Watchman, what is left of the night?"
... The watchman replies, "Morning is coming, but also the night."
Isaiah 21:11–12

It is night in many parts of the world; there is dense spiritual darkness—witchcraft, sorcery, Satanism. There are the primitive religions of voodoo, paganism, and occultism that even in our so-called enlightened times and places are practiced.

"Darkness covers the earth and thick darkness is over the peoples," wrote Isaiah. But he added, "The LORD rises upon you and His glory appears over you. Nations will come to your light, and kings to the brightness of your dawn" (Isaiah 60:2–3).

Apart from Jesus Christ, the Light of the world, there is no hope. In the mountainous country of Seir, south of the Dead Sea, where the descendants of Esau lived, people turned to the seers and asked, "Watchmen, what is left of night?" They wanted to know what the prospects were for deliverance from sin and its burdens. The best their spiritual leaders could say was, "Morning is coming, but also the night." With the return of the night, those who sit in the darkness of sin and all its manifestations—ignorance of the true God, idolatry, immorality—have no hope until they come to the Light—Christ, the Savior of the world.

Christians have ample reason to thank God for the coming of Jesus Christ as the Light of the world. This is what God did through His Son: "He has rescued us from the dominion of darkness and brought us into the kingdom of the Son He loves, in whom we have redemption, the forgiveness of sins" (Colossians 1:13–14). What glorious Good News to shine throughout the world!

PRAYER SUGGESTION

In your prayer, glorify God by thanking Him for the gift of His Son, the Light and the salvation of all people.

In Partnership with God

As God's fellow workers we urge you not to receive God's grace in vain. ... I tell you, now is the time of God's favor, now is the day of salvation. 2 Corinthians 6:1–2

In 1735 the Swedish botanist Linnaeus published his great scientific work, *Systema Naturae*, in which he classified plants according to genus and species. The saying began: "God created, and Linnaeus systematized."

In His church, God assigns roles. Paul told the Corinthians that he planted the seed of the Gospel, Apollos watered, but God made it grow (1 Corinthians 3:6). For God's Word to be properly proclaimed and applied, church workers are needed. The apostle reminded Titus that he was to remain on Crete to, "straighten out what was left unfinished and appoint elders in every town" (Titus 1:5).

As far as our salvation is concerned, Christ has completed it. We can add nothing. We are fully redeemed by Jesus' blood shed on the cross. Now there is work for us to do, not to earn salvation but to serve the Lord in whatever situation He places us.

Our response is to do good works for the glory of God, for the good of our neighbor, and for the joy of knowing that we fulfill a purpose in life. It is always time to spread the glad tidings of salvation in Christ, as the prophet Zechariah urged, "Say to the Daughter of Zion, 'See, your king comes to you'" (Matthew 21:5).

The apostles faithfully did what Christ commanded—they preached His Gospel to the world. We too praise our Lord by what we say and do. We confess our faith in Him when we share what we have with others. We give our witness by our actions and words, and by what we leave undone: the works of a sinful world.

PRAYER SUGGESTION

Give thanks to Christ for making you a partner in the spreading of the Gospel.

God's Witness of Himself

He has not left Himself without testimony. Acts 14:17

In Feodor M. Dostoevsky's novel *The Brothers Karamasov*, one of the brothers calls himself an atheist, but he talks about God all the time.

This may also be true of self-declared atheists here and now. They claim God doesn't exist yet they work overtime to prove it. Perhaps they have tried to put God into the little box that is human reason. Not being able to do this, they go on to deny His existence. All the while it is true what David stated in Psalm 14:1: "The fool says in his heart, 'There is no God.'"

The problem Paul and his associates encountered during their missionary trips was not atheism but idolatry. In Lystra, where Paul had healed a lame man, the people thought that Zeus and Hermes had come to them in the persons of Paul and Barnabas. But the apostle taught that God had given witness of Himself as their provider of food and other necessities.

Apart from God's revelation of Himself in nature, He has made Himself known in Holy Scripture. There He assures us that He is the heavenly Father who sent His Son to redeem us from sin and its penalties and to make us His children. Through the Gospel and the sacraments, the Holy Spirit bears witness in our hearts that, believing in Christ as our Savior, we are at peace with God.

There is no room for unbelief in any religion. The writer to the Hebrews declared, "Without faith it is impossible to please God, because anyone who comes to Him must believe that He exists and that He rewards those who earnestly seek Him" (11:6).

PRAYER SUGGESTION

Give thanks to God for having revealed Himself as the Father of Jesus Christ and your Father.

Christians as Stewards

He who has been stealing must steal no longer, but must work, doing something useful with his own hands, that he may have something to share with those in need. Ephesians 4:28

Buried in St. Louis's New St. Markus Cemetery is Etienne Cabet, the leader of the communist society, the Icarians. It was one of some 200 utopian communities in America. They nearly all failed. People expected too much from such idealistic societies.

The first Christians, we are told, "had everything in common" (Acts 2:44). Many sold their possessions and put the money into a common fund. God had not commanded such an arrangement. In fact, when He commanded, "You shall not steal" (Exodus 20:15), He presupposed the existence of private property. What God does require is that His people be faithful stewards of all that He gives them. All we have is entrusted to us for furthering God's kingdom. In this respect, the Jerusalem Christians set a good example, not that we should relinquish our goods and enter into a communal lifestyle, but that we use our proceeds to God's glory and for the good of people, including ourselves.

It is interesting to note that Paul did not advocate communism. He stressed (in 1 Thessalonians 4:11–12, 2 Thessalonians 3:12, and the text above) that all people who are able should work manually and mentally to earn their own livelihood. He gave a highly spiritual incentive for this work ethic: that we "may have something to share with those in need."

Christ Jesus gave Himself into death for our salvation. How can we do anything else but give ourselves to Him, helping His brothers and sisters as their need requires?

PRAYER SUGGESTION

Ask the Lord Jesus in prayer to strengthen you in the conviction that all you are and have are at His disposal.

One Purpose amid Variety

There are different kinds of gifts, but the same Spirit.
1 Corinthians 12:4

The Bible sometimes compares people with flowers, usually to illustrate the brevity and fragility of life. One can also make the point that, like flowers, people come in a wide variety. They vary in the way they look and the places they are found. And they vary in their talents and spiritual gifts worked by the Holy Spirit.

It is a beautiful father or mother who pass on to children the proper use of spiritual possessions that come with the saving faith in Jesus Christ. Those are beautiful children who love, honor, and obey their parents. Those are beautiful disciples of Christ who proclaim His Gospel. St. Paul quoted this from Isaiah: "How beautiful are the feet of those who bring good news" (Romans 10:15). One can say that not only are their feet beautiful but also their hands, their words, their minds. Yes, how beautiful are those who do works of love in the Savior's name! How beautiful are those who are clad in "garments of splendor" (Isaiah 52:1). That means that by faith they are dressed in the robe of Christ's righteousness.

It is a part of the beauty of God's people that they serve with the variety of gifts given them by the Holy Spirit. Paul mentioned some: "To one there is given through the Spirit the message of wisdom, to another the message of knowledge, ... to another faith, ... to another the gifts of healing" (1 Corinthians 12:8), and so forth. The Holy Spirit has but one purpose in distributing the spiritual gifts in so great a variety, and that is that Christians not only profess but also proclaim that "Jesus is Lord" (1 Corinthians 12:3). What a privilege!

PRAYER SUGGESTION

Ask the Holy Spirit to assist you in properly using the gifts He has entrusted to you for the sake of Jesus, your Savior.

God Gives the Humble a Lift

He has brought down rulers from their thrones but has lifted up the humble. Luke 1:52

Hsuan T'ung, the last emperor of China, abdicated in 1912. In 1959, the People's Republic pardoned him and let him return to China, where he spent the rest of his days working as a gardener.

The world has witnessed the downfall of mighty rulers many times before. "As Nubuchadnezzar was walking on the roof of the royal palace of Babylon, he said, 'Is not this the great Babylon I have built as the royal residence by mighty power and for the glory of my majesty?' The words were still on his lips when a voice came from heaven, 'This is what is decreed for you, King Nebuchadnezzar: Your royal authority has been taken from you. You will be driven away from people and will live with the wild animals; you will eat grass like cattle'" (Daniel 4:28–32).

How quickly God can bring down the proud and powerful! As the psalmist warned, "Do not put your trust … in mortal men, who cannot save. When their spirit departs, they return to the ground; on that very day their plans come to nothing" (Psalm 146:3–4).

Who alone saves? It is Jesus Christ, the Son of God, who by the work of His hands, the travail of His soul in the Garden of Gethsemane, and His death on the cross restored what Adam and Eve forfeited: childhood of the heavenly Father and the inheritance of eternal life.

St. Paul opened his letter to the Philippians with this: "Your attitude should be the same as that of Christ Jesus" (Philippians 2:5). It brings us back to the text: "[God] has lifted up the humble." It is an implied plea for God do the lifting up.

PRAYER SUGGESTION

Ask the heavenly Father to give you the humble mind of Jesus Christ and to help you walk in His steps.

Needed: Patience and Persistence

Let us not become weary in doing good, for at the proper time we will reap a harvest if we do not give up. Galatians 6:9

Theodor Geisel, who used the pen name Dr. Seuss, wrote some 45 books that have become children's classics. He said once that his first manuscript was published only after 28 publishers rejected it.

How often should you try if at first you don't succeed? Much depends on what it is you are trying to do. Or we may ask: How often should we rise again after falling into sin or failing to do what is right? No limit can be set for this. We should repent and in faith turn to God for forgiveness *every time*. God calls us to patience: "Let us throw off everything that hinders and the sin that so easily entangles, and let us run with perseverance the race marked out for us" (Hebrews 12:1). This says that we are to put forth effort after effort to overcome pet sins and to avoid the temptations over which we trip so easily.

In the above text, the apostle urged his readers to persevere in doing good, promising that God will bless our efforts in due time. He added, "Therefore, as we have opportunity, let us do good to all people, especially to those who belong to the family of believers" (Galatians 6:10). Spouses, parents, and children are encouraged never to give up on one another, but to bear their mutual burdens. Let them address their problems in love, continuing their efforts even when positive results are not immediately evident.

Imagine where we would be if God gave up on us for our recurrent sinning! For the sake of Jesus Christ, whose redeeming, reconciling merit is ours by faith, God forgives us richly and reinstates us as His dear children every day.

PRAYER SUGGESTION

Ask God, in Jesus' name, to bless your words and deeds as you give support to someone in need.

Believing What the Book Says

He who did not spare His own Son, but gave Him up for us all—how will He not also, along with Him, graciously give us all things? Romans 8:32

Many people speak of their Christian faith in vague terms. But Filipe Alou, manager of the Montreal Expos, was forthright: "I believe everything the Book says. I believe in the great sacrifice that God made of His Son for my sins."

This is a clear confession of faith in Jesus Christ, as Savior. This is the faith that saves. Jesus Himself declares, "Whoever believes in Him shall not perish but have eternal life" (John 3:16).

In Philippi, after an earthquake had opened all the prison doors, the excited jailor asked Paul and Silas, "'What must I do to be saved?' They replied, 'Believe in the Lord Jesus'" (Acts 16:30–31). We can be sure that before they baptized him and his family, the disciples explained what Jesus had done for the salvation of all—that He died on the cross and that He rose from the dead on the third day.

We do not have first-hand witnesses like Paul and Silas present to preach on Christ's redemption and resurrection. But we do have their words on record that bear witness to Jesus and to His atoning, life-giving work. As Alou had manuals to guide him in his work as a baseball team manager, so he also has the Word of God to instruct him on the way to eternal life. The important thing is not just to *have* it but to *follow* it.

In Romans chapter 8, Paul drew a conclusion from the promise and premise of Christ's great sacrifice. If the heavenly Father did this much, will He not also in Jesus' name grant us what we need and pray for?

PRAYER SUGGESTION

Ask the Lord Jesus to renew daily your faith in His great gift to you so you will trust in Him also to give you lesser gifts.

The Indwelling God

I pray that [of His Father's] glorious riches He may strengthen you with power through His Spirit in your inner being, so that Christ may dwell in your hearts through faith. Ephesians 3:16–17

The word "enthusiasm" has interesting roots. It comes from the Greek *en* (in) and *theos* (God). Its origin reflects a religious philosophy of paganism that a person who mustered great fervor and energy for a cause (enthusiasm) did so because of a god within him. Another belief in some pagan philosophies was the blending of the divine with the human, allowing the human being to say that he was god. What presumption!

The Bible teaches the indwelling of the Triune God in believers. This divine indwelling in Christians is totally different from pagan enthusiasm, however. The apostle clearly stated that God's presence in our hearts comes "through faith." This is faith in the atoning merit of Jesus Christ as our Savior. It is created and sustained only through the means of grace: Word and sacraments. It is not based on human feelings or emotions but on the truths of God's Word.

Yes, enthusiasm is important in Christendom—enthusiasm for missions, for Christian education, for spiritual growth in the people of God, growth in young and old. It is our joy to be enthusiastically and energetically involved in God's work. In the Old Testament we read of the rebuilding of the walls of Jerusalem under Nehemiah. Why this progress? He wrote, "for the people worked with all their heart" (4:6).

PRAYER SUGGESTION

Pray to Father, Son, and Holy Spirit dwelling within you to strengthen you for personal tasks and for the mission of the church.

Our Partnership in the Gospel

I planted the seed, Apollos watered it, but God made it grow.
1 Corinthians 3:6

In a book published in 1735, Swedish botanist Carolus Linnaeus was the first to classify plants and animals by giving them two names.

God gives people work to do in His kingdom. He put Adam into the Garden of Eden "to work it and take care of it" (Genesis 2:15), to "'rule over the fish of the sea and the birds of the air and over every living creature that moves on the ground'" (Genesis 1:28). Man was to be the caretaker of God's creation, and eventually Linnaeus helped by providing a way to better understanding.

Can man be a co-worker with God? We are incapable of coming to faith in Jesus Christ by our own reason or strength. Neither can we create faith in another person. It is the Holy Spirit who, through the Gospel, kindles faith in cold hearts so Jesus is acknowledged as the Savior. Human effort is totally ruled out.

Yet the faithful have work to do. Paul told his readers that he, as the pioneer missionary, sowed the seed of God's Word. After him others, like Apollos, did the irrigating. God called them to this work. Like Linnaeus, Paul clarified and to some extent systematized the teachings of the Bible, thus helping us to distinguish between sin and grace, Law and Gospel, justification and sanctification. But all the while it was God who made the seed of faith grow. It is God who, through His Word, makes the seed sprout and grow into a harvest of faithful service.

God extends to us a partnership by calling us to proclaim His Gospel, to teach it, and to live it in our daily lives. What a privilege to be "God's fellow workers" (2 Corinthians 6:1)!

PRAYER SUGGESTION

Ask the Holy Spirit to bless the preaching of Christ's Gospel in the world and the testimony we give by our personal words and deeds.

Righteous in God's Eyes

"This man [tax collector] ... went home justified before God."
Luke 18:14

The eighteenth-century Scottish poet, Robert Burns, wished that some power would "the giftie gie us to see ourselves as others see us." As it is, most people see themselves only through their own eyes.

David spoke of the wicked person who has "no fear of God before his eyes." Lacking the right relationship to God, "in his own eyes he flatters himself too much to detect or hate his sin" (Psalm 36:2). The Pharisee praying boastfully in the temple was such a person—spiritually blind, self-centered, unwilling and unable to see himself as others did, and especially as God does. The result was self-righteousness.

The publican was different. He acknowledged himself to be a sinner. He came to see himself as God saw him. Quite apart from his sins as a tax collector, he knew he had transgressed all of God's Ten Commandments in thoughts, words, and deeds. Truly penitent, he, despite his refusal to raise his eyes to heaven, did in his heart look up to God. He asked God to be merciful to him. And he went home justified by faith that God, in His righteousness, did have mercy on him.

We do well to follow those who appreciate it when others sincerely and truthfully call their attention to spiritual shortcomings. It helps us to arrive at a proper self-evaluation. It is critical that we see ourselves as forgiven people having God's full approval for Jesus' sake. This is in Robert Burns's expression a "giftie" only God can give. "It is by grace you have been saved, through faith—and this not from yourselves, it is the gift of God" (Ephesians 2:8).

PRAYER SUGGESTION

Ask God to give you full understanding of what it means to be forgiven for Jesus' sake and to see yourself in this light.

Standing in Jesus' Shadow

He must become greater; I must become less. John 3:30

Few people know who Hannibal Hamlin was. In 1861, he was elected vice president of the United States. Had Abraham Lincoln been assassinated in his first term, Hamlin would have been president. Standing in the shadow of Lincoln, he fulfilled his function, however unimportant his place in history seems now.

If anyone ever stood in the shadow of another it was John the Baptist. It was his role to be the Messiah's herald and to stand in Christ's shadow after His public ministry began. In the context of this passage, John used a beautiful illustration, saying that Christ was the bridegroom—the one to whom the bride belongs—and he only the best man. He said his joy was complete in seeing that Jesus was fulfilling His mission as the Lamb of God taking away the sin of the world.

John the Baptist was faithful to his God-given assignment, although it meant standing in Christ's shadow and, later, imprisonment and execution. But as he decreased in his work, he gained in stature in the sight of God. Jesus said, "there has not risen anyone greater than John the Baptist" (Matthew 11:11). Then, to emphasize that good standing before God is not a matter of human merit but of divine grace, He added, "Yet he who is least in the kingdom of heaven is greater than he" (Matthew 11:11).

In deep humility, yet with great joy, we prepare our hearts to adore Christ Jesus. Part of this joy is our willingness to let Him be the Lord while we cheerfully serve Him however we can. It is a line we can all repeat after John: "[Jesus] must become greater, I must become less."

PRAYER SUGGESTION

Ask the Savior to help you to be faithful to Him in every circumstance, never hesitating to give full glory to Him.

We Are Christ's Guests

Then Jesus directed them to have all the people sit down in groups on the green grass. Mark 6:39

A boy who had just come from a Sunday school class was asked what the lesson was all about. He replied that it was about lazy people—"about a multitude that loafs and fishes." It is true. In the account of the feeding of the 5,000, the people did nothing to earn their daily bread.

The multitude had come together in a lonely and remote place. They were in no position to engage in a "do it yourself" scramble for food. The people were our Lord's guests. And Jesus directed His disciples to have the people sit on the grass to be served a meal.

Our spiritual sustenance comes from Jesus Christ just as completely and miraculously. It is a miracle of divine grace that by the water and Word of Holy Baptism faith is given us, and by the consecrated bread and wine of Holy Communion Christ's true body and blood are imparted for our spiritual growth in Him. It is most astounding that the simple Gospel message of our Lord's cross and empty tomb, which is folly and an offense to human reason, is the wisdom of God and the power of God whereby those who hunger and thirst after righteousness are fully satisfied.

Divine grace means that we are Christ's guests. We come to His Holy Meal empty handed. Salvation is God's outright gift—we contribute nothing. The Good Shepherd, who laid down His life on our behalf, leads us to the "green grass" of His Word, providing all we need for our spiritual nurture. We sing, "The Lord's my Shepherd, I'll not want; He makes me down to lie In pastures green; He leadeth me The quiet waters by."

PRAYER SUGGESTION

Express your gratefulness to the Savior for having you as His guest and for providing for all your needs.

Our Witness to the Whole World

*"You will be My witnesses in Jerusalem, and in all Judea and
Samaria, and to the ends of the earth." Acts 1:8*

The anthem of the U.S. Marines describes the geographical
range of their service: "From the halls of Montezuma to the shores
of Tripoli."

Shortly before His ascension, Jesus indicated the scope of His
disciples' missionary activity. Our Lord viewed the growth of the
Gospel in ever-widening circles. The starting point was Jerusalem,
where the Holy Spirit was poured out on the disciples on
Pentecost and where the Christian church was founded.

The circles of expansion were Judea, which surrounded
Jerusalem, and Samaria to the north. The persecution of
Christians that began when Stephen was martyred drove the dis-
ciples to regions beyond. We read: "Those who had been scattered
by the persecution in connection with Stephen traveled as far as
Phoenicia, Cyprus and Antioch" (Acts 11:19).

The growth of Christ's church continues. It has not been
completed because these places have been evangelized. Our Lord
says to every generation: "You will be My witnesses ... to the ends
of the earth." To this day all of Christ's followers can teach all
nations the Word of salvation and baptize them in the name of the
Triune God. He who suffered and died for the sins of all mankind
says "The Christ will suffer and rise from the dead on the third day,
and repentance and forgiveness of sins will be preached in His
name to all nations, beginning at Jerusalem" (Luke 24:46–47).

It is our privilege to be Christ's witnesses wherever we are in
this world and to send missionaries to places beyond our reach.

PRAYER SUGGESTION

*Ask the risen and ascended Savior to equip you to be His witness at
home, at work, in school, and in your community.*

Reconciliation before Sundown

Do not let the sun go down while you are still angry. Ephesians 4:26

Edgar A. Guest, a popular poet of the previous century, wrote: "I do not want to stand with the setting sun And hate myself for things I've done."

One of the things to leave undone, according to the Apostle Paul, is letting the sun set on one's anger. Anger, if unattended, can lead to hatred. Such an emotional wound needs healing; it should not be allowed to fester.

In cases where anger is justified—and there is such a thing as righteous anger—care needs to be exercised that it does not become a sin. The possibility of righteous anger becoming unrighteous always exists. That is why the apostle stressed the urgency of reconciliation before much time passes.

Jesus spoke similar words in His Sermon on the Mount: "If you are offering your gift at the altar and there remember that your brother has something against you, leave your gift there in front of the altar. First go and be reconciled to your brother; then come and offer your gift" (Matthew 5:23–24).

The incentive for seeking reconciliation before sundown is the great truth that the heavenly Father did not permit the sun to set on Good Friday until Jesus had effected the reconciliation of sinners, announcing it with these words on the cross: "It is finished" (John 19:30). All was fulfilled; peace between God and sinners was restored. St. Paul taught, "God was reconciling the world to Himself in Christ, not counting men's sins against them" (2 Corinthians 5:19).

It is by faith that the reconciling work of Jesus Christ—full righteousness—is credited to us.

PRAYER SUGGESTION

Give thanks to Christ for reconciling mankind to God so you can live in peace with others.

Marriage: What God Intended

"What God has joined together, let man not separate." Matthew 19:6

Sometimes humans can learn from God's other creatures. Jesus said that we could learn not to worry about the future from the birds of the air (Matthew 6:26). But there is more to be learned from birds. Some, such as cardinals and mourning doves, mate for life. It is not so among people.

The failure of a marriage gives great cause for concern. It affects not only the marriage partners but also other family members. Divorce is very common. When one Hollywood marriage lasted only 39 days, a humorist said they must have thrown "minute rice" on the couple after the ceremony.

"It was not this way from the beginning" (Matthew 19:8), Jesus declared, referring to the practice that Moses, a *civil* lawgiver, granted certificates of divorce to people who want to terminate their marriage. He stressed God's original intent that marriage last until death ended it. What God explicitly stated in His Word (Exodus 20:14), He also revealed as a principle of nature. Jesus said: the Creator in the beginning made them "male and female" (Genesis 1:27), making it the natural thing for a young man to leave his parental home and "be united to his wife" (Genesis 2:24).

St. Paul wrote eloquently about the best marriage glue there is—love. He told husbands and wives to love each other "just as Christ loved the church and gave Himself up for her" (Ephesians 5:25). True love in marriage has its roots in the redeeming love of Jesus Christ, our Savior.

PRAYER SUGGESTION

Pray that the union of—and the unity in—marriage everywhere may be strengthened by the self-sacrificing love of Christ.

Spiritual Renewal

[He] satisfies your desires with good things so that your youth is renewed like the eagle's. Psalm 103:5

Eagles were included on the insignia of ancient military branches. It may have been due to such precedents that the United States designated the bald eagle as its national symbol.

Eagles are birds of prey. They excel in strength, flight, and vision. David had something else in mind when he compared himself to an eagle. Like other birds, eagles molt, shedding their feathers. During this time the eagle is inactive, after which it becomes active again. It has renewed vitality and soars through the sky once more.

So it was with David in his spiritual life. He was down, but God raised him up; God renewed him with "good things." The Lord satisfied David's desires with the promises of His Word—forgiveness of sins, new spiritual life, and eternal life.

We, too, are in need of such renewal. God renews us through: the Gospel and the sacraments. St. Paul wrote: "[God] saved us through the washing of rebirth and renewal by the Holy Spirit" (Titus 3:5). He reminded the Colossians to keep on ridding themselves of the old self with its practices and putting on the new self, "which is being renewed in knowledge in the image of its Creator" (Colossians 3:10). This is not a one-time exercise but something Christians do every day in the newness of life.

What words of praise the psalmist has for his renewal at the hands of God! For the sake of Christ, the promised Savior, God forgives all sins. As Christians, we can be assured that times of distress are followed by God's life-renewing blessings in Christ Jesus.

PRAYER SUGGESTION

Join David in giving thanks to God for His renewing grace in Christ and for all His blessings that renew your life.

Full Coverage in Christ

All have sinned and fall short of the glory of God, and are justified freely by His grace through the redemption that came by Christ Jesus.
Romans 3:23–24

Article I of the U.S. Constitution, in the section dealing with the apportionment of people for their representation in Congress, declares that Native Americans were not to be counted and that a slave should be regarded as three-fifths of a person. Fortunately such distinctions were changed when Amendment XVI provided for equal treatment as citizens for "all persons born or naturalized in the United States." With God things are different. His statements will never be amended.

All people without exception are sinners. God's promise of grace fulfilled in Jesus Christ is likewise unchanged. God tells: "There is no difference, for all have sinned and fall short of the glory of God" (Romans 3:22–23). The way of salvation is also unchanged: All are declared just through faith in Christ's redemption (Romans 3:24).

In every age, some claim people achieve glory through effort of their own. If that were true, we could quit believing in Christ as the Savior, for people could save themselves, partially or totally.

As human sinfulness remains constant, so does our need for God's saving grace in Christ remain constant. God's new covenant with us, which is the charter of our salvation, offers full coverage. None is excluded; none is told that he is only fractionally redeemed (perhaps three-fifths) and that he must make up the rest himself. There is no balance due, as though Christ pays a certain amount of your debt and you are responsible for the rest. No, Jesus died to bring each one of us salvation full and free.

PRAYER SUGGESTION

"Redeemer, come! I open wide my heart to Thee; here, Lord, abide."
Amen.

Young People, an Asset

Don't let anyone look down on you because you are young.
1 Timothy 4:12

Some people consider teenagers a liability. But a wiser person called them "the generation in escrow." In the future those teens will be adults, justifying every "investment" made in them.

Timothy, who was St. Paul's right-hand man, was the product of a mixed marriage. His mother, Eunice, was a Christian, his father an unconverted Greek. This could have been a problem for young Timothy but it wasn't, mostly because his mother, assisted by his grandmother Lois, took up the slack. The apostle took note of the "sincere faith" (1 Timothy 1:5) of Eunice and Lois and that they had taught Timothy the truth of salvation from the Holy Scriptures "from infancy" (2 Timothy 3:15). The psalmist asked, "How can a young man keep his way pure?" The reply: "By living according to Your Word" (Psalm 119:9). That is what Timothy did. Believing in Christ as his Savior, he had the strength and wisdom to live in accordance with his faith.

Some people may have thought Timothy too young to be a pastor and, therefore, that they need not take his admonitions to heart. Paul encouraged him to "be a good minister of Christ Jesus" (1 Timothy 4:6), teaching both Law and Gospel. He was not to let anyone intimidate him on account of his youth. God's Word is God's Word, regardless of who teaches it.

We can reserve judgment of teenagers and remember that many are like Timothy, sincere in their belief in Jesus Christ as their Savior and willing to dedicate their lives to Him. We can look up to (not down on) them, thanking God for them.

PRAYER SUGGESTION

Express your thankfulness to God for having blessed Christ's church with faithful teenagers as His precious gifts.

A Prophet Who Profits

You, my child, will be called a prophet of the Most High; for you will go on before the Lord to prepare the way for Him. Luke 1:76

Several years ago, the nation was stunned to learn of huge profits gained by some TV evangelists through their ministries. While it is proper to use the media for proclaiming the Gospel and while it is proper to draw salaries (1 Timothy 5:18), the point should always be to profit the hearers and viewers spiritually.

Old Testament prophets foretold of the coming of the great Prophet, the Messiah. Moses said, "The LORD your God will raise up for you a Prophet like me" (Deuteronomy 18:1). The prophets of old told of the ransom—the redemption, the forgiveness of sins—to come through Him who was not only David's descendant but also his Lord. "[God] said [this] through His holy prophets of long ago" (Luke 1:70), Zechariah declared. God revealed this in the Old Testament, given by inspiration.

Then, as the New Testament opens, we find Zechariah prophesying that his newborn son, John, would be the "prophet of the Most High" and would "go ... before the Lord to prepare the way."

Jesus Christ is that great Prophet, towering over all prophets. By word and deed He proved Himself as the promised Messiah who had come to redeem sinners and to effect reconciliation with God. This redemption is ours, as Scripture teaches, "through faith in Jesus Christ" (Romans 3:22).

Because this Prophet profits us so greatly "through the tender mercies of God," we cannot but exclaim with Zechariah, "Praise be to the Lord, the God of Israel, because He has come and has redeemed His people" (Luke 1:68).

PRAYER SUGGESTION

Give thanks to the Lord Jesus for being the great Prophet, proclaiming and conveying the great blessing of full salvation in Him.

God Gives Strength to the Weak

[God] chose the lowly things of this world and the despised things—and the things that are not—to nullify the things that are, so that no one may boast before him. 1 Corinthians 1:28–29

If flowers could speak, some, hardy peonies or dramatic roses, might boast and others, violets that grow wild, might whisper.

Everywhere in God's creation we see counterparts to the meek violet: tiny finches, little mice, delicate butterflies. Numbered among them are human beings. "All men are like grass and all their glory is like flowers of the field" (40:6). We are weak and easily destroyed. However, many people pretend this isn't so.

Paul found people who made great pretense of their wisdom, oratory, and nobility. They despised the apostle because, in their view, his presence was weak and his speech contemptible. They pronounced as foolishness the preaching of Christ's cross. Why should they desire forgiveness when they denied their sin? Why worship a Savior who, in great weakness and shame, was nailed to a cross?

This attitude prompted Paul to put things into perspective. Human frailty, he pointed out, underscores the might and mercy of God. Because we are imperfect humans, we can't achieve salvation on our own. It becomes evident that salvation is the work of God's grace in Jesus Christ. No one can claim an I-did-it-myself salvation.

As Christians we acknowledge that Christ "has become for us wisdom from God—that is, our righteousness, holiness, and redemption" (1 Corinthians 1:30). We can speak of having strength, but it comes from God. We can boast, but we "boast in the Lord" (1 Corinthians 1:31). Meek violets that we are, we survive because our life, for time and eternity, comes from God.

PRAYER SUGGESTION

Thank the heavenly Father for His abiding Word and for granting us salvation through faith in Jesus Christ, the personal Word.

A Famine of the Word

"I will send a famine through the land—not a famine of food or a thirst for water, but a famine of hearing the words of the LORD."
Amos 8:11

Famine uproots people and drives them to move to other lands. Overlooking Cobb Harbor, from which many people of Ireland left during the 1847 potato famine, is a statue of a young mother and her two sons going to join the husband and father who was already in the United States.

As serious as a food famine is, it is exceeded by another kind—the famine of God's Word. It is written, "Where there is no vision [no divine revelation], the people perish" (Proverbs 29:18 KJV).

Amos took the people of Israel to task for neglecting the Word of God. They observed feasts, yes, but without piety and devotion. Those who were rich sought to increase their wealth at the expense of the poor, selling "the righ-teous for silver, and the needy for a pair of sandals" (Amos 2:6). All of this aroused God's anger: "'The days are coming,' declares the Sovereign LORD, 'when I will send a famine through the land—not a famine of food or a thirst for water, but a famine of hearing the words of the LORD.'"

We have lived through years when Europe's largest country and its surrounding republics suffered a true famine of God's Word. Atheism was taught; the teaching of Christianity was stren-uously forbidden. Thanks be to God that the communistic regime fell, marking the end of the famine of God's Word in some countries. However, many mission fields remain.

May we continue to cherish His Word, assured that it will feed our faith in Jesus Christ, the bread of life.

PRAYER SUGGESTION

Ask God to grant us the continual use of His Word and the sacraments, that through them we may be nurtured and strengthened.

God's People: Comforters

Comfort, comfort My people, says your God. Isaiah 40:1

The apostolic church, in keeping with its God-given rights, appointed people to work in areas of specific need. Among these were almoners who assisted the poor, exorcists who drove out demons, healers who visited and prayed over the sick, and so on.

One appointment that is edifying to all is that of consoling, comforting, encouraging, and exhorting the downcast. St. Paul said, "If a man's gift ... is encouraging, let him encourage" (Romans 12:6–8). What wonderful work people can do in any distressful situation: death and sickness, suffering, persecution, poverty, spiritual temptation, and doubt!

It is certainly pleasing to God that comfort be brought to His sorely tried people. He declared, "Comfort, comfort My people. ... Speak tenderly to Jerusalem, and proclaim to her that her hard service has been completed, that her sin has been paid for, that she has received from the LORD's hand double for all her sins" (Isaiah 40:1–2). The message of forgiveness and peace with God through the atonement of the suffering Servant, the Messiah, was the comfort brought by God's Old Testament spokesmen.

"Comfort, comfort My people" is a most appropriate Lenten text. Forgiveness in Christ, the Lamb of God, is the comfort that pastors bring to the ailing and failing members of the church. In this they have the assistance of elders and deacons in the congregation who pray for the sick (James 5:14–15). And not only they but all members of the church bring words of hope and cheer to sorrowful and suffering brothers and sisters in the faith. That is how we can strengthen one another in the communion of saints.

PRAYER SUGGESTION

Ask the Holy Spirit, our Comforter, to keep us in the fellowship of faith, that we may be comforters to one another in Jesus' name.

Water for the Spiritually Thirsty

"Come, all you who are thirsty, come to the waters." Isaiah 55:1

Advice is freely given to people who travel to foreign lands. For instance, they are counseled to drink plenty of water to avoid dehydration, yet they are reminded to be aware of impure water that may cause sickness.

The same points can be made about spiritual water. First, there is the invitation to the thirsty, to those who would hear Him "that your soul may live" (Isaiah 55:3). Urged to come are those whose souls thirst for the living God much "as the deer pants for streams of water," (Psalm 42:1–2). Isaiah invited them to satisfy this thirst with the Word of God. This is the living water Jesus offered to the Samaritan woman at Jacob's well.

Isaiah's invitation is repeated in Revelation 22:17 where the spiritually thirsty are invited to come and "take the free gift of the water of life." Without this living water we are spiritually dehydrated.

It is likewise necessary, as with the above advice to travelers, to check the purity of the water. As we travel through life, we should be concerned about false doctrine. Isaiah referred to prophets who give in to the wishes of hearers who say, "Give us no more visions of what is right! Tell us pleasant things, prophesy illusions" (30:10). This is a sure way to get "thirst quenchers" that seem to offer momentary refreshment but that bring no peace with God.

Of His Gospel, Jesus says, "The water I give him will become in him a spring of water welling up to eternal life" (John 4:14). Those who receive the water of salvation joyously share it with others.

PRAYER SUGGESTION

Pray to the Lord Jesus to give you a fresh supply of the living water He offers.

Cause to Celebrate

*"He calls his friends and neighbors together and says,
Rejoice with me; I have found my lost sheep!" Luke 15:5*

To celebrate means to rejoice together, perhaps for a birthday, or wedding. It is a good time to invite family members who may have dropped out of things. To open the door to an estranged person puts the Lord's kind of an adventure into the occasion.

Recovering a lost sheep was an important event among Palestinian shepherds. More than head counts or property values were involved. At stake was a living being—a beloved lamb that the shepherd knew by name. To find it and restore it to the flock marked the triumph of the shepherd's love and concern.

To be sure, there is joy in heaven over every one of Christ's people here on earth, the 99 who remain true to their Savior. The Lord and His angels are happy over their faithfulness, their spiritual growth, their continuance in the flock to which the Good Shepherd ministers. But there is also joy—exceedingly great joy—over one sinner who repents and returns to Christ's church.

Why this great joy? It means the recovery of a human soul worth more than all the material wealth of the world. It means the reinstatement of a person for whose redemption Jesus Christ shed His precious blood.

If someone's turnaround occasions great joy in heaven, shouldn't we on earth rejoice likewise and, as our Lord's parable states, arrange for party time? Shouldn't we work harder at bringing straying sheep back into Christ's fold? Shouldn't we be more concerned about backdoor losses? God help us to retain those we have and to regain the ones conspicuous by their absence!

PRAYER SUGGESTION

Let your prayer be an intercession for someone who is a spiritual drop-out.

Heaven—What Is There

There will be no more night. They will not need the light of a lamp or the light of the sun, for the Lord God will give them light.
Revelation 22:5

The ancient Egyptians believed in life after death. That is why they put into their tombs things the dead would supposedly need in the afterlife: food, clothes, and even servants.

Christendom teaches "the resurrection of the dead and life of the world to come" (Nicene Creed). But it does not presume that the coming life in heaven is a continuation of the present life on earth. Earthly things will not be needed. Instead of telling us what things will be present in heaven, the Bible says more about what will *not* be there: no death or mourning, no crying from pain, no night, no sunlight or lamplight, no temple for God's people, for "the Lord God Almighty and the Lamb are its temple" (Revelation 21:22).

Heaven is described as an extraordinary place. The New Jerusalem is not like any earthly city we know. It is clean and beautiful, its streets paved with gold, precious stones everywhere. This is symbolic language, of course. Life in heaven is so different from our earthly life that literal language and human imagination cannot begin to describe its realities.

There are, however, biblical descriptions to which we can cling. Jesus said that heaven is a *place*. There is the Father's house of many rooms, where Jesus has prepared a place for us. And our bodies "will be like His [Christ's] glorious body" (Philippians 3:21).

To be in the presence of our heavenly Father as children reconciled and redeemed by the Lamb of God—that is heaven in brief.

PRAYER SUGGESTION

Pray that God, for Jesus' sake, may preserve in you the glorious vision of eternal life to come.

How Good Is Our Heavenly Father?

"Ask and it will be given to you; seek and you will find;
knock and the door will be opened to you." Matthew 7:7

Jesus tells of fathers who act as responsible providers. He calls them "evil," but added that even they know how to give good gifts to their children, not giving them stones for bread nor snakes for fish.

In this part of His Sermon on the Mount, Jesus is speaking about prayer. Drawing an analogy, He reasons: If even sinful fathers heed the requests of their children, "how much more will your Father in heaven give good gifts to those who ask Him!" (Matthew 7:11). Both the Giver and the Gift are far superior to what is human.

How wonderful are the gifts of the heavenly Father! First He gave His Son to lay down His life for the whole world of sinners. Then He, together with the Son, gives the Holy Spirit so we might be brought to faith and receive the gifts of forgiveness, peace with God, and a bond that unites us with Him and with one another as redeemed and baptized members of His family.

If fathers, although sinful and estranged from God, willingly supply their families with the necessities of life, think how much more Christian fathers can do! They can and will provide not only earthly bread but also spiritual nourishment from Him who is the bread of life, Jesus Christ. They will look to their children's four-fold growth: mental, physical, social, and spiritual, as it is said of Jesus that they may grow as Jesus grew "in wisdom and stature, and in favor with God and men" (Luke 2:52).

PRAYER SUGGESTION

Give thanks to the heavenly Father for all His gifts to you, including a Christian father who taught you to love Christ.

God's Double Choice

[The Lord] said to me,
"You are My Son; today I have become Your Father." Psalm 2:7

At the baptism of Jesus, the heavenly Father said, "You are My Son, whom I love; with You I am well pleased" (Mark 1:11). At Jesus' transfiguration the same heavenly voice said, "This is My Son, whom I have chosen; listen to Him" (Luke 9:35). Isaiah spoke of the Messiah as the Servant. He wrote, "'You are My witnesses,' declares the Lord, 'and My Servant whom I have chosen, so that you may know and believe Me and understand that I am He'" (Isaiah 43:10). Peter testified that Jesus was God's Son, the Chosen One, quoting Isaiah: "See, I lay a stone in Zion, a chosen and precious Cornerstone" (1 Peter 2:6).

If Jesus of Nazareth is the Father's Chosen One, and that He is, we need not look for another. He is God's Son who died and rose again for our salvation. Of this we are sure.

Also important is God's choice of us as His sons and daughters. This eternal election is inseparable from the Father's choice of Christ: "In Him we were also chosen, having been predestined according to the plan of Him who works out everything in conformity with the purpose of His will, in order that we, who were the first to hope in Christ, might be for the praise of His glory" (Ephesians 1:11–12).

In brief, the Father chose Christ, and in Him, without any merit or worthiness on our part, God chose us to be His children. In the Bible, God assures us of our salvation. Adhering to Jesus Christ by faith, and faithfully using the means of grace, we will certainly prevail, for God has chosen us in Christ.

PRAYER SUGGESTION

Pray that the Holy Spirit may make you certain that God is your Father and that Christ, His Son, is your Savior.

What Is Christ's Kingdom?

Jesus went into Galilee, proclaiming the good news of God. Mark 1:14

Answers to the question posed in the title above vary. Some equate it with social work. Others think of it in political terms. Even the apostles asked, "Lord, are You at this time going to restore the kingdom of Israel?" (Acts 1:6).

During His hearing before Pontius Pilate, our Lord did indeed declare that He had a kingdom, but He was quick to explain, "My kingdom is not of this world" (John 18:36).

The word "king*dom*" indicates that Christ has *dom*inion and that He reigns. He rules through Word and Sacrament. These are the media through which the Holy Spirit, sent by Christ, creates and sustains faith in us. As Jesus opened His public ministry, He said, "The time has come. ... The kingdom of God is near. Repent and believe the good news!" (Mark 1:15). Because Christ, through Word and Spirit, reigns in the hearts of people, His kingdom is invisible, but nevertheless very real.

Christ's kingdom is also pictured in the Bible as a *realm*. It is the holy Christian church. As a realm, Christ's kingdom has defined boundaries. It is by faith in Christ's redeeming merit that people enter it. It is more an organism—Christ's body of which the believers are the members—than an organization. In this realm Christ provides spiritual leadership through ordained pastors.

Christ's kingdom of grace as both a reign and a realm merges into the kingdom of glory. The latter is where the church militant becomes the church triumphant. The hymn verse states, "The saints on earth and those above But one communion make, Joined to their Lord in bonds of love, All of His grace partake."

PRAYER SUGGESTION

Pray that Christ, through His Word and Spirit, may keep you a member of His kingdom.

Taking a Loss, Getting a Gain

"Remember Lot's wife!" Luke 17:32

In His talk about the end times, Jesus declares that people will not expect His coming. "It was the same in the days of Lot. People were eating and drinking, buying and selling, planting and building" (Luke 17:28). They did not expect the burning of Sodom. The people of Noah's time did not expect the Flood. So it will be prior to Christ's second coming.

"Remember Lot's wife!" Jesus says. Why did she want to go back? We don't know; she may have sought something relatively minor but she lost something major: her life.

"Remember Lot's wife" is a fitting Lenten reminder. Christ's salvation, so dearly bought at the price of His own blood, is a spiritual blessing far exceeding what this world offers. So we remember the pious women mentioned in the Lenten account. They gave up personal convenience to be close to Christ. They were the last at the cross and the first at the tomb on Easter morning. Who were they? Mary Magdalene, Salome, the mother of James and John, and others. We also remember Mary and Martha, who supported the ministry of Jesus, adhering to faith in Jesus' Word and work.

Further, we may say, "Remember Pilate's wife!" She urged her husband not to "have anything to do with that innocent man" (Matthew 27:19). Tradition has it that she became a Christian. If she did, you can be sure that she gave up many things: her social position, political advantage, financial resources. She would have taken losses for such a gain.

Jesus is our priceless treasure. May we always remain faithful to Him regardless the cost!

PRAYER SUGGESTION

Pray that the Spirit of God enables you, through the Gospel and the power of your Baptism, to find your highest good in Jesus.

Cause or Effect?

Then Jesus said to her, "Your sins are forgiven." Luke 7:48

An all-important point is brought up in Jesus' words to the woman who anointed His feet: Is her act of love the cause or the effect of God's forgiveness of her sins?

If the *cause*, then salvation can be said to depend on the loving works a person does. But if it is the *effect*, then all the emphasis is on God's prior act of forgiveness by grace, for Christ's sake, through faith. Then our love is the result of God's great love to us in Christ, as the apostle wrote, "We love because He first loved us" (1 John 4:19).

Forgiveness is ours by God's "*grace* ... this not from yourselves, it is the gift of God—not by works, so that no one can boast" (Ephesians 2:8–9).

Forgiveness is ours because of Christ's atoning work—for His sake, in other words. All "are justified [declared just by God] freely by His grace through the redemption that came by Christ Jesus" (Romans 3:24).

Forgiveness is ours through *faith*, faith being the hand that accepts Christ's merit and makes it its own: "We maintain that a man is justified by faith apart from observing the Law" (Romans 3:28).

Saved by amazing grace, for the sake of Christ, through faith—that is what the Gospel is all about. Jesus, the true substance of the Gospel, showed on many occasions that He was a master teacher in applying this grace after the Law had done its work.

PRAYER SUGGESTION

Pray to the Holy Spirit to lead you into all truth so you may firmly believe in Christ as your Savior and find joy in following Him.

Lift up the Cross

Carrying His own cross, [Jesus] went out to the place of the Skull.
John 19:17

One of the best-known photographs from World War II shows the United States Marines raising the flag on Mount Suribachi in the Pacific on February 23, 1945.

Another mount on which something of the highest significance was raised was the place of the Skull, or Mount Calvary. Lifted up there was the cross. On that cross our Lord was nailed, not for crimes He had committed but for the sins of the whole world. He was the Lamb who was sacrificed for the sins of all.

What shall we do with Christ's cross raised on Good Friday? Representations of it have appeared on countless church altars and lifted high on steeples. It appears in artwork that hangs on walls in places of worship, education and business, and in homes. Crosses are worn as jewelry or woven into clothing as well.

The cross symbolizes that out of the curse of sin has come the love of God in surrendering His own dear Son to save us. Flags are raised in every battle, but Christ's cross needed raising only once, for "we have been made holy through the sacrifice of the body of Jesus Christ once for all" (Hebrews 10:10).

The cross is a symbol of great relevance to Christians. Our Savior calls on us to carry our personal crosses as we follow Him. That is what we are doing as His disciples. Furthermore, we raise Christ's cross as we spread His gospel everywhere—on mountaintops, in the valleys, on the plains. In the words of the well-known hymn, we encourage one another to "Lift high the cross, the love of Christ proclaim Till all the world adore His sacred name."

PRAYER SUGGESTION

Ask your loving Savior to enable you to continue raising His cross wherever you live and work.

One Way of Salvation

We maintain that a man is justified by faith
apart from observing the Law. Romans 3:28

When someone presents opposite points of view, he may say, "On the one hand ..." then say, "On the other hand... ."

There are many times that two viewpoints are appropriate—economic theory, politics, court—but the Christian religion is not one of them. True, there are things the Bible neither commands nor forbids, and in those areas we have freedom of choice. A case in point is the worship service. God does not prescribe an exact order of worship, but He does want us to exercise good judgment.

What are areas of doctrine where God speaks plainly and leaves no room for choice? We know, for example, what Holy Scripture teaches concerning the second Person of the Trinity. Jesus is the Christ, the Son of God, true God and true man. One cannot say that He was a mere human of great moral principles and nothing more.

What about the way of salvation? Can one say yes to St. Paul's statement: "Since we have been justified through faith, we have peace with God through our Lord Jesus Christ" (Romans 5:1) and add to it that we are justified (fully or in part) by good works? People in Galatia did this when they advocated a "both-and" Christianity, that is: "We are saved by *both* faith *and* good works or the deeds of the Law, such as circumcision." But this philosophy is works-righteousness and has no place in Christian beliefs.

How thankful we can be that salvation, forgiveness, and peace with God do not rest on what we are able to do but are entirely the work of Christ!

PRAYER SUGGESTION

Give thanks to God for having spoken clearly through the prophets and apostles in matters of faith.

The Folly of Sin, the Wisdom of Faith

"The ox knows his master, the donkey his owner's manger,
but Israel does not know, My people do not understand." Isaiah 1:3

A bird known as the shearwater was taken by plane from England to Boston, where it was released. It knew how to find its way back; after 12 days it was back in its nest in England.

The prophet Isaiah commented on animal instinct. We sometimes speak of horse sense. This is because in days past, horses were known to find the way home even under cover of darkest night, in heavy snow, or in dense fog when landmarks were obscured and riders could not find the way.

How do we explain that human beings, endowed with a mind and everything that goes with it—reason, judgment, intelligence, memory—sometimes sink below base animal instinct? Why should people so deprive themselves of good sense as to stagger from one sin to another, becoming so lost that they must ask others to show them the way home (not only their earthly home but their heavenly one as well)?

God tells the reason for human folly: "Ah, sinful nation, a people loaded with guilt, a brood of evildoers, children given to corruption!" (Isaiah 1:4). All this comes about when people "have forsaken the LORD, ... spurned the Holy One, ... turned their backs on Him" (Isaiah 1:4).

Because of the foolishness of the human race, God in His mercy sent His Son to redeem us from the folly, fallacy, and fault of sin. This Jesus Christ, in the words of Paul, "has become for us wisdom from God—that is, our righteousness, holiness and redemption" (1 Corinthians 1:30).

PRAYER SUGGESTION

Ask the Holy Spirit to grant you the wisdom and knowledge to be a true disciple of Jesus.

The River of Salvation

You give them drink from Your river of delights. Psalm 36:8

Rivers have played a significant part in the history of humankind. They supply water for transportation, irrigation, drinking. For some, as poet Langston Hughes stated in *The Negro Speaks of Rivers,* "water symbolizes freedom, justice, and power."

The River Jordan is frequently mentioned in the Bible. John the Baptist used its water to baptize people, including his own cousin, Jesus of Nazareth. John's baptism was temporary and was replaced by the Baptism Jesus instituted in the name of the Triune God.

Baptism is a means of grace, a sacrament. As such it offers, transmits, and seals all that Jesus earned for us as our Savior: forgiveness of sins and eternal salvation. One could say, to use Hughes's expression, that Baptism brings freedom from sin, justice (or righteousness in God's sight), and power to lead a Christian life. God's grace is abundant, like the water in a flowing river. Through the faith created and confirmed in Holy Baptism we are spiritually refreshed.

By itself, water, whether applied by pouring, washing, sprinkling, or immersing, does not have the power to wash away sin and produce faith. The power to do this rests in the Word of Christ and the power of the Holy Spirit.

We can rejoice in our Baptism daily and rise to the newness of life in Jesus Christ, the risen One. We thank our Lord for making us His own through the Sacrament He instituted.

PRAYER SUGGESTION

Ask the Holy Spirit's help so you can honor and keep your baptism covenant with the Triune God.

Childhood Memories

"Train a child in the way he should go, and when he is old he will not turn from it." Proverbs 22:6

A song has it, "How dear to my heart are the scenes of my childhood, When fond recollection presents them to me." The events of childhood are long remembered.

Because young minds and memories are so receptive and retentive, youth is an ideal time for Christian teaching. In Christian homes and schools, character building goes hand in hand with nurturing the Christian faith. Christian living is a fruit of faith inculcated from God's Word. Paul reminded Timothy, "From infancy you have known the Holy Scriptures, which are able to make you wise for salvation through faith in Christ Jesus" (2 Timothy 3:15).

Through Holy Baptism we bring our children to Jesus Christ, their Savior. The faith engendered in this sacrament is nurtured through the teaching of God's Word, first the simple scriptural truths, comparable to milk, then with doctrine, the meat and potatoes of our spiritual diet.

Many grown-up Christians confess that they found delight in their childhood because they had come to know Jesus, the children's Friend. He bore all their sins and griefs and through His promises of new life and of the eternal life to come brought them happiness. These pleasant memories bespeak thankfulness to their Christian parents as well.

"Oh, blest that house; it prospers well! In peace and joy the parents dwell, And in their children's lives is shown How richly God can bless His own."

PRAYER SUGGESTION

Give thanks for your Christian education and pray to the Lord Jesus to nurture you in the faith.

Counting the Cost

"Anyone who does not carry his cross and follow Me cannot be My disciple." Luke 14:27

When the *Titanic* sank in the north Atlantic on April 15, 1912, it carried 2,200 passengers but had lifeboats for only 800. What miscalculation!

Jesus set the record straight with regard to calculating the cost of discipleship. Following Him is no picnic. It means loving Him more than one loves members of the family. It means receiving the same kind of hatred, contempt, and physical abuse heaped on Him.

Jesus cites cases of miscalculation—a man who had miscalculated the cost of building a tower and a king who underestimated the cost of a military campaign. Serious financial losses as well as ridicule followed. Jesus set the price of following Him high: "Any of you who does not give up everything he has cannot be My disciple" (Luke 14:33).

Jesus counted Himself in the cost of His redemptive ministry. Prior to His arrest in Jerusalem, He announced that He would be mocked, flogged, and crucified, adding, "On the third day He will be raised to life!" (Matthew 17:23). The outcome—Christ's resurrection and our guaranteed salvation—made the sacrifices worthwhile.

How thankful we are that Christ did not use *Titanic* arithmetic in providing salvation for only a few! St. Paul wrote to the Corinthians, "He died for all, that those who live should no longer live for themselves but for Him who died for them and was raised again" (2 Corinthians 5:15). We have no problem now in counting the cost of discipleship. We count it a privilege.

PRAYER SUGGESTION

Pray that the Holy Spirit may enable you to count purpose, meaning, and joy in the cost of your discipleship to Jesus Christ.

Set Free from Sin and Satan

Jesus was driving out a demon that was mute. Luke 11:14

In *The Phantom of the Opera,* a hideously deformed man lives under the stage of a Paris opera house and harasses the performers. He excludes only Christine, a young soprano in the opera company, with whom he is in love.

In Jesus' time, people were harassed by demons; our Lord drove out many of them. In a parable, He stressed the need of the liberated person to make sure that the ousted evil spirit cannot re-enter him. If the demon returned, he would bring others with him. Who are these demons? Jesus didn't say, perhaps they were "demon rum," drugs, sexual immorality, and other evils Jesus mentioned in Matthew 15:19. These demons, if "personalized," can destroy a person and can make the human heart a home base from which to operate as they seek to destroy others.

Many a talented person is kept from achieving his goals because he is heavily influenced by evil forces. But once Jesus sets him free from sin and Satan, the freed person can be assured that the door to his heart remains sealed to these unwelcome forces.

How important that we take these words of Jesus to heart: "Blessed rather are those who hear the Word of God and obey it" (Luke 11:28). Yes, blessed are all who believe in Jesus Christ, for He loves us so much that He laid down His life for our salvation. When Jesus is our abiding Friend, there is no room for demons in our hearts and minds. What blessed deliverance! Our Lord has set us free from sin and Satan!

PRAYER SUGGESTION

Give thanks to Jesus for redeeming you, asking His help so you can remain free.

True Freedom: God's Free Gift

You have been set free from sin and have become slaves
to righteousness. Romans 6:18

Before slaves in the United States were freed, many tried to escape. For example, Henry "Box" Brown had himself packed into a crate and shipped from Richmond to Philadelphia. Regardless of the means, escapees were never assured of freedom.

Through Adam and Eve we became the slaves of sin. All their descendants live with the same insecurity: complete freedom from sin cannot be achieved by what is done or undone. Even a man such as Saul, a Pharisee, could not break free from sin. He told the Philippians that he kept all the rules of the Pharisees and achieved a legalistic righteousness that was faultless. But he was not faultless in the sight of God. Later, as St. Paul the apostle, he understood true freedom from the slavery of sin and from the fear of death. It was the gift of God's free grace. Christ had fully and effectively set him free, for "God made Him who had no sin to be sin for us" (2 Corinthians 5:21).

Now we are free as well. But we do not live in a vacuum. We are free not only *from* something but *for* something. By faith in Christ we are declared righteous. This means all our sins are forgiven. We are a new creation in Christ, and consequently we are willing to serve Him by doing the works of righteousness.

This is the only way to be free. Trying to run and hide from God won't work. Trying to earn our own righteousness is out of the question—we could never be assured of real freedom. But how different it is to have our emancipation proclaimed and effected by God Himself! On this freedom alone can we rely!

PRAYER SUGGESTION

Tell the Lord Jesus that you gladly enlist in His service, for in Him you have received the righteousness that God accepts.

God's Word, a Power in Today's World

I am not ashamed of the Gospel, because it is the power of God for the salvation of everyone who believes. Romans 1:16

A sociology researcher at Penn State University said, "Today there are no boundaries. Nothing is forbidden. Television emphasizes the deviant so that it becomes normal."

This trend, accelerated by the misuse of the invention, dates to where God established a boundary for obedience: "You are free to eat from any tree in the garden, but you must not eat from the tree of the knowledge of good and evil" (Genesis 2:16–17).

The Lord's words were perfectly clear and Adam understood their meaning. But along came Satan to obscure the boundary. He convinced Eve, who persuaded Adam, that their choice should not be restricted. By obeying Satan rather than God, our first parents declared: "We are free to do as we please; we have the right ..."

The media opens the door wider still to sinful license. Television is blamed for making deviant behavior seem acceptable. People who defend this are advised to give equal time to what Holy Scripture says. In his letter to the church in Rome, St. Paul traced the growth of moral degeneration. He declared that persistent disobedience led to divine judgment. God "gave them over" to deviant behavior—to idolatry and sexual perversion (Romans 1:24).

But the apostle did not give up. He confidently declared the power of the Gospel in bringing salvation to all who believe. The Word of God points to Jesus Christ as having obediently fulfilled all righteousness for us and as having suffered death on the cross for our redemption. Now we are willing and able to live to the glory of God, always in conformity to His holy will.

PRAYER SUGGESTION

Pray that God, for Jesus' sake, will through the Gospel give you the strength to live as becomes His people.

Getting to Know Jesus Better

O Hope of Israel, its Savior in time of distress, why are you like a stranger in the land, like a traveler who stays only a night?
Jeremiah 14:8

A newspaper columnist, having delivered an address at a social function, was on his way home on the train. He was surprised that some of the passengers called him by name. Had he become a celebrity? When he got home, he discovered that he had forgotten to remove his nametag.

Jesus wore a nametag. The tag told who He was: "the King of the Jews." One might wonder why this identification was necessary. Was Jesus not well known after raising Lazarus from the dead? Did He not ride into Jerusalem amid public acclaim? Was not the whole city stirred up because of His arrest, arraignments before the Sanhedrin and Pontius Pilate, and the noisy procession to Mount Calvary?

What we have here is a paradox, a yes-and-no situation. Yes, many in Jerusalem recognized Jesus, but they really didn't *know* Him. To some He was an impostor, a troublemaker, or a mere teacher and would-be healer. To a relatively few was the Messiah and Son of God revealed. As for the majority, this was true, as St. John wrote, "He was in the world, and though the world was made through Him, the world did not recognize Him" (John 1:10). He remained a stranger and a traveler just passing through.

So the nametag on the cross was necessary. It was also truthful. The label upheld Jesus' testimony before Pilate, "You are right in saying I am a king" (John 18:37). Our Lord is indeed our true Messiah and King. And since He is, we are happy to know Him through Word and sacraments.

PRAYER SUGGESTION

Implore the Holy Spirit to reveal Christ Jesus more clearly to you as you study God's Word.

A Wind-Resisting House

The winds blew and beat against that house; yet it did not fall.
Matthew 7:25

While Margaret Mitchell was writing *Gone with the Wind,* she and her husband lived in a ground-level apartment her husband called "The Dump." (At that, this Atlanta, Georgia, apartment was much better than the borrowed stable where Jesus was born.)

"Be it ever so humble, there's no place like home," wrote John Howard Payne in "Home, Sweet Home." What keeps a house from becoming a dump? The character of the people living in it makes all the difference. The home of Joshua, an Israelite leader, was blessed because the head of it resolved, "As for me and my household, we will serve the Lord" (Joshua 24:15).

The beauty of Christian homes today, from humble cottages to pretentious palaces, does not lie in the location, architecture, or furnishings, but in the exercise of faith in Jesus Christ. We sing: "Oh, blest the house, whate'er befall Where Jesus Christ is all in all."

The Christian home is a hall of mirrors reflecting the love and forgiveness that Jesus procured by His sacrifice on the cross and His rising from the tomb. The apostle Paul wrote, "Be kind and compassionate to one another, forgiving each other, just as in Christ God forgave you" (Ephesians 4:32).

Christian homes, however humble, will stand long after mansions built on greed have been blown away by the winds of change and decay. This is a good time to ask ourselves: In what kind of home do we live? Is it, thanks to Christ's presence, a place where we can prepare for the Father's house of many rooms?

PRAYER SUGGESTION

Give thanks to God for homes throughout the world that are based on the words of Jesus and on His redeeming work.

The Burden of Unbelief

Who has believed our message and to whom has the arm of the LORD been revealed? Isaiah 53:1

In Greek mythology, Apollo gave Cassandra the gift of prophecy. When she disobeyed him, he ordained that she would continue to prophesy but that nobody would believe her. You may have experienced instances when you knew you were telling the truth but others didn't believe you. Isaiah knew what that was like. When he spoke God's Word about the Messiah, he wondered who believed him.

Certainly Jesus encountered rock-hard unbelief. There was the time that even His own people in Nazareth refused to believe He was the Messiah (Luke 4:16–30). People who were mourning at the home of Jairus laughed scornfully at Him although He raised Jairus's daughter from the dead (Matthew 9:23–26). And to Nicodemus Jesus said, "I have spoken to you of earthly things and you do not believe; how then will you believe if I speak of heavenly things?" (John 3:12).

Throughout His ministry, Jesus was met with unbelief. At the end of His time on earth, He was rejected by His followers, betrayed by own His disciples, and forsaken by all of them.

Christ suffered especially on Good Friday when people rejected His message. Every step of the road to Calvary was paved with unbelief. He confessed before high priest and council that He was the Christ, the Son of the Highest, and before Pilate He testified to the truth of His spiritual kingdom—but no one would believe Him. For every Christian since, it comes down to this: Do we believe it? God grant that we do!

PRAYER SUGGESTION

Give thanks to Jesus for speaking the truth and to His Spirit for leading you to believe it.

The Dimensions of Christ's Love

To grasp how wide and long and high and deep is the love of Christ.
Ephesians 3:18

When Marco Polo returned to Venice after traveling to the Far East, he astounded the Europeans with descriptions of what he saw, including his claim that China's Yangtze River was so wide in places that he could not see the opposite shore.

Sometimes our troubles seem like that—too wide, too long, and too deep to see the other side. The Bible tells of people who were inundated by troubles. Job, for example, knew such afflictions. When troubles befall us, we can recall the perseverance of Job and we can take comfort that "the Lord is full of compassion and mercy" (James 5:11).

We can also draw strength from the power that exceeds the pressure of all earthly affliction: God's love for us in Christ. We can sing, "Oh, the height of Jesus' love, Higher than the heav'ns above, Deeper than the depth of sea, Lasting to eternity! Love that found me—wondrous thought—Found me when I sought Him not."

This truth is based on the testimony of one who was found by Jesus, although he was not seeking Him. Paul knew firsthand the dimensions of Christ's love. He wrote that we may try to grasp its dimensions, but Christ's love for us is beyond our comprehension. It is a love that "surpasses knowledge" (Ephesians 3:19). In Christ "we have redemption through His blood, the forgiveness of sins, in accordance with the riches of God's grace" (Ephesians 1:7).

Yes, Christ's love is beyond comprehension. Like the Yangtze, it is so wide, so long, so deep that we cannot take it all in. This is a reality that we gratefully accept in faith, thanks to the working of the Holy Spirit.

PRAYER SUGGESTION

Give thanks and praise to your Savior for His boundless love.

Slaying with the Tongue

Come, let's attack him [Jeremiah] with our tongues and pay no attention to anything he says. Jeremiah 18:18

The Olympics in Sarajevo contrasted with another international event that occurred there. In 1914 Francis Ferdinand, archduke of Austria, and his wife were murdered in Sarajevo, an act that precipitated World War I. Throughout the rest of the world, assassin Gavrilo Princip was regarded as a villain; but in Sarajevo he was hailed as a hero and a statue was erected in his honor.

Jeremiah's enemies carried out a different kind of assassination. These inhabitants of Judea and Jerusalem resented the prophet's message from God and decided, therefore, to destroy the messenger with slander and threats.

So much more so than Jeremiah, Jesus was the victim of character assassination. Amid lies and deceit, the King of kings was betrayed into enemy hands. The assassin did not use a sword to deliver Jesus to His death. He attacked Jesus with the tongue when he asked the authorities, "What are you willing to give me if I hand Him over to you?" (Matthew 26:15).

One might think that Christ's killers would have deemed Judas a hero for turning over Jesus to them. But they didn't. To them, Judas was a disposable tool that was cast away after the job was done. Their words to him when he tried to return the 30 pieces of silver showed their contempt for him. Even if there were statues in Jerusalem, Judas would never have rated one.

People today continue to attack Jesus with the tongue, and whenever they do, they crucify Him anew. In contrast, Christians "call on [Jesus] in every trouble, pray, praise, and give thanks."

PRAYER SUGGESTION

Express your gratitude to the Lord Jesus for having endured all insults and injuries for your salvation.

Be a Blessing Where You Are!

As they [those blessed by God] pass through the Valley of Baca,
they make it a place of springs. Psalm 84:6

Stations built along an early railroad in British Columbia were
named Portia, Lear, Romeo, Juliet, and the like because Andrew
McCulloch, the chief engineer, liked Shakespeare. In the evenings
he would recite the bard's writings to railroad workers in their
camps. It was a cultural treat in wilderness country.

God's people are an influence for good where they live and
work—and wherever they travel. The writer of Psalm 84 visualized
them and their doings as fresh water in a desert. The Israelites,
including Jesus, would travel to Jerusalem three times a year for
the major festivals. These trips can be compared to our life's journey to the house of the Lord—both the church we attend here and
God's house in heaven.

Because Christians have peace with God through the merit
and mediation of Jesus Christ, they not only receive rich blessings
from God but they *become* a blessing. Christians are comforters, to
one another and to mankind as a whole. In the valleys of mental
and spiritual depression, Christians become springs of fresh water;
they share the Word of God, the water of life.

Andrew McCulloch brought Shakespeare and a bit of culture
into unsettled country. Think what our world would be like if
every Christian were similarly enthused about sharing Jesus Christ
and His Gospel of salvation! Then the "Valley of Baca" throughout
the world becomes a spiritual garden. We can help this to happen
today—speak a kind word, do someone a favor, say a prayer of
intercession—to brighten the valley where we are.

PRAYER SUGGESTION

Pray that God leads you to someone with whom you can share the
Gospel of Christ.

Achieving Tongue Control

Consider what a great forest is set on fire by a small spark. The tongue also is a fire, a world of evil among the parts of the body. James 3:5–6

The word "curfew" has interesting roots. Today it means that people should be off the streets at a certain hour. In Europe, long ago, it meant to cover the fire—from the French *covrir,* to cover, and *feu,* fire. At a designated hour, people were to go indoors, cover the hearth fires, and go to bed.

Uncontrolled fire can destroy everything in its path. In our spiritual lives as well, little sparks can set off huge fires. St. James spoke of the destructive force of peoples' tongues. Although it is a small part of the body, the tongue can do much evil: it "corrupts the whole person [and] sets the whole course of his life on fire" (James 3:6). Both the innocent and the guilty suffer—the intended victims, their families and friends, and those with evil words.

We have the example of Jesus, who guarded His tongue, especially during His trial: "When they hurled their insults at Him, He did not retaliate; when He suffered, He made no threats" (1 Peter 2:23). When the truth was at stake, however, He readily testified before the Sanhedrin and before Pontius Pilate.

The example of Jesus would be of little benefit if we didn't have the motivation and might to use our tongues aright. Thank God that we do have the desire and power to do so, for the Holy Spirit gives us this desire through our faith in Jesus' redeeming merit. Our hearts are changed. Evil desires, so often expressed in hateful words, yield to love. And we seek to bank the fires of evil desires in our hearts. It is a spiritual curfew.

PRAYER SUGGESTION

Ask the Lord Jesus to make you willing and able to speak only the truth in all of life's situations.

In the Footsteps of the Servant

[He] made Himself nothing, taking the very nature of a servant.
Philippians 2:7

After John Quincy Adams left the presidency, he served 18 years with distinction in the House of Representatives. An ardent Christian and public servant, he was willing to continue serving his country after leaving the country's highest-ranking office. He didn't consider it a demotion to move to a lower position.

Christ's followers are willing to serve even when it means social or financial setback. Would two brothers who ran a successful business willingly take non-paying jobs? James and John did. Would a rich tax collector take an assignment that offered no income? Matthew did. Would the wife of the manager of a king's household sacrifice her position to serve a pauper? Joanna did. Would a brilliant, ambitious student leave his distinguished mentor to become an itinerant preacher? Paul did.

For centuries Christians have taken a demotion to live as servants. This is following in Jesus' footsteps. As Paul said, "He humbled Himself and became obedient to death—even death on a cross!" (Philippians 2:8). The humiliation of Jesus was ultimate servanthood.

But Jesus is more than an example to us, He is also our equipper. Through the Holy Spirit, He gives us gifts and abilities to fulfill God's will. He made us the recipients of all God's spiritual blessings: reconciliation and peace, forgiveness and life eternal. And as the beneficiaries of the fullness of divine grace, we are deeply moved. In Martin Luther's words, "that I may be His own, and live under Him in His kingdom, and serve Him in everlasting righteousness, innocence, and blessedness."

PRAYER SUGGESTION

Say to the Lord Jesus that you are unspeakably thankful for your salvation and that you will gladly be His disciple and servant.

Healing for Broken Families

All this is from God, who reconciled us to Himself through Christ and gave us the ministry of reconciliation. 2 Corinthians 5:18

The U.S. Civil War certainly was not civil. Adding to the misery was the hatred and heartache that destroyed relationships. This situation affected many families, even the nation's first family. Mary Todd, wife of the Northern President Lincoln, had one brother and three half-brothers who fought for the South. It took a lot of healing to reunite the remnants of war-torn families.

Family divisions occur over wars, politics, money, power, or property, and also over religion. Our Lord said: "I did not come to bring peace, but a sword" (Matthew 10:34). Then quoting from the prophet Micah, He said: "I have come to turn 'a man against his father, a daughter against her mother, a daughter-in-law against her mother-in-law—a man's enemies will be the members of his own household'" (Matthew 10:35–36).

The rejection of Jesus Christ as God's Son and the Savior of sinners brings such tensions into the home, the family, the larger relationship. That, of course, is not our Lord's fault, nor that of those faithful to Him. Jesus is the great peacemaker. He wants to reconcile people to one another and to "reconcile both of them to God through the cross, by which He put to death their hostility" (Ephesians 2:16).

At the foot of Christ's cross, people of faith can lay aside their differences and become one family of God. Bitterness, anger, slander, and malice, said the apostle, are gone. Love builds bridges. "Be kind and compassionate to one another, forgiving each other, just as in Christ God forgave you" (Ephesians 4:32).

PRAYER SUGGESTION

Ask that Christ's peace may keep your family united in love and in the common bond of faith in Him.

God Watches over Us

The LORD will watch over your coming and going both now and forevermore. Psalm 121:8

Legend has it that on March 19, the swallows return to San Juan Capistrano, an old Spanish mission in southern California. The birds spend winters elsewhere and return home each spring. For some, the departure of the swallows is a sad event.

People may be saddened by the passing of other things—fading flowers, falling leaves, harvested fields. It hurts when dear friends depart or when their love turns cold. Some parents suffer from "empty-nest syndrome," forgetting that it is proper for children to grow up and strike out on their own.

Another cause of distress may be our own need to leave the familiar and embark on new endeavors. Employment opportunities may call for a move that causes anxiety. Young people going to college can become disconcerted. Persons who cannot care for themselves may be bewildered by a move to a care facility. At such times, people may feel that friends and family have left them like the swallows leave San Juan Capistrano.

Whatever the situation in which God's people find themselves, one thing is sure: God is with them and remembers them. Psalm 121 is a beautiful reminder of God's promise to watch over us.

Our divine Maker and Preserver is also our Redeemer in Christ Jesus, our Savior. God sent His beloved Son into the world to redeem all its inhabitants *from* sin and the fear of death. He also redeemed them *for* something—for a purposeful life here and now and for eternal life. So when the swallows leave us and we see change all around, we can be assured of God's unchanging love for us and His constant presence with us.

PRAYER SUGGESTION

Say a prayer along the lines of the hymn, "Abide with Me."

People Are Worth Saving

Whoever turns a sinner from the error of his way will save him from death and cover over a multitude of sins. James 5:20

Abortion, stem cell research, euthanasia, life support. Medical ethics are hot topics. When asked whether measures should be taken to lengthen human lives, world-renowned physician Dr. Michael DeBakey replied, "It will be most unfortunate if we ever decide that a human life is not worth saving."

Physical health is closely related to *mental* and *spiritual* well-being—this because of the close union of a person's body, mind, and soul. This truth is reflected throughout Holy Scripture. St. James, well acquainted with all aspects of human nature, declared, "Is any one of you sick? He should call the elders of the church to pray over him and anoint him with oil in the name of the Lord" (James 5:14). Prayers of faith go well with basic remedies.

James referred to saving sinners by using the means God puts at our disposal for this very purpose: the Law, the Gospel, the sacraments. He urged that Christian admonition be always spoken in love. He referred to the reality of sin—how temptations lead us into sin and how sin then grows: "Sin, when it is full-grown, gives birth to death" (James 1:15).

But God does not want sinners to die; He wants them to live. To this end He sent the Lord Jesus Christ into the world to die for the sins of all. The Savior's blood covers all sin.

When we speak God's truths to wayward people, we are throwing them a lifeline, God's own life-support system. We are showing our love for our Lord when we deem highly the people for whom Christ died and work toward their total well-being.

PRAYER SUGGESTION

Give thanks to God for every sinner who repents and believes in Jesus as Savior.

A Change of Vocations

"Come, follow Me," Jesus said, "and I will make you fishers of men."
Mark 1:17

Sometimes changing vocations is for the better. Case in point: John Newton, author of "Amazing Grace" and other hymns, was a pastor. But before that he engaged in African slave trade. All vocational changes involving Christians, while perhaps not as dramatic as Newton's, are nevertheless significant. Take brothers Peter and Andrew and James and John, who were fishermen. Our Lord recruited them for a new vocation—fishers of people. Their net for catching people for Jesus was His Gospel.

After Christ's ascension and the outpouring of the Holy Spirit at Pentecost 10 days later, the apostles became full-time missionaries. Their vocation then was to be Christ's witnesses to the world, testifying that salvation from sin and death is found only in the crucified and risen Christ.

Some Christians in our time also feel called to leave what they are doing—to quit their day jobs—so they can concentrate all their energies on missions. They become full-time fishers of people. But it is not our Lord's will that we all do this. Some of Christ's disciples continue in their roles as fishermen, farmers, mechanics, business executives, teachers, nurses, secretaries, and housewives. In so doing, we fulfill the overall Christian vocation of being Christ's witnesses wherever we live and work. We are followers of Jesus, serving Him by serving our fellow human beings and helping to build His kingdom from our particular vantage points. We, too, are "fishers of men."

PRAYER SUGGESTION

Pray that Christian missionaries throughout the world may win many souls for Christ, the world's Savior.

Meeting Jesus on the Road

A very large crowd spread their cloaks on the road, while others cut branches from the trees and spread them on the road. Matthew 21:8

Jesus met many people on the road: beggars, parents pleading for His healing of their sick children, prospective disciples. It was enthusiastic followers such as these who decorated the road to Jerusalem with cloaks and branches.

The invitation is also extended to us, in the words of the hymn: "Come, let us meet Him on the road And a place for Him prepare." The Lord of Palm Sunday and Easter is on His way, and in spirit we go forth to meet Him on the road.

After he met Jesus on the road to Damascus, Saul the Pharisee became a chief proclaimer of the very faith he had set out to destroy. What a blessing to the world the apostle Paul became after Jesus met him on the road! When Paul approached Rome, he was met by Christians who came from the city "as far as the Forum of Appius and the Three Taverns" (Acts 28:15). Another "road experience" happened near Jerusalem after the Resurrection. It involved Cleopas and his friend, who were joined by the Stranger as they walked. The men said later, "Were not our hearts burning within us while He talked with us on the road and opened the Scriptures to us?" (Luke 24:32).

Let us go forth in faith as we travel the road of life. He who travels with us on this journey is the Way, the Truth, and the Life— the only road to the heavenly Father.

PRAYER SUGGESTION

Ask the Savior to accompany you on all journeys you must make, especially on the one great journey that is your life.

Spiritual Riches

"Blessed are you who are poor, for yours is the kingdom of God."
Luke 6:20

After the 1849 discovery of gold in California, there was a great exodus westward. During the long, hazardous trek to dreamed-of fortune, prospectors made many choices. One was at a place called California Junction. There were two signs. One said, "To Oregon." The other, attached to rocks painted golden, said, "To California." The majority followed the latter sign.

Jesus was well aware of the sin of covetousness and spoke about it many times. During the Sermon on the Plain (Luke 6:20–49), He "stood on a level place," where, so to speak, He leveled with His hearers on many topics of everyday living, including wealth. He opened with the beatitude, "Blessed are the poor in spirit" (Matthew 5:3).

Our Lord was saying, in effect, that spiritual poverty brings great riches: the kingdom of God. Spiritual poverty means having no great works to show, no high standing, no merit of which to boast. It is, however, a poverty that is rich in faith that looks to Jesus Christ for salvation, rich in repentance and its fruits. In the temple, the boasting Pharisee was a spiritual pauper, but the publican, who said, "God, have mercy on me, a sinner" (Luke 18:13), was spiritually rich. He "went home justified before God" (Luke 18:14).

Jesus' disciples had forsaken all and followed Jesus. They were physically poor, but in Jesus they were rich in the forgiveness of sins and they had peace with God. St. Paul wrote, "the kingdom of God is ... righteousness, peace and joy in the Holy Spirit" (Romans 14:17). God grant that we can say "Amen!" to this.

PRAYER SUGGESTION

Ask the Holy Spirit that you may be enriched in all spiritual treasures: forgiveness, the fruit of the Spirit, the promise of eternal life.

Christ, the Bedrock of Faith

No one can lay any foundation other than the one already laid, which is Jesus Christ. 1 Corinthians 3:11

In the mid 1800s, engineers knew that building a bridge across the Mississippi River would be difficult due to the unstable riverbed. James B. Eads overcame this problem when he sank granite piers all the way to the bedrock, as far as 90 feet down. Eads Bridge is still in use.

Faith in Christ can be compared to a bridge in that it would be very unstable if built on the shifting sand of human opinion. No one realized this more than the apostle Paul. He called himself a master builder because, at his conversion, he came to realize that Jesus Christ was the only solid rock on which to build the church. The other apostles taught the same. Peter, quoting Isaiah concerning the "chosen and precious cornerstone" (1 Peter 2:6), added his own testimony: "To you who believe, this Stone is precious" (1 Peter 2:7). Peter was a good witness. He confessed in the presence of the Lord, "You are the Christ, the Son of the living God" (Matthew 16:16). And in his epistle to the church in Corinth, he explained why Christ is the basis of our faith: He redeemed us, not with perishable things like silver and gold, but with His precious blood as the Lamb of God (1 Peter 1:18–19).

Holy Scripture bears witness to the certainty of our faith because Jesus Christ is its sure foundation due to His redeeming sacrifice and resurrection from the dead. The bridge to God is secure because it rests not on the shifting sand of a riverbed but on the solid rock of God's own promise. We can trust in Christ as the only bridge to the Father.

PRAYER SUGGESTION

Give thanks to the Holy Spirit for His assurance through the Gospel that Jesus Christ is the solid Rock on which we stand.

Christ's Messengers on the Move

"Go into all the world and preach the Good News to all creation."
Mark 16:15

"Neither snow nor rain, nor gloom of night, stays these couriers from the swift completion of their appointed rounds." A motto of U.S. postal carriers, these words were originally spoken to describe the messengers of ancient Persia.

The couriers Christ sent out were His apostles. He told them, "You will be My witnesses in Jerusalem, and in all Judea and Samaria, and to the ends of the earth" (Acts 1:8). These emissaries would not have succeeded had they been "fair weather" witnesses. The fact is that these dedicated men, as even their enemies admitted, carried the message that turned the world upside down: the news of Christ's redeeming death and His resurrection.

A most important event in the conversion of the Gentile world was the apostleship of Paul. This messenger of Christ could truthfully say he worked harder than all of them. The exalted Christ called him directly: "This man is My chosen instrument to carry My name before the Gentiles and their kings and before the people of Israel" (Acts 9:15). Paul could not be stopped—not by imprisonment, beatings, stoning, shipwrecks, and other forms of persecution (2 Corinthians 11:23–29).

Nothing has changed. The Lord Jesus still sends His messengers into the world. Their mission hasn't changed. They are to tell everyone that Christ Jesus came into the world to save sinners from sin, death, and the devil. We are all participants in the church's mission. No rain, snow, nor gloom of night can keep us from completing our appointed assignment.

PRAYER SUGGESTION

Pray that the Lord Jesus will continue to send many messengers of God's saving grace into all the world.

The Practice of Continual Prayer

Be joyful always; pray continually; give thanks in all circumstances, for this is God's will for you in Christ Jesus. 1 Thessalonians 5:16–18

The saying goes, "If you fail to pray when the sun shines, you may not know how to pray when the clouds come."

Paul's urging that we "pray continually" does not call for all-day and all-night prayer marathons. We have to allow time for other things: eating, resting, sleeping, building relationships with one another. Besides, long-winded praying is beset by temptations, such as falling into thoughtlessness. Jesus tells us to avoid "babbling like pagans" (Matthew 6:7).

Paul meant that we can pray regularly and diligently on schedule (as we rise, eat, and go to sleep); we can also pray silently and spontaneously (as we work, shop, drive). And he said we are free to do this any time throughout the day.

Closely related to prayer, as St. Paul explained, is joyfulness, for from such a state of mind prayers of thanksgiving flow more readily. In all circumstances, thanksgiving is in order. It improves one's mood and, more important, it is God's will. God is pleased when His children, redeemed by Christ and reconciled to the Father through His death on the cross, come before Him with praise.

The habit of diligent prayer prepares us for times of trouble when prayer is especially needed. How sad the situation of King Saul when, filled with fear of the large Philistine army, "he inquired of the LORD, but the LORD did not answer him" (1 Samuel 28:6). It was too late. His unbelief and neglect of prayer took their toll.

God tells us to pray continually, while there is still time. Then we will also readily call upon Him in the day of trouble.

PRAYER SUGGESTION

Ask the Lord God to grant you His Holy Spirit so you may be enabled to pray faithfully in Jesus' name.

Healing Water

[God] saved us through the washing of rebirth and renewal by the Holy Spirit. Titus 3:5

Many city names include the word "Springs." People might visit Hot Springs or Eureka Springs in Arkansas, or Excelsior Springs in Missouri, to drink or bathe in the mineral water for physical healing.

Our Lord Jesus used water for spiritual healing when He instituted the Sacrament of Baptism. The Word and the waters of Baptism heal spiritually because the Holy Spirit works through it. It causes a sinner, even a very young one, to come to saving faith. In Baptism, the water and the Word flow like a refreshing, healing spring, bringing with it all that our Savior earned for us on the cross: forgiveness of sins, life, salvation, spiritual renewal.

Baptism is "the washing of rebirth and renewal by the Holy Spirit." For those who are Christians already, Baptism confirms faith, completing the new birth of which Jesus spoke to Nicodemus. What is this new birth? The Holy Spirit makes the baptized, believing person a new creation, yielding the fruit of the Spirit: love, joy, peace, patience, kindness, goodness, faithfulness, gentleness, self-control. The power of Baptism in fruitful living is depicted in the psalms, where the person who loves God's saving Word is compared to "a tree planted by streams of water, which yields its fruit in season" (Psalm 1:3).

When Saul the Pharisee was still suffering from the shock of his conversion at Damascus, the disciple Ananias laid his hands on him and baptized him. His baptism was definitely Christ's healing water for a spiritually sick man.

PRAYER SUGGESTION

Give thanks to the Triune God, into whose name you were baptized, for making you one of His beloved children.

Old Heresies in New Dress

Some of them went to the Pharisees and told them what Jesus had done. John 11:46

Someone said, "A great many people suppose they are thinking when they are really rearranging their prejudices."

Such "thinking" is mirrored in the hostility of the scribes and Pharisees toward Jesus. They disliked Him from the start because He threatened their position. The high priest Caiaphas said it openly, "If we let Him go like this, everyone will believe in Him, and then the Romans will come and take away both our place and our nation" (John 11:48).

Jesus' opponents rearranged their prejudices to suit their argument. When He forgave a man his sins, they said He was blaspheming for only God could forgive sins. When He cast out a demon, they said He was in league with Beelzebub. When He healed a man on the Sabbath, they accused Him of working on the Sabbath, a violation of the law. Before Pontius Pilate they expressed a whole new set of prejudices: "We have found this man subverting our nation. He opposes payment of taxes to Caesar and claims to be Christ, a king" (Luke 23:2).

In today's society, "new thinking" or "new religion" is often just a rearrangement of old prejudices against Christianity. Old heresies in a new dress. Christians today are criticized for the same things first-century opponents complained of: causing disunity in the nation, opposing lucrative but ungodly trends, neglecting the needs of life in this world for life in the world to come, and so on.

Christians will not rearrange their beliefs because of what the world says. They stand firmly with Jesus Christ and rely on His unchanging Word.

PRAYER SUGGESTION

Thank the Lord Jesus for His unchanging love for all mankind.

God's Deeds in Our Behalf

It will now be said of Jacob and of Israel, "See what God has done!"
Numbers 23:23

The first message sent via modern media was, "What hath God wrought!" Samuel Morse, inventor of the telegraph, used these words to acknowledge God's hand in the historic event.

Here is another example of God's hand in history: The book of Numbers records the efforts of Moabite King Balak to have a witch doctor stop the Israelites from entering his country on their way to the Promised Land. The witch doctor, Balaam, realized that God was blessing Israel and it was futile to put a curse on His children. Balaam even uttered a Messianic prophecy: "A Star will come out of ... Israel" (Numbers 24:17). Centuries later, the high priest Caiaphas condemned Jesus to die for the people (Mark 14:53–64). The evangelist John concurred that Jesus would die for all mankind (John 11:49–50).

Such passages prove that God lets nothing stand in the way of His will. He works through pious persons in government—Queen Esther in Persia and Daniel, the prime minister of Babylonia. Sometimes His power causes ungodly potentates to yield to Him. As necessary, the Lord declares His truths through unbelievers.

"What hath God wrought" has special meaning in our lives. His great deeds for our salvation are crowned with His Son, Jesus Christ, who lived a life of obedience for us, died for us, and rose from the dead for us as foretold. From the Father and the Son came the Holy Spirit to found the church and make us members of it by giving us saving faith. One divine promise remains: Christ's return in glory to take us home to the Father in heaven.

PRAYER SUGGESTION

Give thanks to God for having worked the wonders of His grace for your salvation in Christ Jesus.

The Mother Stood Her Ground

Near the cross of Jesus stood His mother. John 19:25

Indeed, Mary stood her ground. When she and Joseph found the 12-year-old Jesus in the temple after spending days searching for Him, Mary stood in amazement bordering on anger: "Son, why have you treated us like this?" (Luke 2:48).

Mary stood with anxiety in her heart as she observed Jesus in His ministry. "While Jesus was still talking to the crowd, His mother and brothers stood outside, wanting to speak to Him" (Matthew 12:46).

Mary stood at the cross, watching her son die. She had walked on the way of sorrows, the *via dolorosa,* to Calvary and saw that Jesus had been stripped of His clothes, beaten and bloodied, and nailed to the cross. There she heard her son's last words. She also heard the enemies ridicule Him. This day was most painful for her. The prophecy of aged Simeon at Jesus' presentation in the temple had come true: "A sword will pierce your own soul" (Luke 2:35).

Her son, God's Son, was dying. Who would redeem Israel and all mankind? What had become of the angel's words at the Annunciation: "He will be great and will be called the Son of the Most High" (Luke 1:35)? When next we read of her, she was in the upper room with the disciples, waiting, praying, and preparing for the coming of the promised Holy Spirit.

But *stabat mater*—Mary stood. She had faith that God would stand behind His promise to grant salvation through promised Christ. And so it is with us. We have our sorrows, but we stand certain in the promises of God.

PRAYER SUGGESTION

Ask Jesus to turn your pains and sorrows into joy because He lives.

Growth from Small Beginnings

He told them another parable:
"The kingdom of heaven is like a mustard seed." Matthew 13:31

Probably no two persons from the past would be more astounded than Wilbur and Orville Wright at the growth of the airplane industry. In 1903, these brothers were the first Americans to successfully fly a heavier-than-air craft powered by a motor. Few human enterprises have so phenomenal a growth.

The kingdom of heaven had a small beginning but phenomenal growth, like a tiny mustard seed growing into a large tree. At first, relatively few belonged to this kingdom—the early patriarchs, the poor in spirit, those who waited for the Messiah. Then Jesus came to change everything. He came to die for sinners. And, having completed this work, He rose from the dead and ascended into heaven. Then came the Holy Spirit, imparting great strength to the apostles. The converts in Jerusalem became the mother church of Christendom. (It should be noted that lay Christians played a great part in bringing the Gospel to all the world.)

At first Christians were persecuted but by the middle of the fourth century A.D., the Roman emperor, Constantine the First, professed the Christian faith. Through the centuries God has continued to lead many people into His church.

We can take the Teacher's lesson of the mustard seed into our daily lives and learn from it. Something we may be doing—starting a family, a new job, starting a Christian mission with only a handful of members—may have meager beginnings. But we have the right, on the basis of our Lord's promises, to trust that He will bless our efforts so even the tiniest of seeds will grow into trees.

PRAYER SUGGESTION

Ask the Holy Spirit to grant His blessing on the preaching of Christ's Gospel throughout the world.

The Unchanging Price

You are not your own; you were bought at a price.
Therefore honor God with your body. 1 Corinthians 6:19–20

Nathaniel Currier and James Ives made over 8,000 prints depicting life in the 1800s. They sold some of their pictures for five cents each. Now authentic original Currier and Ives prints may sell for $20,000 or more.

We have become accustomed to rising prices. There is, however, one price that remains constant: the price Jesus Christ paid for our redemption. That price cannot be reckoned in terms of gold or silver; it was—and still is—"the precious blood of Christ, a lamb without blemish or defect" (1 Peter 1:19).

The Son of God paid this price for each sinner—for one weak in faith (1 Corinthians 8:11) and one who is strong; for the penitent thief on the cross (Luke 23:43); for the Pharisee who became St. Paul (Galatians 2:20); even for Judas, the betrayer. The price was paid for every person in every land.

The price Jesus paid is not only unchanging, it is the same for every sinner. Unlike a Currier and Ives print, our worth in God's sight does not change. Small children are dear to the heart of Jesus, who receives and blesses them in Holy Baptism. When they grow older and become fathers and mothers, grandfathers and grandmothers, they are still of the same value.

"You are not your own." We belong to Christ, who bought us. We are mindful also of the cost of our redemption, prompting us to honor and serve God with our bodies, souls, and minds—our total selves. None of us, however old or weak, is worthless. Instead we put a high value on ourselves, for if we are precious in God's sight, we are precious indeed.

PRAYER SUGGESTION

Thank the Lord Jesus for having paid the price of your redemption.

The Voice of Conviction

"We cannot help speaking about what we have seen and heard."
Acts 4:20

Someone has written that the Old Testament prophets were "called by God and overcome by His Word." Jonah was a reluctant prophet. When God called him to preach the Word in Nineveh, he went in the opposite direction. But Jonah could not escape God. He was "overcome by His Word." The prophet Isaiah, on the other hand, responded to the Lord with, "Here am I. Send me!" (Isaiah 6:8). Jonah was a draftee, but Isaiah was a volunteer.

The apostles were likewise called by the Lord and overcome by the Word. They were not overpowered in the sense that they went into the world like robots. Their call to the ministry was gladly heeded for they had seen the miracles of Jesus and heard the Word of the Lord. They were "overcome" in the sense that having seen and heard the risen Savior, they were fully persuaded and convinced. They fully believed that Jesus was the Lamb of God sacrificed for the sins of the world. Could they be threatened into silence? No! Peter and John told the religious authorities, "We cannot help speaking about what we have seen and heard."

Throughout the centuries God's spokesmen have been committed to His Word. At the Diet of Worms, 1521, Martin Luther refused to recant. He told Emperor Charles V that he was "overcome by the Scriptures."

How about us? Through the power of the Holy Spirit, we can repeat the words of St. Paul, "Christ's love compels us" (2 Corinthians 5:14). We do not go forth as "talking heads" but as people so full of gratitude and conviction that we gladly speak for Christ.

PRAYER SUGGESTION

Pray that the Holy Spirit might deepen your conviction concerning Jesus Christ and His salvation earned for all.

Creeks and the River

Do not put your trust in princes, in mortal men, who cannot save.
Psalm 146:3

When people in Missouri speak of the "big river," they do not mean the mighty Mississippi. They mean the Missouri, a good-sized creek that can become rampant and cause floods.

There is a parallel here that can be applied to people. Throughout history were those who thought of themselves as mighty rivers but were really creeks. Hitler and Mussolini fall into that category, as do Pharaoh, Nero, Herod, and Genghis Khan. They all thought they were big rivers.

How foolish are humans who think they are God! "Do not put your trust in princes, in mortal men, who cannot save. When their spirit departs, they return to the ground; on that very day their plans come to nothing" (Psalm 143:3–4). Pharaoh's plan to keep the children of Israel enslaved came to naught. Herod did not succeed in destroying the Christ Child. Nero sought to wipe out Christianity. Genghis Khan—whose name meant "lord of lords"—swept over Asia and Europe with his marauders but he never became a world conqueror. Human creeks cannot be the River that God is.

There is only one King of kings and Lord of lords. Enemies cannot destroy Him and His Gospel. He outlasts them all. Gamaliel of the high council in Jerusalem was right when he spoke to his colleagues of the apostles' message: "If it is from God, you will not be able to stop [it]" (Acts 5:39). Christianity is certainly "of God," proclaiming the salvation gained by the Crucified One who rose from the dead. God "gave Him the name that is above every name" (Philippians 2:9). To Him be all glory!

PRAYER SUGGESTION

Pause to give praise to Jesus and to promise Him your total loyalty.

A Fountain of Tears

Oh, that my head were a spring of water
and my eyes a fountain of tears! Jeremiah 9:1

Why was Jeremiah crying? The prophet wished he had an unlimited supply of tears so he could sufficiently lament the downfall of Jerusalem and the kingdom of Judah. Soon Nebuchadnezzar would lead many people into Babylonian captivity. But the onslaught had already begun, and Jeremiah cried "for the slain of my people" (Jeremiah 9:1). God's judgment would come because the people, led by their priests and princes, were engaged in what the one true God hates the most: idolatry.

But Jeremiah did more than weep. He offered comfort. He declared, "Because of the LORD's great love we are not consumed, for His compassions never fail. They are new every morning" (Lamentations 3:22–23). This comfort was based on the merit of the prophesied Messiah.

Many others have shed bitter tears. David declared that his tears stained the scroll on which God keeps His record. God has not promised that His children would be without grief; just the opposite. Jesus said to His disciples, "You will weep and mourn while the world rejoices" (John 16:20). But He also said, "Your grief will turn to joy" (John 16:20). This is the comfort of Christians: Nothing "will be able to separate us from the love of God that is in Christ Jesus our Lord" (Romans 8:39).

Are there tears in your life? Are they many or few? Take courage! God keeps track of your tears. He assures you that every promise of His enduring grace—forgiveness, peace, and life eternal—is yours because of the reconciling work of Jesus Christ, who carried all our griefs and sorrows to the cross for us.

PRAYER SUGGESTION

Thank Jesus for bearing all your sins and griefs to Calvary's cross.

A Sorrowful Spring Turned Bright

"We are going up to Jerusalem, and everything that is written by the prophets about the Son of Man will be fulfilled." Luke 18:31

After a long winter, spring is welcomed. The song "April in Paris" describes such "charms of spring" as "chestnuts in blossom" and "holiday tables under the trees."

It was spring in the Holy Land when Jesus led His disciples to Jerusalem for Passover. En route to the Holy City, Jewish pilgrims would have seen wildflowers in bloom and fields ready for planting. But our Lord looked beyond the beauties and foresaw agony and affliction. He knew it was His last Passover celebration and He tried to prepare His disciples for what lay ahead.

It is amazing how clearly the man Jesus discerned the future. He not only read the signs of the times as His enemies sought to kill Him, He recalled what the Old Testament Scriptures foretold about the Messiah's suffering and death. He told His followers specifically how He would be handed over to the Romans, mocked, insulted, abused, flogged, and ultimately executed. Especially clear was the prophecy of Isaiah: "He was pierced for our transgressions, He was crushed for our iniquities; the punishment that brought us peace was upon Him, and by His wounds we are healed" (Isaiah 53:5).

Yet Christ's resurrection was also foretold: "After the suffering of His soul, He will see the light of life" (Isaiah 53:11). Jesus told His disciples that He would rise again on the third day. But the dire prediction—as well as the promise of His triumphant resurrection—was beyond the disciples' understanding.

When we look at what our Lord and Savior accomplished to give us time and eternity, it is always springtime in our souls.

PRAYER SUGGESTION

Give thanks for what Christ has done to bring life into the world.

God Is Unchanging

Its place remembers it no more. Psalm 103:16

A group with historic interests wanted to preserve the boyhood home of poet T. S. Eliot. However, the house no longer existed—it had been razed to make room for a parking lot.

Things like this are quite common in our world. Historic sites yield to commercial buildings. Urban change is especially evident in depressed areas and major commercial areas. Change is all around. We see the transience of all things mundane. Human beings don't last either. They pass away like wildflowers along the road. The place where they grew is easily obliterated.

Perhaps you know people who made a homecoming trip, maybe for a class reunion, for genealogical research, or for an anniversary of a church to which they once belonged. How many people remember them? How much has changed?

We expect change. But we do not despair. Much in this world is like quicksand, but God is our Rock. From everlasting to everlasting, He is God. He was there before He created the mountains and the oceans. They may change, but not their Creator. He is unchanging not only in His being but also in His Word. Jesus said that His words, which were the words of God, will still be there when heaven and earth pass away. God stands behind every promise pertaining to our well-being here on earth and to our eternal salvation in heaven.

Like Father, like Son! "Jesus Christ is the same yesterday and today and forever" (Hebrews 13:8). So unchangeable is His love that prompted Him to lay down His life for all sinners. Tell yourself it is true: Jesus loves me dearly!

PRAYER SUGGESTION

Pray that amid the many changes in life you may remain firm in your faith in Jesus Christ.

Is It the Same Christ?

Jesus said, "Do not hold on to me,
for I have not yet returned to the Father." John 20:17

Is a remodeled house the same house or is it a different one? Is the glorified body of the resurrection the same body or a different one? The answer is that it is both, as we learn from the risen Christ.

When Jesus appeared to the disciples after Easter occasions, He was the same Lord they had known before. To prove it, He ate in their presence. Yet His body was different—it was glorified. And His mission on earth during the 40 days between His resurrection and ascension was different from what it had been before.

These truths emerged from the tomb on Easter morning. Upon recognizing Him, Mary Magdalene assumed that the same familiarity that had previously prevailed between Jesus and His followers would be continued. But Jesus headed this off when He said, "Do not hold on to Me." Jesus would not have her touch Him. Instead, He sent her on a mission: "Go instead to My brothers and tell them, 'I am returning to My Father and your Father, to My God and your God'" (John 20:17).

The message Mary delivered explains why Jesus said she shouldn't touch Him: "I have not yet returned to my Father." He was telling her that a relationship much closer than bodily contact is coming. Since Jesus returned to the heavenly Father and sent the Holy Spirit as Counselor, we have lived in very intimate communion with Him. He lives in our hearts, and we in Him. So, is it the same Christ who died for us and rose again? Yes, but He is our Friend in a much fuller sense.

PRAYER SUGGESTION

Express your gratitude to the risen Christ for His love that took Him to the cross for your salvation.

Worship with Bells On

The gold bells and the pomegranates
are to alternate around the hem of the robe. Exodus 28:34

Bells have played a prominent part in the lives of Christians. A popular song refers to "church bells" ringing at a wedding. English poet John Dunne referred to the slow, solemn peels of a bell to announce a death: "Never send to ask for whom the bell tolls; it tolls for thee." On a more joyful note, Henry W. Longfellow's carol opens with: "I heard the bells on Christmas Day."

Bells were also used in Old Testament worship. The Lord prescribed to Moses that the high priest's vestments were to be adorned with bells so the tinkle would alert worshipers to the priest's entry into the Holy Place, where he would sprinkle a lamb's blood on the mercy seat. This sacrificial act of the high priest on the Day of Atonement foreshadowed the sacrifice the Lamb of God would bring for the sins of all.

The verse above gives insight into a difference between the Old and New Testaments. God's ceremonial law prescribed ever so many things, not only pertaining to the Sabbath and to circumcision, but down to the details of the high priest's robe. As New Testament people, we are accustomed to exercising freedom as to the design and use of a pastor's vestments, the order of worship in church services, and the like. We have freedom in such things because God has neither commanded nor forbidden them in the New Testament. But any freedom is always to be used responsibly.

That is why the prescribed bells on Aaron's robe remind us indirectly of Paul's words to the Galatians: "It is for freedom that Christ has set us free" (Galatians 5:1).

PRAYER SUGGESTION

Give thanks to God who, for Jesus' sake, has freed us from bondage to the Law, asking Him that we may never mislead others by our freedom.

The Day of Salvation Is Now

"What do you see, Amos?" he asked.
"A basket of ripe fruit," I answered. Amos 8:2

God uses whatever it takes to make a point. To Amos, He used visual aids: a swarm of locusts, fire, a plumb line, and a basket of fruit. The prophet introduced the vision of the fruit with: "This is what the Sovereign LORD showed me" (Amos 8:1).

The word "ripe" indicates that the fruit is highly perishable. The point God makes is this: "The time is ripe for my people Israel; I will spare them no longer" (Amos 8:2). As ripe fruit quickly perishes, so shall God's judgment come instantly on all who reject His grace.

During His ministry, Jesus stressed the need for repentance and for believing the Gospel, for the kingdom of God was at hand (Matthew 4:17). The kingdom does not stand still. Hearers of the Word ought not think that tomorrow or next week, next month or next year is soon enough to heed it. If the Gospel is neglected or rejected, the opportunity is lost. "Now is the time of God's favor, now is the day of salvation" (2 Corinthians 6:2).

Even during the bitterest hours of His Passion Jesus gave witness to God's judgment on unbelief: telling the Sanhedrin that the Son of Man would come as their Judge, telling the mourners to shed no tears for Him but for themselves lest God's judgment come on them. At the same time our Lord proclaimed God's saving grace. He proclaimed it to the dying thief who repented. And He proclaimed it in the strongest terms possible when on the cross He gave His life as a ransom for all.

The vision we see is not one of rotting fruit, but of Christ's redemption as the fruit of His labors in our behalf.

PRAYER SUGGESTION

Give thanks to the Lord Jesus for granting us the time of salvation.

Lost and Found

The LORD God called to the man, "Where are you?" Genesis 3:9

One of the puzzles of American history is the fate of colonists on Roanoke Island, off the North Carolina coast, in 1585. When supply ships came five years later, no one greeted them. The settlement established by Sir Walter Raleigh had vanished.

Long before this, God established the first human family—the first colony, if you will—in the Garden of Eden. But when the Lord came to the garden one evening, Adam and Eve were not there to welcome Him. The Lord found them hiding in the bushes, trying to avoid Him because their sin caused them to have bad consciences.

Despite their sin, God did not abandon our first parents. Nor does He forsake their many offspring. He takes the initiative in tracking them down. He seeks the sinners; it is not the sinners seeking God. In Jesus' parable, it was all up to the shepherd to find the lost sheep.

Yes, the great miracle of divine love did take place. God came to earth in the person of His Son, Jesus Christ, seeking the lost. And God found them, not sparing His own Son but giving Him up for the salvation of all. In the words of the hymn, this is the extreme dimension of God's grace: "Love that found me—wondrous thought—Found me when I sought Him not."

What does it mean for us to be found by God? Unlike our first parents hiding in the bushes, we are found in our homes, communities, and churches, gladly doing God's will and serving the least of Christ's brothers. We do not hide, for our conscience is at rest. We have peace with God through our Lord Jesus Christ.

PRAYER SUGGESTION

Pray to the heavenly Father that you may be ever willing to look for lost sinners and guide them home to Him.

Three Kinds of Trees

They might be called trees of righteousness, the planting of the LORD, *that He might be glorified. Isaiah 61:3 KJV*

Evergreen trees stand out in every season; even in winter they show their life by their greenness. By way of contrast, many other trees are barren in winter, their leaves having fallen to the ground. If you didn't know better, you'd think they were dead. But they are very much alive, conserving sap and strength for the winter. Of course some trees without foliage are dead. By and by they will fall down or someone will cut them down and use them as firewood.

People can be compared to trees. In fact, the Bible does this in several places. The prophet Isaiah said that some people are like the lofty cedars of Lebanon. Christians who meditate on God's Word and grow in faith are, as the psalmist said, like trees planted by streams of water that yield fruit in season. But faithless and loveless people are like dead trees. They have no other future than to be cut down and burned up.

Dear to God are those who are ever-green, ever-bearing. He blesses them and makes them a blessing to many. Our Lord cautions us regarding people who seem like dead trees, without foliage or fruit. He does not want us to cut them from the membership of the church. He tells us to remember that He will, with the sunshine of His grace, nurture them and cause them to grow in faith and bear spiritual fruit again.

Through our Baptism, God has grafted us to Him. He causes our faith to live and makes us "trees of righteousness." He sent His Son, Jesus Christ, to die on the tree and to earn our righteousness. In Christ is the life we need.

PRAYER SUGGESTION

Ask the Spirit of God to enlighten and energize you through the Gospel so you may be a spiritual fruit-bearing tree.

Helping the Helpers

I ask you, loyal yokefellow, help these women who have contended at my side in the cause of the Gospel. Philippians 4:3

The ground caved in, trapping a workman. For 13 hours firemen and paramedics worked to free him. During this time, Red Cross and Salvation Army volunteers cared for the rescue workers by serving them food and drink.

In Philippi, St. Paul labored to set people free from the cave-in of sin by proclaiming the Gospel of salvation in Jesus Christ. While he was doing this, he was assisted by people who had come to faith. The apostle wrote this of the faithful who were helping him: "[All] the household of Stephanas were the first converts in Achaia, and they have devoted themselves to the service of the saints" (1 Corinthians 16:15).

Jesus Christ, the Son of God, came into the world to be everyone's Rescuer, Helper, Redeemer. The hymn writer called Him "Help of the helpless." While He was preaching and teaching about the kingdom of heaven, there were women, Mary Magdalene among them, who were of help to Him and to His followers.

An evangelism hymn tells what Christians can do if they cannot speak like angels or preach like St. Paul. They can help helpers. And they certainly can pray, and by their prayers hold up the arms of their pastors, as Aaron and Hur did for Moses in a battle with the Amalekites.

Here is a tribute to the otherwise unknown mother-in-law of Peter: After Jesus cured her of a fever, "she got up and began to wait on Him" (Matthew 8:15). A response to Jesus' love for her, she was helping the helper and those with him.

PRAYER SUGGESTION

Ask for God's help in finding opportunities for rendering service wherever it is needed.

Christ, Our Permanent Treasure

"You earn wages, only to put them in a purse with holes in it."
Haggai 1:6

In Greek mythology, Zeus punished Tantalus for revealing secrets he had entrusted to him. In the afterlife, Tantalus had great thirst and hunger but food and water were always just out of reach. From this comes the verb "tantalize," that is, to be tormented by not getting what one wants or to find one's expectations unfulfilled.

Jesus speaks of those whose faith is choked by the "the deceitfulness of wealth" (Matthew 13:22). Such was the experience of people who returned to Jerusalem from captivity in Babylon. They lost interest in building God's house and were more concerned with their own (Haggai 1:4). Personal wealth was more important than God, but there was no blessing on their financial gains. How tantalizing it was to earn wages only to lose them!

Wealth cannot provide happiness and security. No one learned that better than Judas Iscariot, who betrayed his Lord for 30 pieces of silver. He held a considerable treasure, but it did not bring peace. On the contrary, Judas was miserable in his wealth. He even tried to return the money, saying, "I have sinned … for I have betrayed innocent blood" (Matthew 27:4), but to no avail. Judas threw the money away and hung himself.

Riches, when sought for their own sake, are tantalizing. Only in Jesus Christ can we find real wealth. He is our treasure, priceless and permanent. Not with gold and silver, not with dollars and diamonds, but with His own precious blood He redeemed us from sin, making us God's beloved children and the heirs of eternal life. Believing in Him, we have lasting and true treasure.

PRAYER SUGGESTION

Ask that Jesus may teach you to rest your faith solely on His saving merit and thus find security for time and for eternity.

The "If" Is Removed

If only for this life we have hope in Christ,
we are to be pitied more than all men. 1 Corinthians 15:19

After the *Titanic* struck an iceberg on April 14, 1912, Anna Turga was told to go to a higher deck. But she was cold and decided to go to a lower deck where it was warmer. She was subsequently saved. Years later her son wrote, "The decision turned out to be crucial. Most of the people on the upper deck drowned."

So often life seems to depend on "if," on certain conditions. This is especially true of events on which our eternal salvation depends. What if Christ had not risen from the dead? St. Paul wrote what the results would have been: the dead would not rise, all hope would be lost, our faith would be futile. There would be no Easter—no reason for the things we do as Christians: pray, worship, minister. This also would apply, *"If* only for this life we have hope in Christ, we are to be pitied more than all men."

However, the "if" is canceled and all these outcomes are avoided. Christ did indeed rise from the dead. Christ Jesus "died for our sins according to the Scriptures ... was buried ... was raised on the third day according to the Scriptures" (1 Corinthians 15:3–4). The apostles and many others knew this for sure for they had seen and heard and touched the risen Lord for themselves.

And we rejoice in a faith that is valid. It rests on this promise of Jesus: "I am the Resurrection and the Life. He who believes in Me will live, even though he dies; and whoever lives and believes in Me will never die" (John 11:25–26). It follows, as St. Paul declared, "No matter how many promises God has made, they are 'yes' in Christ" (2 Corinthians 1:20).

PRAYER SUGGESTION

Express your thankfulness to God for validating your faith by raising Jesus from the dead.

Christianity, a Religion of Diligence

It is by grace you have been saved. Ephesians 2:8

Does being a Christian require great effort? The answer is no … and yes, depending on what aspect of Christianity we are considering. When it comes to having God's forgiveness and peace with Him, our efforts are naught. We are saved by grace, not by our own effort. We are reconciled to God by the death of His Son, Jesus Christ. Believing in Him as our Savior, we are the beneficiaries of His atoning work. We can add nothing.

At the same time, it is true that Christianity is not a lazy person's religion. Paul made it clear that salvation is Christ's full and free gift to us and stressed that faith in the Savior means we actively respond through good deeds. Such deeds are the outward evidence of a living faith, proof that we take salvation seriously.

Pay attention to Paul's words: "Continue to work out your salvation with fear and trembling. For it is God who works in you to will and to act according to His good purpose" (Philippians 12:12–13). God the Holy Spirit, who works faith in us through the sacraments and the Scripture, gives us strength and motivation to express our faith in the way we live.

Personal Christianity calls for efforts prompted by love for Christ. It makes us willing to sacrifice and surrender so Christ may be glorified. It prompts us to be diligent in prayer and in every response to God's great gift of salvation in Jesus. Christianity comes easy for those who love the Savior, who invites us: "Come to me … for I am gentle and humble in heart, and you will find rest for your souls. For My yoke is easy and My burden is light" (Matthew 11:28–30).

PRAYER SUGGESTION

Ask the Holy Spirit to give you zeal for activities that further the Gospel of Jesus Christ.

The Ant as a Teacher

Go to the ant, you sluggard; consider its ways and be wise!
Proverbs 6:6

In Aesop's fable about the ant and the cricket, the ant laid up food for the winter while the happy-go-lucky cricket played, saying he must exercise his voice and had no time to work. The result: he was hungry in the winter.

The same lesson was taught by the writer of Proverbs: the ant has "no commander, no overseer or ruler, yet it stores its possessions in summer and gathers its food at harvest" (Proverbs 6:7–8).

Jesus has this to say about timely activities: "Walk while you have the light, before darkness overtakes you" (John 12:35). As for the future, He declares, "Store up for yourselves treasures in heaven" (Matthew 6:20). We are to give thought to the present life but also—and especially—to the hereafter. We cannot by our own worries, works, or effort earn heaven; Jesus has done all that. He secured our future by dying on the cross and rising from the tomb. He opened paradise and will there receive all who believe in Him. What is important is that we make peace with God *now*—now while it is still the day of salvation—by believing in Jesus Christ. Thereby we lay up treasures in heaven and obtain eternal life. Then in this life, with heaven always in view, we live purposefully.

Yet Christians are not self-centered. When a burden is too heavy for a single ant, other ants help carry it. That is what God's people do. They are all members of Christ's body, the church. Paul said, "Carry each other's burdens, and in this way you will fulfill the law of Christ" (Galatians 6:2). The law of Christ is love. When we love others, we want to help.

PRAYER SUGGESTION

Say to the Lord Jesus that you come to Him for the strengthening of your faith so you may be His today, tomorrow, and forever.

In Christ's Kingdom of Peace

The wolf will live with the lamb, the leopard will lie down with the goat, the calf and the lion and the yearling together; and a little child will lead them. Isaiah 11:6

Most artists paint many pictures before they achieve fame. It was different with Edward Hicks, who made his reputation with only one picture: "The Peaceable Kingdom." It depicts animals living peacefully together and William Penn conferring amicably with Native Americans. This painting portrays pacifism—the belief that all problems can be solved peaceably.

The peace Isaiah spoke of is the peace *of* God, which passes all understanding; peace *with* God through the mediation and merit of the Prince of Peace. Isaiah said, "He was pierced for our transgressions, He was crushed for our iniquities; the punishment that brought us peace was upon Him, and by His wounds we are healed" (Isaiah 53:5). Jesus, who suffered under Pontius Pilate, was crucified, died, and was buried, is this Peacemaker. And because He fully gained our reconciliation, God brought Him back from the dead.

The peace of God is guaranteed to affect those who accept it in faith. First, it brings inner peace to the individual. Further, those who are justified by faith, and thus are at peace with God through Christ, may live in peace with one another and be an influence for good. God works through them in promoting peaceful relations in community, country, and the world at large.

Left to their own devices, human beings cannot achieve the kind of peace Hicks depicts in his painting, but Christians, by the power of God working through them, can change animosity into amity. They have been doing it all along.

PRAYER SUGGESTION

Thank the Lord Jesus for reconciling you to God and ask that He help you to be a peacemaker on earth.

Christians as Fishermen

"Come, follow Me," Jesus said, "and I will make you fishers of men."
Matthew 4:19

The Christian symbol ICHTHYS is the Greek work for fish and is used as shorthand for *Jesous Christos Theou Hyios Soter:* Jesus Christ, Son of God, Savior.

Fish were common symbols in the ministry of Jesus. Twice He miraculously multiplied bread and fish into rations for thousands. He blessed Peter with an immense catch of fish. After His resurrection He did the same when seven disciples let down their nets and hauled in 153 fish. Then, on the shore of the Sea of Galilee, the risen Lord took bread and the fish and fed His disciples.

The Bible describes two other miracles involving fish. In one, Jonah was rescued from the sea by this divine act: "The LORD provided a great fish to swallow Jonah, and Jonah was inside the fish three days and three nights" (Jonah 1:17). This event foretold Jesus' death, who said, "As Jonah was three days and three nights in the belly of a huge fish, so the Son of Man will be three days and three nights in the heart of the earth" (Matthew 12:40). The other miracle occurred when, on the Lord's instruction, Peter caught a fish with a shekel in its mouth, which Jesus used to pay His tax.

Since so many people living near the Sea of Galilee depended on fishing for their livelihood, it is no surprise that Jesus recruited His first disciples from among fishermen: the two sets of brothers, Peter and Andrew and James and John. He called them to become spiritual fishermen. All Christians are called to be spiritual fishermen. With the net of the Gospel, they catch people for Christ, who died and rose again to save them. We too are called.

PRAYER SUGGESTION

Give thanks to Christ for making provision for the Gospel to be proclaimed in your midst and calling you to be a spiritual fisherman.

Christ Works through His Church

Then they prayed, "Lord ... show us which of these two you have chosen to take over this apostolic ministry, which Judas left." Acts 1:24–25

Why didn't Jesus personally name a successor to Judas?

Our Savior appointed the 12 apostles to represent the 12 tribes of Israel. He gave to 10 apostles the authority to forgive sins (John 20:21–23), and He entrusted the Great Commission to "the 11 disciples" (Matthew 28:16–20). Yet it was important that His message was carried to the world by *12* men. So why didn't He appoint a replacement for Judas? We don't know. "Who has known the mind of the Lord?" (Romans 11:34)

Yet the risen and ascended Lord did indicate a successor. The 120 followers assembled in the Upper Room prayed that He would show them which of two candidates, Joseph and Matthias, "You have chosen." It was Matthias. Christ did the choosing; He carried out His choice through the members of His church.

Christ is still in charge of the church. He carries out His work through the church's members as, under the Spirit's guidance, they proclaim the Gospel and administer the sacraments. It is through His disciples today that He fulfills His purposes. Christians cannot die for the salvation of others nor can they create faith in them, but they do have the responsibility of telling the world that "In [Christ] we have redemption through His blood, the forgiveness of sins" (Ephesians 1:7). We have the authority—as did the 120 disciples in the Upper Room—to call pastors and teachers to do Christ's work, serving together in His kingdom.

Our Lord did, in fact, appoint a successor to Judas, the apostle Matthias, but He did it through the church.

PRAYER SUGGESTION

Thank the Lord Jesus for continuing to be the Head of His church and for guiding its members through His means of grace.

When Creatures Outranked Their Creator

"Foxes have holes and birds of the air have nests, but the Son of Man has no place to lay His head." Matthew 8:20

When Jesus learned that King Herod wanted to kill Him, He replied: "Go tell that fox, 'I will drive out demons and heal people today and tomorrow, and on the third day I will reach My goal'" (Luke 13:32). He refused to let Herod put a stop to His work.

Jesus would not let His ministry suffer from threats of harm nor from the temptation of wealth, comfort, or ease. He told a would-be disciple that lowly animals had more than He, the eternal Word, the King of kings.

St. Paul underscored Christ's deep poverty and humility: "You know the grace of our Lord Jesus Christ, that though He was rich, yet for your sakes He became poor, so that through His poverty you might become rich" (2 Corinthians 8:9).

All of this—the incarnation of the Son of God, His obedience, His humility and poverty, His suffering and dying—is the Good News of our redemption, as Jesus Himself said, "God so loved the world that He gave His one and only Son, that whoever believes in Him shall not perish but have eternal life" (John 3:16). Jesus, as the sinners' substitute and our Savior, divested Himself of His divine majesty, descending to a standard of living below that of foxes and birds. His redeeming death, in that He drained the cup of suffering to its bitter dregs, is the content of the Gospel we live by. Jesus provided spiritual riches for us when He laid up treasures in heaven for us. These riches include forgiveness, peace with God, life with a purpose now, and eternal life in the world to come.

PRAYER SUGGESTION

Thank the Lord for enriching you with salvation full and free.

New Birth, New Life

We were therefore buried with Him through baptism into death in order that, just as Christ was raised from the dead through the glory of the Father, we too may live a new life. Romans 6:4

Quite often, people who fail get another chance, a new lease on life. A case in point is the Ukrainian mother who brought her three-year-old, nearly blind son to the United States for the cornea transplant that restored his eyesight. She said, "My son was given a second birth, and I with him."

There are second births also in peoples' spiritual lives—the kind of which Jesus spoke when He said to Nicodemus, "No one can enter the kingdom of God unless he is born of water and the Spirit" (John 3:5). New birth was also taught by St. Paul: "If anyone is in Christ, he is a new creation" (2 Corinthians 5:17).

Sometimes this change is very dramatic, a great miracle of divine grace. For many, however, spiritual rebirth is not as dramatic but is, nevertheless, miraculous. Baptized in infancy and given Christian instruction as they grew, they have believed in Jesus Christ as their sole Savior all along, loving and serving Him in response. That was the experience of Timothy, St. Paul's co-worker, to whom the apostle wrote, "From infancy you have known the holy Scriptures, which are able to make you wise for salvation through faith in Christ Jesus" (2 Timothy 3:15).

Regardless when our second birth took place, we are all mindful of the daily washing and renewal of Baptism, as well as the need to rededicate ourselves to Christ every day, rise with Him from the deadness of sin, and "live a new life."

PRAYER SUGGESTION

Let your prayer be marked by thankfulness to God for your spiritual rebirth, and by the resolve to live for Christ every day.

The Heavenly Father Provides

"Consider the ravens: They do not sow or reap, they have no store-room or barn; yet God feeds them." Luke 12:24

Ravens have black feathers and that, in the minds of some, makes them messengers of gloom and doom. At least, Edgar Allen Poe thought so. Having lost his beloved Lenore, Poe let the raven be "emblematical of mournful and never-ending remembrance."

Although ravens are not highly regarded for their beauty or singing ability, they play useful roles in nature and they are often mentioned in the Bible. The account of the great Flood tells how Noah "sent out a raven, and it kept flying back and forth until the water had dried up from the earth" (Genesis 8:7).

In contrast to great waters, the earth suffered from a great drought at the time of the prophet Elijah. The Lord instructed Elijah to stay in the Kerith Ravine, telling him, "You will drink from the brook, and I have ordered the ravens to feed you there" (1 Kings 17:4). The passage goes on to say that these birds brought him bread and meat in the morning and evening.

Jesus points out that the birds are not only providers for others but that God provides for them. The lesson is: God's people are not to worry about the future. They are, to be sure, wise to make plans but they are not to doubt the faithfulness of their Provider.

God, our Creator and Provider, is also our Redeemer. God's Son came to earth to quench the hunger and thirst of the soul by making full restitution for our sins. Through Him we are redeemed from sin and death. A Christmas stanza declares, "Upon a manger filled with hay In poverty content He lay; With milk was fed the Lord of all, Who feeds the ravens when they call."

PRAYER SUGGESTION

Thank God for providing food for your body and spiritual sustenance through the Gospel of Christ.

Jesus, Lamb of God and Lion of God

See, the Lion of the tribe of Judah, the Root of David, has triumphed.
Revelation 5:5

People identify with lions. They form lions' clubs. They want the "lion's share" of just about everything. Prominent persons are "lionized"—treated as celebrities and called social lions. And when someone is brave, he is "lion-hearted."

In the Bible, lions are destructive: "Roaring lions tearing their prey open their mouths wide against me"(Psalm 22:13). In the Bible, the strength of lions was celebrated when Jacob blessed his son, Judah: "You are a lion's cub, O Judah; you return from the prey, my son. Like a lion he crouches and lies down" (Genesis 49:9). In accordance with this prophecy, the tribe of Judah bore the lion on its banner to symbolize royal power.

When Jacob referred to the Scepter that will not depart from Judah (Genesis 49:10), he clearly prophesied the Messiah, the Son of David. Jesus, triumphant over sin, death, and the devil, has great power and privilege in heaven—He can open the scroll and its seven seals to reveal the counsels of God and turn them to the good of His church. The Lamb of God, that suffered and was sacrificed for the sin of the world, is now the Lion.

Because Jesus triumphed, the "roaring lion"—the devil—has no power over us (1 Peter 5:8). Because he is still "looking for someone to devour" (1 Peter 5:8), we need to be watchful and alert. Peter cautioned, "Resist him, standing firm in the faith" (1 Peter 5:8). Satan's kingdom is destroyed, but clean-up continues. Thanks be to God that we are safe in Christ's kingdom!

PRAYER SUGGESTION

Say a prayer of praise to Jesus Christ for His great victory over Satan and sin and for taking you into His kingdom of grace.

Idol Worship, Idle Worship

"Worship the Lord your God, and serve Him only." Matthew 4:10

Idolatry—the worship of idols, visible and invisible, material and immaterial—is folly. The prophet Hosea emphasized this in telling the Israelites that wooden gods cannot help them: "They consult a wooden idol and are answered by a stick of wood" (Hosea 4:12).

Would it make a difference if the idol were jade or gold? Not at all. The worship of a manmade idol is idle worship. Hosea suggested that idol worship indicates idleness in would-be worshipers, who chose a religion of convenience. He wrote that their false sacrifices are performed under trees "where the shade is pleasant" (Hosea 4:13).

Idolatry takes many forms. It can be practiced in a place where no statues or figurines of gods are present. Whatever a person regards as his highest good, that is his substitute for God. This can be many things: wealth, pleasure, quest for fame, even the kind of self-fulfillment that puts one's ego first. Idolatry is involved when people become caught up in philosophies. Even atheism, the very denial of the existence of God, can become a religion, and somewhere in that scheme of things is the concept of one's highest good.

Whatever the idol, it cannot deliver; it lets people down. Fulfillment comes only from worshiping and serving the Lord, our God. He is our highest good. In Jesus Christ, His Son, He imparts His saving love to us, accepting us as His redeemed children and heirs. We have what no money can ever buy: peace with our heavenly Father, purpose in life, and assurance of eternal life with Him.

PRAYER SUGGESTION

Implore God, for Jesus' sake, to help you trust more fully in Him as the only true God and to serve Him.

Jesus, the More Excellent Redeemer

[Christ] entered the Most Holy Place once for all by His own blood, having obtained eternal redemption. Hebrews 9:12

The expression "holy cow" is more than an epithet in India—it is a statement of faith. Cattle have long had a place of importance in pagan religions. Ancient Egyptians worshiped Apis, the sacred bull, because of his connection with the god Ptah. The Israelites, during their long sojourn in Egypt, may have soaked up this form of idolatry as evidenced by their worship of the golden calf. The psalmist highlights the folly of this: "At Horeb they made a calf and worshiped an idol cast from metal. They exchanged their Glory for an image of a bull" (Psalm 106:19–20).

God is not pleased with thoughtless, faithless, and mechanical offerings that reject true repentance and faith in the Messiah as the sinner's Substitute. "The multitude of your sacrifices—what are they to Me. ... I have no pleasure in the blood of bulls and lambs and goats" (Isaiah 1:11). Hand in hand with gross misunderstanding went ingratitude, as the prophet said, "The ox knows his master, the donkey his owner's manger, but Israel does not know, My people do not understand" (Isaiah 1:3).

The religion of the Israelites called for animal sacrifices as atonement for sins. This shedding of blood prefigured the outpouring of the holy, precious blood of Jesus Christ. But for New Testament people, it is not the blood of animals, only the blood of Jesus Christ that redeems, cleanses, and purifies us from all sin. This truth is stressed in hymn verses: "Not all the blood of beasts On Jewish altars slain Could give the guilty conscience peace Or wash away the stain.—But Christ, the heavenly Lamb, Takes all our sins away; A sacrifice of nobler name and richer blood than they."

PRAYER SUGGESTION

Give thanks to the Savior for paying the price for your redemption.

God Is Holy and Wholly Good

When the kindness and love of God our Savior appeared,
He saved us. Titus 3:4

A man who was as much a philosopher as a psychologist, Carl Jung had difficulty reconciling the goodness of God with evil. One interpreter declared that Jung viewed God as "at least three-fourths good." If that were true, God is one-fourth evil. And if that were so, God's holiness is totally corrupted. We know what a little evil can do. One cannot speak of the contents of a glass as three-fourths pure and one-fourth poison.

God is totally good: "Good and upright is the LORD" (Psalm 25:8). For God to be good means evil cannot dwell with Him or in Him. Evil is of the devil; God is holy, the very antithesis of evil. Since God is good, He has all the other qualities that go with it: "compassionate and gracious ... abounding in love and faithfulness" (Exodus 34:6).

God imparts His goodness to us, His redeemed children who are created in His image. Although sin is still in us, all our sins are forgiven for Jesus' sake. Our death sentence is changed because God's Son died in our place: "The wages of sin is death, but the gift of God is eternal life in Christ Jesus our Lord" (Romans 6:23).

Jesus Christ is the communicator of the goodness of God; He is also a participant in it. Like the heavenly Father, so also the Son is holy and wholly good. He calls Himself the Good Shepherd who cares for us and provides us with all we need for body and soul. That is why we can say with confidence: "Surely goodness and love will follow me all the days of my life, and I will dwell in the house of the LORD forever" (Psalm 23:6).

PRAYER SUGGESTION

Pray that by the power of God you may grow more and more into the likeness of Christ, both in goodness and holiness.

The Descending Dove

He saw the Spirit of God descending like a dove and lighting on Him.
Matthew 3:16

Because the Creator gave doves a homing instinct, they were often trained to be couriers. For example, Noah sent out doves and they returned to the ark, their home, one with a "freshly plucked olive leaf" in its beak (Genesis 8:11).

At the baptism of Jesus, the Holy Spirit took the form of a dove and descended on Jesus. Just as a dove instinctively returns home, God the Holy Spirit sought Jesus as the third Person of the Trinity. "God anointed Jesus of Nazareth with the Holy Spirit and power" (Acts 10:38). Thus was our Lord empowered to begin His ministry of preaching, teaching, and healing.

Doves were also significant earlier in Jesus' life on earth. At His presentation in the temple, a Jewish tradition, an impoverished Joseph and Mary offered "a pair of doves" in lieu of a lamb (Luke 2:24). These doves were given to "redeem" Jesus as the firstborn.

The dove figures especially prominent on Pentecost when the apostles were filled with the Spirit, just as Jesus had promised. They now had the wisdom and strength to begin preaching the Gospel all over the world. Throughout history, artists have depicted this manifestation of the Holy Spirit as a dove.

It is still the time for Jesus' work—building up of His church—to continue. The Holy Spirit prompts and motivates Christians throughout the world to speak of full and free salvation in the Savior. "Spirit of truth and love, Life-giving, holy Dove, Speed forth Thy flight; Move on the water's face, Bearing the lamp of grace, And in earth's darkest place Let there be light."

PRAYER SUGGESTION

Ask the Holy Spirit to enter your mind and heart with the comfort of the Gospel.

Out of Sight, Out of Mind

You will tread our sins underfoot and hurl all our iniquities into the depths of the sea. Micah 7:19

The government and private industry both are charged with disposing the radioactive and toxic waste of nuclear energy. In our spiritual lives, we are confronted with the problem of dealing with the contamination and poisonous waste of our sin.

The prophet Micah announced the judgment of God, and he also proclaimed the Lord's mercy, expressing the latter with great wonderment: "Who is a God like You, who pardons sin and forgives the transgression of the remnant of His inheritance? You do not stay angry forever but delight to show mercy. You will again have compassion on us; You will tread our sins underfoot and hurl all our iniquities into the depths of the sea" (Micah 7:18–19).

With God, who is righteous and regards sin as an abomination, it is not simply a matter of merely getting our sins out of sight. That would be a cover-up, which conflicts with His holiness. The Lord disposes of our sins by putting their guilt and penalty on Jesus, the Sin-Bearer, who carried them to Calvary's cross. St. Paul wrote, "[God] forgave us all our sins, … He took it away, nailing it to the cross" (Colossians 2:13–14).

The Bible speaks of God's full-forgiving grace in many ways: posting a notice that the debt is paid, treading our sins underfoot, hurling our iniquities into the sea, putting our sins behind His back. God assures us that for Jesus' sake, whose merit and mediation are ours by faith and sacrament, all our sins are completely and forever out of His sight and mind. In Christ we are reconciled. We are God's children and the heirs of eternal life.

PRAYER SUGGESTION

Thank the heavenly Father for casting your sins into the sea because Jesus atoned for them.

Straying Sheep Have a Searching Shepherd

We all, like sheep, have gone astray, each of us has turned to his own way; and the LORD has laid on Him the iniquity of us all. Isaiah 53:6

In Isaiah's text, we note the all-inclusive expressions: "we all" and "each of us." People are depicted here not only as a flock from which a sheep is sometimes missing; the text states that all are lost and can't find the way home.

God in His mercy made provision for erring sinners to be saved. From heaven came God's Son to be the true Shepherd. He also came as the Lamb of God. What did He have to do to be our Savior? Was it enough for Him to merely point the way to salvation? Would it suffice for Him to teach us a few lessons, equip us with snappy slogans, and suggest several exercises to help us live a moral life? Would we be able to take it from there and, on our own, get to heaven? No, that—and a thousand more things—would not be enough to qualify Him as the Good Shepherd.

What would it take then? Jesus reconciled us to God when He gave His life on the cross and rose from the grave as proof that our salvation was accomplished. The prophet Isaiah, moved by the Holy Spirit, envisioned this hundreds of years prior to the events. He said, "The LORD has laid on Him the iniquity of us all."

With our redemption completed, down to the crossing of every "t" and the dotting of every "i," the prophet points out that there is more. As our Good Shepherd, Jesus continues to look after us, interceding for us and sending forth His ministers. Isaiah stated it well: "He tends His flock like a shepherd: He gathers the lambs in His arms and carries them close to His heart; He gently leads those that have young" (Isaiah 40:11). All glory be to Christ!

PRAYER SUGGESTION

Express your gratitude to the Lord Jesus for His care for you.

The Kingdom of Little Children

"Let the little children come to Me ...
for the kingdom of God belongs to such as these." Mark 10:14

A touching story is Harper Lee's *To Kill a Mockingbird*. Our heart goes out to six-year-old Scout. She is a good child and spends her first years in a good home. But Scout cannot remain in her little world. She is exposed soon enough to prejudice and hatred. But her upbringing serves her in good stead. When she is exposed to evil, she knows how to cope with it and turn it to good.

Jesus had a lot to say about children—for example, He noted that they are an example to adults in their simple and sincere faith in Him. He said, "The kingdom of God belongs to such as these." When the disciples needed a lesson in humility, He placed a child in their midst and said: "Unless you ... become like little children, you will never enter the kingdom of heaven" (Matthew 18:3).

Because children are sincere, many regard them as innocent and thus in no need of Holy Baptism. Our Lord tells us, however, that they from the beginning add actual sin to the original sin in which they were conceived and born. Jesus died also for the sins of children; He loves them and wants them in His kingdom.

Jesus cautions us to avoid setting a bad example or causing children to sin. He wants us to teach them what is good and true by both precept and example. He wants all adults, particularly parents and teachers, to help children make the transition from the protected world that is the home to the larger world of their developing personal and social lives. Sooner or later they have to come to grips with the evil around them.

Christ is pleased when we teach children—and when we learn from them—for of such is God's kingdom.

PRAYER SUGGESTION

Ask God to give you sincere faith and never doubt Jesus' love.

The Refreshing Grace of God

Then will the lame leap like a deer,
and the mute tongue shout for joy. Isaiah 35:6

The prophet Isaiah used as an example the agile and nimble leaping of a deer to describe the joy expressed by people who are healed from their sin and its consequences.

Here is another comparison: "As the deer pants for streams of water, so my soul pants for You, O God. My soul thirsts for God, for the living God" (Psalm 42:1–2). Deer get hot and thirsty during a pursuit; then they long for a drink of cooling water.

People, too, are at times pursued and harassed by their enemies, especially by the enemies of the soul. We sometimes speak of these enemies as "the world." Another enemy is the alter ego in us that we call the sinful flesh. The latter can tempt us to carnal sins as well as doubts in heart and mind. After wrestling with these enemies, we long for living water.

Thank God that such water exists! From whom is this wonder water available? From Jesus Christ alone, who declared, "The water I give him will become in him a spring of water welling up to eternal life" (John 4:14). Both statements are true: Jesus is Himself the Living Water, and the Gospel He wants us to drink and to share with the world's thirsty souls is also living water. It was in great agony that our Savior procured living water for us. It required that He be crucified and, in great pain of body and of spirit to exclaim, "I am thirsty" (John 19:28).

We are now the blessed ones. The Gospel of His redemption renews and refreshes us and quenches the thirst of our soul. We want all people to hear, to have, to hold it, and to drink of it.

PRAYER SUGGESTION

Ask the Lord to lead you to a friend, a neighbor, or a relative whose soul longs for the Word of God.

A Guest Bearing Gifts

All of them were filled with the Holy Spirit and began to speak in other tongues as the Spirit enabled them. Acts 2:4

On Pentecost, the Holy Spirit was poured out on the apostles, endowing them with power and many gifts. These gifts included the ability to speak in other languages, as well as knowledge of the Word of Christ, which the Spirit restored to their memories.

The Spirit still comes to the church and to individuals. And when He does, He brings many gifts—more than we can count. The prophet Isaiah mentions seven of them: The Spirit Himself, wisdom, understanding, counsel, power, knowledge, and the fear (or reverence) of the Lord.

These are gifts the Holy Spirit bestows on Christians today. In the confirmation rite, this is said to the catechumens: "God, the Father of our Lord Jesus Christ, gives you His Holy Spirit, the Spirit of wisdom and knowledge, of grace and prayer, of power and strength, of sanctification and the fear of God."

The Spirit Himself is the greatest of these gifts for He converts us, bringing us to faith in Christ, our Lord and Savior. A "little Pentecost" occurs with every individual conversion.

Besides giving us Himself, the Spirit gives *wisdom*, making us wise unto salvation; He gives us *understanding*, the ability to distinguish properly concerning things; He gives us *counsel*, or good advice from the Counselor, for ourselves and to share with others; He gives us *might*, the power to prevail in and through faith; He gives us *knowledge*, knowing and believing in the true God and in Jesus Christ, whom He has sent; and finally, He gives us *fear*, which is not terror but proper respect for God and His Word.

PRAYER SUGGESTION

Give thanks for the Holy Spirit, the heavenly Guest who comes, bringing choice gifts.

Jesus, the Door to God's Kingdom

"Indeed, it is easier for a camel to go through the eye of a needle than for a rich man to enter the kingdom of God." Luke 18:25

Camels are known for their burden-bearing ability, especially in hot and dry climates.

Jesus referred to camels in His teachings. He upbraided the Pharisees for being falsely conscientious, telling them, "You strain out a gnat but swallow a camel" (Matthew 23:24).

Today's text was addressed to a young man who had asked what he must do to inherit eternal life. Jesus reminded him of the Ten Commandments. But the man brushed them aside with the remark, "All these I have kept since I was a boy" (Mark 10:20). He believed God's Moral Law applied only to actions. The young man had not committed adultery, had not murdered anyone, had not stolen, had not dishonored his parents, and the like. What he didn't understand was that the Commandments apply to thoughts and desires, and not only to spoken words and deeds.

Our Lord clearly saw this man's self-righteousness and told him to sell everything and distribute the proceeds to the poor. Then he could follow Jesus. This did not suit the questioner at all. Wealth was his god; his heart clung to his possessions. A man in such a spiritual condition could not be Christ's disciple nor enter the kingdom of God. The simile of a camel's inability to pass through the eye of a needle makes this truth very plain.

How does anyone, rich or poor, enter God's kingdom and enjoy eternal life? Only by faith in Jesus Christ as our Redeemer from sin and the power of death. Jesus Himself declares that He is the only Way to the Father.

PRAYER SUGGESTION

Ask the Lord Jesus to keep you from covetousness and to strengthen your faith in Him.

The Noble Woman

She is clothed with strength and dignity; ... She watches over the affairs of her household. ... Her children arise and call her blessed; her husband also, and he praises her. Proverbs 31:25, 27–28

Christian wives and mothers play important roles in upholding home, church, and country. The last chapter of Proverbs pays tribute to women as such.

In our time, many women are employed outside the home. This takes nothing away from their "strength and dignity" as pillars in the family. Husbands and children lend willing hands to get the work done: cleaning, shopping, cooking. Yet the greater responsibility in the home still rests on shoulders of the wife and mother. She "watches over the affairs of her household."

The woman described in Proverbs was by no means a housebound slave. She was a business woman who was responsible for making and selling items produced in her cottage industry and for business transactions such as dealing with real estate: "She considers a field and buys it" (Proverbs 31:16). If she had servants in the home, she supervised them as the family manager. The family budget she drew up included provision for the needy. Little wonder that her children and husband called her blessed!

New Covenant women are priestesses in the home and, if employed outside the home, are Christ's servants in the workplace and builders of His church. They are first-class members of Christ's body, the church. They gladly serve Him in and out of the church, in every aspect of their lives because they know and believe that He died for them and gave them a place of honor in His kingdom.

PRAYER SUGGESTION

Give thanks to God for the women of Christ's church and for the part they play in our lives.

The No and Yes of Parenthood

Train a child in the way he should go, and when he is old he will not turn from it. Proverbs 22:6

In the chapel of Fredericksborg Castle in Denmark hangs Hendrik Krack's painting *Jephthah and His Daughter.* Jephthah, a judge in Israel, had vowed that he would sacrifice to God the first person he met at his homecoming if God would give him victory over an invading enemy. Jephthah won. But the first person he met was his one and only daughter. Nevertheless, he kept his vow.

Fathers are usually very fond of their daughters, providing for them, paying for their college education, and giving them into marriage without sparing the costs. There are exceptions, of course. In the story *On Golden Pond,* a crotchety father is not on good terms with his daughter. Sometimes it is daughters who contribute to strained relations with their fathers.

In any event, neither parent should make foolish or improper vows with regard to their children. Christian parents care for their children and teach them to love Jesus Christ, who gave His life for their salvation. But parents cannot live the children's lives for them. They should not prematurely commit their children to a certain vocation when it is not yet evident that they are fitted for it. They should not make irrevocable vows that could harm their children's future.

In one respect to be sure, all parents know they tread on safe and solid ground—that is, bringing up their children in the truths of God's Word, reminding them of their Baptism, instilling in them love for the Savior, and living their own lives as faithful Christian servants. God will surely bless such a parent-child relationship.

PRAYER SUGGESTION

Thank God for faithful fathers, asking the Holy Spirit for spiritual strength to enable children to grow up in Christ, their Savior.

God's Word, Twice-told

In the past God spoke to our forefathers through the prophets at many times and in various ways, but in these last days He has spoken to us by His Son. Hebrews 1:1–2

One may read Hawthorne's, *Twice-told Tales.* The word "tale" cannot be used for anything God has said, but "twice-told revelation" can be, for God gave us His Word in the Old Testament as prophecy and in the New Testament as fulfillment.

Old Testament prophets openly proclaimed God's Word. God communicated with His people "in various ways," that is, through prophetic writings, dreams and visions, signs and wonders, or in direct address as when He spoke directly to Moses and Samuel.

We can say that the many revelations of God amounted to just one prophecy that Isaiah 53 so clearly states: The Son of God would be born as a baby to keep the Law people had transgressed and to take upon Himself the complete load of sin and atone for it.

The Lord God, ever generous, spoke for a second time in the New Testament through the words and events marking the fulfillment of this prophecy. He spoke through Jesus Christ, the Word personified. What more effective way for God to speak than through His own Son, through Christ's very work and witness?

The message delivered through Jesus Christ as God's spokesman had one grand theme: "God so loved the world that He gave His one and only Son, that whoever believes in Him shall not perish but have eternal life" (John 3:16). To that end, Jesus named apostles whom He endowed with the Holy Spirit so they correctly spoke and wrote the Word of God. The New Testament is God's second message—the message of fulfillment. Praise the Lord!

PRAYER SUGGESTION

Ask the Holy Spirit to continue to open your heart and mind to the truths of Holy Scripture and its testimony of Christ.

The Divine Counselor Is Promised

"The Counselor, the Holy Spirit, whom the Father will send in My name, will teach you all things and will remind you of everything I have said to you." John 14:26

Have you ever tried to move a heavy sofa or a long table by yourself? It's not easy. First you take hold of one end and move it, then you move to the other end and shove. The job is much easier when another person helps. This is the image in the Greek verb for what the Spirit does for those who have come to faith in Christ. He "helps us in our weakness" (Romans 8:26)—literally, "together with us He takes hold of the other end" to move the burden.

It is only the Holy Spirit who, through the Gospel, brings us to faith in Jesus Christ as our Savior. "No one can say, 'Jesus is Lord,' except by the Holy Spirit" (1 Corinthians 12:3).

The Holy Spirit, whom Jesus sent, continues to work in us after we have come to faith. He is the Counselor, or Paraclete, literally "one who is called to someone's aid." We have the image of the Spirit taking hold on the other end.

As Counselor, the Spirit *consoles*. He imparts the comfort, consolation, and peace implicit in the forgiveness of sins. As Counselor, the Spirit also *teaches*. A teacher cannot do the learning for the pupil—he or she can only present, remind, encourage. The Spirit *enlightens*; He helps us solve problems. He keeps on *teaching* us that our salvation is found in Christ alone. He helps us *recall*; as Jesus said, He "will remind you of everything I have said to you." What Jesus said to His disciples then He says also to us now.

Our Lord left His disciples through death's door and later ascended into heaven. But in His place came another Comforter, the Holy Spirit. How well for us that He came!

PRAYER SUGGESTION

Ask for the continued indwelling of the Holy Spirit in your heart.

A People Repossessed

You are not your own; you were bought at a price.
Therefore honor God with your body. 1 Corinthians 6:19–20

Repossession is a familiar concept. We speak of a repossessed automobile, for example, as having been taken back and given a new owner. In the days of slavery, even humans were bought and sold. The idea that people could be the property of other, equally mortal, people is repulsive to us today. Yet we can think of our relationship to God as one of repossession. Our heavenly Father reclaims us and is our new owner and master.

It was not always so. We were once possessed by someone else. In the New Testament gospels, we read of afflicted people whom Jesus freed from demonic possession. In the region of the Garasenes, for example, He ordered an evil spirit out of a man. This person recognized his new Lord and *begged* for the privilege of following Him. This was a man repossessed. His mission from this time forth was to tell what great things God had done for him.

It is unlikely that any of us have been in such a transition, yet as Christians we are a repossessed people. Before our baptism into Christ, we were owned by the devil. In Holy Baptism, we were asked, "Do you renounce the devil and all his works and all his ways?" Through our godparents, or we ourselves, we replied that we did. Then and there we came under a new owner: the Lord, Jesus Christ.

Such repossession is of the greatest significance for Christians, which is the point Paul made in the above reading. We are no longer the slaves of sin. We are a repossessed people, bought with a price: our Savior's holy, precious blood.

PRAYER SUGGESTION

Tell the Lord Jesus that you gladly live in His kingdom and willingly serve Him.

Equal Status

You are no longer foreigners and aliens, but fellow citizens with God's people and members of God's household. Ephesians 2:19

The busiest day at Ellis Island in New York Harbor was April 17, 1907, when 12,000 immigrants were admitted into the U.S.

God had His own chosen people in the Old Testament: the descendants of Abraham, with whom God established a solemn covenant. He was their God and they were His people. This Old Testament "church" had its pre-sacraments: circumcision and the Passover, plus many other rites and ceremonies.

But Israel was disobedient, which nullified the old covenant. God issued a new covenant for the creation of a new church, a new fellowship of believers, a communion of saints. The birthday of the New Testament church came when the Holy Spirit was poured out on the apostles on Pentecost. On that day, 3,000 were baptized and became the nucleus of Christ's church.

The first members of the Christian church were Jews. But Jesus was clear that He wanted Gentiles included in this church as well, and instructed the apostles to teach all nations and to baptize them in the name of Father, Son, and Holy Spirit. Paul was Christ's chosen instrument to carry the Gospel of Christ's salvation to the Gentile world. It was Jesus' directive to assimilate into church membership people who had been pagan. This is the apostle's concern in the text above. The newcomers, believers in Christ's death and resurrection for their salvation, enjoyed equal status with the original citizens in God's kingdom, the Jewish Christians.

The same is true of relationships in the local congregation. Newcomers, regardless of their origin of birth, are always welcome. They enjoy equal membership as life-long members.

PRAYER SUGGESTION

Thank the Savior Jesus Christ for making you a member of His church.

The Knowledge To Be Revealed

What we will be has not yet been made known. But we know that when He appears, we shall be like Him, for we shall see Him as He is.
1 John 3:2

When we enter the realm of faith and spiritual things, a whole world of questions opens up: what God is like, how we stand in God's sight, whether our prayers are heard.

John opened this chapter with an exclamation of wonder concerning God's great love. The heavenly Father lavishes His love on us—it is not trickled down to us or given sparingly—but *lavished*, poured out and over in great abundance. That love is centered in His Son. Jesus, as Mediator, stepped into the sin-created breach and reconciled us to God. Thanks to His atonement (*at-one*-ment), God accepts us as His children. Baptized into communion with the Triune God, we savor divine grace. We have a foretaste of eternal life. We know quite well what our present status is. We are God's people whose life is blest, whose prayers are heard, whose purpose in life is to live under Christ in His kingdom and serve Him.

But what about the future? Who will we be in the life to come? While much has not been revealed to us in God's Word, there is something we do know: "When He appears, we shall be like Him." Our Lord rose from the dead with a glorified body. When He reappears at the end of time, we shall see Him in His glory and our bodies will likewise be glorified. The apostle Paul stated, "We [shall] bear the likeness of the Man [Second Adam] from heaven" (1 Corinthians 15:49). And, "As in Adam all die, so in Christ all will be made alive" (1 Corinthians 15:22).

Yes, in Christ we have received much, and there is more to come!

PRAYER SUGGESTION

Ask the Savior Jesus Christ to sustain and strengthen your faith in His salvation.

Tricked into Disobedience

The woman said, "The serpent deceived me, and I ate." Genesis 3:13

Satan, the father of lies, is a real-life troublemaker. The devil knows how to trick people into doing things that have dire consequences. For instance, his outright deception induced Eve to disobey God and commit an act resulting in her death. Satan "masquerades as an angel of light" (2 Corinthians 11:14).

The devil tried similar tactics on Jesus, the Second Adam, when he tempted Him to disobey and defy God, and thereby destroy God's salvation plan. But as true God, Jesus saw through the scheme and overcame the Tempter.

Scripture finds no fault with innocent, playful tactics such as children playing jokes on one another. But it condemns "dirty tricks." Such an act was committed by Jacob and his mother, Rebekah, when they tricked nearly blind Isaac into thinking he was blessing Esau when he was actually blessing Jacob (Genesis 27). Later in life Jacob was given a taste of his own medicine when his father-in-law-to-be tricked him into marrying Leah when it was Rachel he really wanted as his wife (Genesis 29).

St. Paul gave us good instruction: "Each of you must put off falsehood and speak truthfully to his neighbor, for we are all members of one body" (Ephesians 4:25). As Christians we all belong to Jesus Christ and are members of His body, the church. We who have come to have faith in Christ are a new creation. We have put off the old self and are "created to be like God in true righteousness and holiness" (Ephesians 4:24).

Tricks that reflect goodwill and innocent humor add levity to life, but we need to always beware of Satan's tactics.

PRAYER SUGGESTION

Thank God for dealing truthfully with you in His Word and for sending Jesus as Savior.

Reversing One's Course

They only heard the report: "The man who formerly persecuted us is now preaching the faith he once tried to destroy." Galatians 1:23

The woman designated "Roe" in the 1973 Supreme Court case *Roe v Wade* that opened the door to legal abortion had a change of heart. She was baptized into the Christian faith in 1995.

Saul the Pharisee also had a change of heart. Once a man who breathed "out murderous threats against the Lord's disciples" (Acts 9:1), he was converted on the Emmaus Road and baptized by the disciple Ananias. Eventually Paul proclaimed the saving faith in Christ with the same zeal he once directed toward its destruction.

Many people whom the Holy Spirit brings to faith in Christ reverse their course and try to make amends for their wrongdoing. The jailer at Philippi, after his conversion, washed and dressed the wounds of Paul and Silas that he himself had inflicted. Zacchaeus, having acknowledged the identity of Jesus Christ, no longer cheated and stole, but said, "I give half of my possessions to the poor, and if I have cheated anybody out of anything, I will pay back four times the amount" (Luke 19:8). True conversion effects change, for the Holy Spirit gives us new hearts and minds.

To say "Jesus is Lord" is a creed that people cannot make on their own. It is the work of the Holy Spirit coming into human hearts through the Gospel. Their lives will reveal a new lifestyle. Paul declared, "If anyone is in Christ, he is a new creation; the old has gone, the new has come!" (2 Corinthians 5:17)

On Pentecost, the Holy Spirit descended with power, giving birth to the Christian church. Little "pentecosts" still occur when sinners, having come to faith, confess their sins and promise to amend their lives. May it ever be so.

PRAYER SUGGESTION

Praise God for bringing people to faith in Jesus through the Gospel.

Life, God's Gift

The LORD God formed the man from the dust of the ground and breathed into his nostrils the breath of life, and the man became a living being. Genesis 2:7

Suicide has been described as a "permanent solution to a temporary problem." It is contrary to God's will and the purpose for which a human is born. Life comes from God and it has three distinct aspects: physical, spiritual, and eternal.

The Book of Genesis narrates the bodily creation of Adam. God gave him and all his descendants eyes, ears, and all his members, his reason and all his senses. The Creator gave him a heart that beats, lungs for breathing, a brain for thinking and reasoning, a voice to speak and to sing praises to his Maker.

The life God creates and sustains is not only physical and mental but spiritual as well. This is the inner life, the life of faith and godly knowledge that consists in living in communion with God. This gift makes a person a new creation in Christ Jesus, by whose Word and Spirit that individual has come to rely on Jesus for salvation. John imparts tremendous meaning in these words: "In Him was life, and that life was the light of men" (John 1:4).

A third perspective of the total life God gives is eternal life. It is the unending life, lived without interruption in the immediate presence of our Creator in heaven. "Now this is eternal life: that they may know You, the only true God, and Jesus Christ, whom You have sent" (John 17:3). To know God intimately means we will abide in His presence eternally.

When we consider life in all its dimensions, we realize how precious a gift of God it is. Dare we despise it, abuse it, or terminate it as we see fit? Indeed not!

PRAYER SUGGESTION

Praise God for having fearfully and wonderfully made you.

An Important Little Prayer

One day Jesus was praying in a certain place. When He finished, one of His disciples said to Him, "Lord, teach us to pray, just as John taught his disciples." Luke 11:1

It is said, "Sometimes a little flower goes unnoticed in the shadow of a giant oak." Such is the case with a little prayer in Luke's gospel: "Lord, teach us to pray." It is overshadowed by the great prayer immediately following. In fact, it was in response to this little prayer that Jesus taught His disciples the Lord's Prayer.

Let there be no mistake: the Lord's Prayer is a perfect prayer, covering all our spiritual and physical needs. But this excellence should not cause us to overlook the little prayer tucked away before it: "Lord, teach us to pray."

Jesus still answers this request. By example and precept, He teaches us to pray confidently. He teaches us to pray in His name, for He is the Reconciler who made peace with God on our behalf. He tells us: "Come confidently before your heavenly Father and simply state your needs, or the needs of another person, in your own words. Tell the Father that Jesus sent you."

Jesus gave instruction in prayer on other occasions. After cursing the barren fig tree, He told His disciples that they could pray with power, saying, "I tell you, whatever you ask for in prayer, believe that you have received it, and it will be yours. And when you stand praying, if you hold anything against anyone, forgive him, so that your Father in heaven may forgive you your sins" (Mark 11:24–25). Again, Jesus said, "I will do whatever you ask in My name, so that the Son may bring glory to the Father. You may ask Me for anything in My name, and I will do it" (John 14:13–14).

Jesus will also be our prayer instructor if we but ask Him.

PRAYER SUGGESTION

Ask the Lord Jesus, seated at God's right hand, to teach you to pray.

The Holy Spirit: Heavenly Dew

"When He, the Spirit of truth, comes, He will guide you into all truth." John 16:13

Nothing is as refreshing as water. Because the Holy Spirit gives new spiritual life to the arid desert of the human heart, He can be compared to heavenly dew. That is why in a Pentecost hymn we sing: "O gentle Dew, from heaven now fall With power upon the hearts of all, Thy tender love instilling."

Our Lord taught that the Spirit of truth would come to bear witness to Him through the Word of God. The Spirit and the Word always go together. As Jesus said, "The Spirit gives life. ... The words I have spoken to you are spirit and they are life" (John 6:63). The Word, like the Holy Spirit, is gently refreshing and yet powerful, as Moses declared in Deuteronomy 32:2, "Let my teaching fall like rain and my words descend like dew, like showers on new grass, like abundant rain on tender plants."

As the heavenly Dew, the Spirit gives life and renews us as He creates and confirms faith in the redeeming, merits of Jesus Christ.

We note from Jesus' words that the Spirit does not *compel* anyone to accept the truth He speaks. Rather, He *impels*, persuades, counsels, comforts, and *guides*. He opens hearts and minds to an appreciation and understanding of God's saving love in Christ. He furthers Christian growth, enabling us to bear the fruit of faith. This He could not accomplish in us if He came down as a gully-washer or as rain in bucketfuls. Yet He is not weak, not ineffective, not tolerant of sin. Jesus brings this out by saying that "He will convict the world of guilt in regard to sin, and righteousness, and judgment" (John 16:8). He is hard on out-and-out unbelief, but for Christians He is heavenly Dew.

PRAYER SUGGESTION

Give thanks to the Spirit for refreshing you through the Word.

Correcting Misdirected Zeal

They [Israelites] are zealous for God,
but their zeal is not based on knowledge. Romans 10:2

George Orwell, an English socialist, thought socialism and communism would solve society's problems. But then Orwell had a change of heart. He discovered that communism meant total control (totalitarianism) of a person. Disillusioned, he wrote the novel *1984* that featured the all-watching, all-controlling Big Brother.

No one is better qualified to articulate misdirected zeal than Paul. As Saul the Pharisee, he persecuted the church. He was "a Hebrew of Hebrews;" in regard to the law, a Pharisee; as for zeal, persecuting the church; as for legalistic righteousness, faultless. It took a complete conversion, in a way similar to an Orwellian about-face, to direct him on his way as Christ's apostle.

Not just Pharisees, all people are—by nature—inclined to presume salvation and peace with God is based on good works. But even the most earnest striving for righteousness is futile. The hymn writer spoke for all: "Could my zeal no respite know, Could my tears forever flow, All for sin could not atone; Thou must save, and Thou alone." How then are we to achieve righteousness? The gospel of Paul provides the answer, "Christ is the end of the Law so that there may be righteousness for everyone who believes" (Romans 10:4). Our Savior, Jesus Christ, "gave Himself for us to redeem us from all wickedness and to purify for Himself a people that are His very own, eager to do what is good" (Titus 2:14).

God's people do indeed desire to serve God with good works, but this is a response caused by the Holy Spirit as He changes our hearts and creates in us faith in Christ's merit and mediation. As a fruit of this faith is a new zeal to serve God and others.

PRAYER SUGGESTION

Ask for stronger faith in your Redeemer and great zeal to do His will.

The Dignity of Daily Life

Whether you eat or drink or whatever you do,
do it all for the glory of God. 1 Corinthians 10:31

Numerous paintings show the Virgin Mary in sublime activities: attending to the infant Jesus, consorting with angels, reigning as the queen of heaven. It was indeed a great honor and an exclusive responsibility to be the mother of God's Son. It is fitting to honor her, which the Christian church does on August 15, the Festival of St. Mary, mother of our Lord. But in her everyday life Mary was a down-to-earth person who honored God by faithfully performing her duties as a wife and mother.

Vocation for many people means supervising the household, serving one another in the family circle. Regardless of vocation, the Lord God requires faithfulness. He wants even our eating and drinking to give Him glory.

Christians have the mind of Christ. They strive to grow in their sanctification so as to make progress in Christ-mindedness. They know what Christ has done for them. He, God's faithful Servant, was obedient to the point of death, even death on a cross, to perfect their salvation. The writer of the letter to the Hebrews stated, "He was faithful to the one who appointed Him, just as Moses was faithful in all God's house" (Hebrews 3:2). This faithfulness is all the more remarkable because Jesus was not God's slave or servant but His co-equal Son.

As God's sons and daughters we strive to be more like Jesus. "Each one should use whatever gift he has received to serve others, faithfully administering God's grace in various forms" (1 Peter 4:10). Mary, the mother of our Savior, is an example for us to use whatever talents we have to serve Him.

PRAYER SUGGESTION

Pray for a greater measure of faithfulness in doing your daily work.

Enrolled in the School of Humility

"Take My yoke upon you and learn from Me,
for I am gentle and humble in heart." Matthew 11:29

Ralph Waldo Emerson, American essayist and poet, said the secret of the scholar is this: "Everyman I meet is my master in some point, and in that I will learn from him."

Jesus had a special quality that we can learn from Him: humility. Jesus taught humility by words but mostly by what He was. He, the Son of God, was born in a stable from a poor virgin. He, the Creator of the universe, had no place to call His own. He, a spiritual King, rode meekly into Jerusalem on a donkey. He, the Savior of all mankind, was crucified and His body was laid in another man's grave. All this was humility personified.

All this comes as no surprise. By His own words, Jesus had come to serve and to give His life as a ransom for all sinners. St. Paul testified that Jesus, the Servant of servants, "humbled Himself and became obedient to death—even death on a cross!" (Philippians 2:8).

Faith in Jesus Christ, as our complete Savior and a Friend whose love constrains us to follow in His steps, enables us to lay aside pride and to put on humility. It is like going to school to learn humility and its related qualities: love, gentleness, sympathy, friendliness.

When He speaks of our taking His yoke upon us, we are not to think of a device laid on the necks of draft animals. It is rather like a tie that binds us tenderly to the One who has borne all our sins. It unites us so closely to Him that, in the words we can "cast all [our] anxiety on Him" (1 Peter 5:7).

PRAYER SUGGESTION

Tell your Lord and Savior Jesus Christ that you want to enroll in His school of humility.

Knowing God through Christ

Anyone who runs ahead and does not continue in the teaching of Christ does not have God; whoever continues in the teaching has both the Father and the Son. 2 John 9

In his poem, "The Church in Dallas," Lewis Chamberlain declared, "God is big in Dallas." But alongside this, he said, "there isn't much of Jesus."

It is true of cities the world over that there is a lot of God but little of Christ. Opinion polls indicate that up to 95 percent of people in the United States believe there is a God, but not nearly that many profess faith in Jesus as God's Son and the Savior.

Apart from Christ, this professed "God" comes close to being a non-god. Certainly He is not professed as the heavenly Father, but as the Supreme Being, a Force, Higher Intelligence, Prime Mover. The true God reveals Himself in Holy Scripture as the Father of our Lord Jesus Christ and, through Him, as the Father of all who believe in the Son as their Savior.

Our Lord declares, "The Father judges no one, but has entrusted all judgment to the Son, that all may honor the Son just as they honor the Father. He who does not honor the Son does not honor the Father, who sent Him" (John 5:22–23). And, "Now this is eternal life: that they may know You, the only true God, and Jesus Christ, whom You have sent" (John 17:3). And in asserting that God is triune, Paul said, "May the grace of the Lord Jesus Christ, and the love of God, and the fellowship of the Holy Spirit be with you all" (2 Corinthians 13:14).

If it is true that there is much of God but little of Jesus, it is a situation dating to the time of St. John. We know what to do when others talk about God but leave out Christ: tell them the truth!

PRAYER SUGGESTION

Thank the heavenly Father for sending His Son to be your Savior.

The Church's Proper Concern

As He [Jesus] approached Jerusalem and saw the city,
He wept over it. Luke 19:41

W. H. Auden, a Christian philosopher, poet, and man of letters, said some people are guilty of "talking of navigation while the ship is going down."

In Jesus' time, people of Jerusalem discussed many topics and engaged in many enterprises. Much of their concern pertained to politics under Roman rule. Paying taxes was another issue. Little was recorded about the spiritual condition of God's people, who under corrupt leadership were like passengers of a ship who were unaware of trouble below the surface of the water.

As members of the New Testament church, we need to be alert lest we celebrate on deck while a leak has sprung below. Many of the problems of the churches to whom John addressed Revelation prevail today: spiritual satiety, blending of God's Word with human wisdom, neglecting the means of grace.

It is still time to take spiritual inventory—of ourselves and of the church at large—and to set in order things that are wanting. It is still time to spread the Gospel, telling people the Good News of salvation in Christ Jesus. It is the time to proclaim what St. Paul wrote: "When the kindness and love of God our Savior appeared, He saved us, not because of righteous things we had done, but because of His mercy. He saved us through the washing of rebirth and renewal by the Holy Spirit, whom He poured out on us generously through Jesus Christ our Savior" (Titus 3:4–6).

It is still time to be encouraged and comforted by Jesus' promise, "Do not be afraid, little flock, for your Father has been pleased to give you the kingdom" (Luke 12:32).

PRAYER SUGGESTION

Ask Jesus to strengthen His church and let His kingdom come.

Living in God's Sunlight

Now in Christ Jesus you who once were far away have been brought near through the blood of Christ. Ephesians 2:13

Edgar Allan Poe was plagued by neuroses and phobias. He would venture out only at night; during the day he stayed indoors with the curtains drawn tight against the daylight.

Some people love both physical and spiritual darkness. "Everyone who does evil hates the light, and will not come into the light for fear that his deeds will be exposed" (John 3:20). Christians have come out of the night of sin and guilt and fear and live in the Sonlight of God's love. Jesus, the Light of the world and the Sun of righteousness, shines on us. Paul testified: God "has rescued us from the dominion of darkness and brought us into the kingdom of the Son He loves, in whom we have redemption, the forgiveness of sins" (Colossians 1:13).

It becomes us as God's baptized and redeemed children to "live a life of love" (Ephesians 5:2) and follow in the footsteps of Jesus, no longer stumbling about in spiritual darkness. We walk in His ways, confident in God's mercy and grace.

How wonderful to live openly and honestly in the light! As God's people we have nothing to hide. Our sins are washed away by the water and the Word—they are forgiven and forgotten. "Who will bring any charge against those whom God has chosen? It is God who justifies. Who is he that condemns? Christ Jesus, who died—more than that, who was raised to life—is at the right hand of God and is also interceding for us" (Romans 8:33–34).

So now we don't have to hide in darkened rooms. We can come out and thrive under the Sonlight!

PRAYER SUGGESTION

Give thanks to God for granting you the light of the Gospel of salvation in Christ Jesus.

Truth That Can Be Known

Jesus said, "If you hold to My teaching, you are really My disciples.
Then you will know the truth, and the truth will set you free." John 8:31

Robert Ingersoll (1833–1899), a lawyer and politician, was agnostic. He asserted that one could not know facts about God, the universe, the destiny of humankind, the hereafter. Agnostics can raise questions, but they have no answers. Ingersoll stated, "Every cradle asks whence? And every grave asks whither?" Agnostics reject the Christian creed yet adhere to creeds of their own. At the burial of a child Ingersoll offered this comfort: "It is better to have loved and lost than never to have loved at all."

Pontius Pilate may not have known about the philosophy of agnosticism, but his question "What is truth?" (John 18:38), shows that he leaned in that direction. His flippant remark came in response to Jesus' words, "Everyone on the side of truth listens to Me" (John 18:37).

Jesus taught the truth concerning sinfulness and where it leads: death. He emphasized the truth of God's saving purpose in sending of His Son: "God so loved the world that He gave His one and only Son, that whoever believes in Him shall not perish but have eternal life" (John 3:16). While we were not present at this conversation, we nevertheless know this truth because it is revealed in Holy Scripture. It can be known, believed, and experienced, as Jesus said, by *doing* the truth instead of merely letting it go. Through the Word of the Gospel, the Holy Spirit bears testimony to the truth of Christ. To be by faith attuned to God's purpose, as made known concerning the atoning work of Jesus, is to be a disciple, free to do God's will—and assured of truth.

PRAYER SUGGESTION

Pray that the Holy Spirit may strengthen you in your conviction that Jesus is the Christ and your Savior.

From Discord to Concord

"He who is least among you all—he is the greatest." Luke 9:48

The ancient Greeks had a legend about the goddess Eris. Angered because she was not invited to a wedding, she created a conflict. Eris threw a golden apple among the guests. The apple had this note on it: "To the fairest." Immediately an argument ensued among those present, each one claiming to be the fairest. And Eris lived up to her title as the goddess of discord.

Among Christ's disciples, discord arose over which of them was the greatest. Jesus used the occasion to teach a lesson in humility. He drew a child to His side, saying that whoever welcomed the child welcomed Him and therewith the Father (Luke 18:16).

There were other times when the apostles jockeyed for position. Pride was at the root of their discord. As they matured in their spiritual lives, they began to overcome the rivalry. In their close relationship with Jesus, who laid aside His divine majesty and became a humble servant, the apostles became more Christlike. After His ascension, they were together with one accord (Acts 1:14).

The formula for concord is always this: Christ is our peace who brings peace. This was the case in the early Christian church when some wanted to adhere to the Old Testament rite of circumcision and to the forbidden foods. St. Paul addressed this, writing that Christ "has destroyed the barrier, the dividing wall of hostility" (Ephesians 2:14). How did He do this? "His [Christ's] purpose was to create in Himself one new man out of the two, thus making peace, and in this one body to reconcile both of them to God through the cross, by which He put to death their hostility" (Ephesians 2:15–16). This, still today, is the formula for concord.

PRAYER SUGGESTION

Pray that Christ, the Head of the church, will be our peace also in the visible church.

All Honor to the Son

"The Father ... has entrusted all judgment to the Son, that all may honor the Son just as they honor the Father." John 5:22–23

Two great errors concerning the person of Jesus Christ are the denial of His true humanity and the denial of His true deity.

Our Lord was not a make-believe man but a true flesh-and-blood person. Holy Scripture teaches that He possessed a true human nature, enabling Him to take every human being's place as He obeyed the Law and as He suffered and died for the sins of all.

The Bible teaches with equal clarity that Jesus, the Son of God, has a divine nature. All that is God's is Christ's as well: divine names, divine attributes, divine works, divine honor and glory. He is in all respects equal with God, one with the Father, without the confusion of Persons. With divine honor and glory, and in complete righteousness and wisdom, He will conduct the judgment at His Second Coming.

Our Lord's first coming was that of Redeemer. "When the time had fully come, God sent His Son, born of a woman, born under law, to redeem those under law, that we might receive the full rights of sons" (Galatians 4:4–5). Jesus carried out this assignment to perfection. On the cross He yielded up His spirit and died only after He could say, "It is finished" (John 19:30).

Our Lord's Second Coming is that of judge of the living and the dead. For those who believed in Him as Savior, He is the deliverer. Since the exalted Christ will exercise the divine function of judging all people, He will be regarded as true God, as the Son equal with the Father.

The church, in addressing itself to Christ, sings: "All glory, laud, and honor, To You, Redeemer, King."

PRAYER SUGGESTION

Tell the Savior that you will honor Him today in work and in rest.

The Triune God Revealed

A voice from heaven said, "This is My Son, whom I love; with Him I am well pleased." Matthew 3:17

Many worship services begin "in the name of the Father and of the Son and of the Holy Spirit," and close with, "Praise Father, Son, and Holy Ghost." Our entire worship is directed to the Holy Trinity.

One of the clear revelations of the Triune God occurred at the baptism of Jesus. As Christ, the second Person of the Trinity, stood in the river Jordan, the Holy Spirit, the third Person, descended from heaven in the form of a dove and settled on Jesus. The Father, the first Person, spoke from heaven: "This is My Son, whom I love."

Another clear reference to the doctrine of the Holy Trinity occurred when Jesus gave us the Great Commission: "Go and make disciples of all nations, baptizing them in the name of the Father and of the Son and of the Holy Spirit" (Matthew 28:19). The apostles centered their teaching in the Holy Trinity. "May the grace of the Lord Jesus Christ, and the love of God, and the fellowship of the Holy Spirit be with you all" (2 Corinthians 13:14).

The Old Testament Scriptures do not directly articulate the doctrine of the Trinity but do so indirectly. For example, the Lord told Moses that the high priest Aaron was to speak this blessing on the people: "The LORD bless you and keep you; the LORD make His face shine upon you and be gracious to you; the LORD turn His face toward you and give you peace" (Numbers 6:24–26).

The revelation of the Holy Trinity is comforting. It tells us not only that God in heaven made us, but He sent His one and only Son to redeem us and through the power of the Holy Spirit we are kept in the saving faith to the end.

PRAYER SUGGESTION

Praise the Triune God, from whom all blessings flow.

Thanking God for Our Hands

I praise You because I am fearfully and wonderfully made.
Psalm 139:14

If ever we were to run out of things to be thankful for—and that is inconceivable—we can thank God for our hands.

Our hands—we need to take good care of them because they come in so … well, "handy." Hands, like other members of the body, can suffer from neglect or overuse. It was an eye-catching article in a newspaper that reported that a composer had written a special work, "A Concerto for Two Left Hands." He wrote it for two pianists whose right hands were suffering from excessive use.

Our hands are God's gifts. David prayed to God, "You created my inmost being; You knit me together in my mother's womb" (Psalm 139:13). God gave us, as Martin Luther has taught us to confess, "eyes, ears, and all my members, my reason and all my senses." We can add to that: "God gave me hands."

With our hands, we can take care of our personal needs: washing and dressing ourselves, eating and drinking. We can do our work with skilled hands. We can sew, as did Dorcas, "who was always doing good and helping the poor" (Acts 9:36). We can make an honest living as artists, artisans, mechanics. Any work with our hands is no disgrace if what we do is honest. "He who has been stealing must steal no longer, but must work, doing something useful with his own hands" (Ephesians 4:28).

What else can we do with our hands? We can lift them up in prayer (1 Timothy 2:8). How appropriate it is to sing: "Take my hands and let them move at the impulse of Thy love." We are thankful that Christ extended His hands on a cross to redeem us.

PRAYER SUGGESTION

Say a brief prayer to thank God for your hands and other members of the body.

Love Speaks Louder Than Words

If I speak in the tongues of men and of angels, but have not love,
I am only a resounding gong or a clanging cymbal. 1 Corinthians 13:1

People are often greatly impressed by dramatic statements, by political speeches, by eloquent sermons. Sometimes it is not the forcefulness of the speaker but the content of the speech that strikes home. This was certainly the case with those who heard the words of Jesus. After His sermon on parables, the people said in their amazement, "Where did this man get this wisdom?" (Matthew 13:54).

It is very proper to voice appreciation when a truth is well stated. Who of us, on hearing Peter's impromptu confession: "You are the Christ, the Son of the living God" (Matthew 16:16), would not have replied, "I wish I'd said that!" The statement, brief as it was, touched all the bases as far as the person Jesus was concerned. Of course, we confess Christ not only by words but also with our lives in which our love speaks—speaks louder than words in many instances.

Love is the essential ingredient in all we do and say. The apostle closed the chapter with these words: "Now these three remain: faith, hope and love. But the greatest of these is love" (1 Corinthians 13:13).

Of a false messiah it could be said, "His words are more soothing than oil, yet they are drawn swords" (Psalm 55:21). But Jesus, as St. Peter confessed, was the Christ, the true Messiah. What a sermon Jesus "preached" when in love He gave Himself into death for our salvation!

PRAYER SUGGESTION

Thank the heavenly Father for having spoken to us through His Son.

God Forgives Our Debts

"As he [the king] began the settlement, a man who owed him ten thousand talents was brought to him." Matthew 18:24

Later in his life, Mark Twain entered into a partnership in a publishing firm that failed, leaving him heavily in debt. Despite his age, Twain increased his efforts as a writer and lecturer until the debt was paid. In contemporary times, singer Willie Nelson was in debt to the tune of 32 million dollars, most of it owed to the Internal Revenue Service. He, too, by strenuous effort, paid off the debt.

How do things stand in our spiritual relationship to God? Can we, by our own best efforts, work off the debts we have in God's sight? In the parable of an unmerciful servant, Jesus teaches that this is impossible.

Our debts before God are all our sins in thoughts, words, and deeds. They are so many that we cannot comprehend the amount. The hymn writer put it like this: "Not the labors of my hands, Can fulfill Thy Law's demands." He went on to say that even if his zeal knew no end and if his tears flowed forever, "all for sin could not atone."

What happens to our debts, past, present, and future? God laid them all on Jesus, the Lamb of God who took away all the sins of the world—even ours. Paul clearly stated, "[God] forgave us all our sins, having canceled the written code, with its regulations, that was against us and that stood opposed to us; He took it away, nailing it to the cross" (Colossians 2:13–14). In other words, God tore up our bills. He marked them all: "Paid for by the blood of Christ."

This promise applies to all who are "alive with Christ" (Ephesians 2:5), to all who trust in Him as their Savior.

PRAYER SUGGESTION

Tell Christ that you appreciate His atoning work and that you are willing to forgive others.

Total Commitment to God

Jesus replied: "'Love the Lord your God with all your heart and with all your soul and with all your mind.'" Matthew 22:37

When Queen Juliana of the Netherlands addressed an audience at Columbia University in New York City, she paid tribute to higher education and to those engaged in it. But she added this caution: "It is the heart and soul that rule the world, not the mind alone, however much the mind may think so."

Christian education is the training of the mind *and* heart. "If you confess with your mouth, 'Jesus is Lord,' and believe in your heart that God raised Him from the dead, you will be saved" (Romans 10:9). Jesus did not separate heart and soul from the mind, but kept them together.

Faith is also a matter of the mind. Before we can believe, we need to know *what* to believe. Unless we possess reason, intelligence, and understanding, it is impossible for the Bible to make us wise or to instruct us "for salvation through faith in Christ Jesus" (2 Timothy 3:15). This saving faith is sustained in us by the Holy Spirit through the sacraments and the Word. The Holy Spirit does this as well in infants and those whose minds are weak.

It is a well-balanced Christian who follows the example of Jesus of Nazareth, who "grew and became strong; He was filled with wisdom, and the grace of God was upon Him" (Luke 2:40). Growth goes with commitment. Queen Juliana's remark has special meaning for Christian parents who seek to bring up their children in the fourfold aspects of growth: spiritual, social, physical, and mental. To do anything less is, as someone has said, sending out sparrows to fight eagles.

PRAYER SUGGESTION

Ask for God's help for your total personal growth, especially for growing in your relationship with Christ.

A Day of Remembrance

I thank my God every time I remember you. Philippians 1:3

A World War II ambulance driver remembered finding a dead GI on a battlefield with a half-eaten candy bar in his hand. The saying, "In the midst of life we are in death" certainly applies to those who face death in battle.

On Memorial Day we honor those who gave their lives for their country. We recall the times and circumstances which made it necessary for citizens to answer the call to duty. If they were members of our Christian families, we feel much closer to them as partners with us in the Gospel.

As we recall the past, especially as we remember our loved ones, we do the next thing: Give thanks. We cannot convey our gratitude to the dead, but we can to those still alive. Above all, we thank God for all His blessings and for giving our country dedicated men and women who offered military support to the land.

The message of Memorial Day applies also to us as Christian citizens. We need confidence, especially in times of peril, that the work God has begun in us, in bringing us to faith in Jesus Christ, He will bring to completion and consummation when we come before Him, either on the day of our own death or on the day of Christ's return. As Christian people, we are involved in "defending and confirming the Gospel" (Philippians 1:7)—the gospel of peace with God through the reconciling work of Jesus Christ, this gift of salvation we accept in faith.

The more we are involved in proclaiming and practicing Christ's gospel of peace with God, the greater will be peace on earth regardless of war.

PRAYER SUGGESTION

Pray with the psalmist that God may make "wars cease to the ends of the earth" (Psalm 46:9).

Good Government

Give Your servant a discerning heart to govern Your people and to distinguish between right and wrong. 1 Kings 3:9

On Memorial Day, a civic occasion, we remember all who have served their country, especially those who made the supreme sacrifice.

It is appropriate at any time of the year to touch on the larger themes of good government and citizenship. Who is a good ruler? The Greek philosopher Plato held that the government should consist of wise and just men who have studied philosophy for many years and assume their rule only with their fiftieth year of age.

Wisdom and experience are helpful assets to those who rule. But other qualifications are needed: an upright character, a reverence for human life, recognition of God's moral law as the basis of manmade laws. Because state and church are legally separate, we cannot insist that all our rulers be Christian. But it is to the good of government and its citizens when our rulers are given to prayer and the study of God's Word.

As citizens, we support the rulers we have elected to public office. We do this because we love God, the supreme Ruler and Preserver of law and order. He is also the Father of our Lord and Savior Jesus Christ.

We pray for all who are in rightful authority, asking that God would guide them. In his last words, King David, the father of Solomon, declared, "When one rules over men in righteousness, when he rules in the fear of God, he is like the light of morning at sunrise on a cloudless morning" (2 Samuel 23:3–4). May our civic leaders use their skills and abilities to provide us with good government. And may all people come to faith in Jesus Christ, the King of kings and Savior of all.

PRAYER SUGGESTION

Ask God to bless our native land and all its inhabitants.

The Two Gardens

Build houses and settle down;
plant gardens and eat what they produce. Jeremiah 29:5

In the seal of the city of Chicago is the phrase, *Urbs in Horto*, a city in a garden. Chicago boasts of beautiful gardens but it is also home to run-down areas that are not so beautiful.

The history of sin and salvation took us into two gardens. The first was Eden where Adam and Eve had a beautiful garden home. But the serpent slithered in, and through it Satan led our first parents into sin. They were evicted from their garden home.

Adam fell into sin in the Garden of Eden. And in another garden, the Second Adam—Jesus Christ—began His descent into agony to atone for sin. In Gethsemane He prayed, suffered, and sweat blood on our behalf. These drops of blood were precursors the blood he shed on Calvary's cross as the world's Redeemer.

Because of the events in Gethsemane, on Calvary, and in the garden tomb, our lives are wholly changed. Thanks to the sanctifying work of the Holy Spirit in us, we are changed from desert into fruitful gardens to the glory of God and the good of mankind. This fruitfulness shows in the homes and communities we make. The prophet Jeremiah told the people in Babylonian captivity to become productive in their everyday activities by living holy lives. They were to dedicate time to building homes, planting gardens, enjoying the produce, marrying, and having families.

We can enjoy our gardens and feel the Lord's presence there. Because we hear the voice of Jesus speaking to us in God's Word, we sense its echo, as C. Austin Miles said so well in his song, "In the Garden": "And He walks with me, and He talks with me, And He tells me I am His own."

PRAYER SUGGESTION

Tell God how thankful you are for what He has done to bless you.

Letting God's Will Be Done

To Him who is able to do immeasurably more than all we ask or imagine, according to His power that is at work within us, to Him be glory in the church and in Christ Jesus throughout all generations, for ever and ever! Amen. Ephesians 3:20–21

John Steinbeck, Nobel Prize-winning author of more than 25 books, studied marine science at Stanford University. He received a "C" in freshman English; this student didn't appear to be an author in the making.

The lives of many people change course. God overrides the intentions of people and causes them to do His will. Truly, man proposes, but God disposes.

Few people have experienced a turn-around like that of Saul of Tarsus. In his misguided zeal as a Pharisee, he persecuted Christians. Then the exalted Jesus called him to be His apostle.

As a Christian you have already undergone a change for you were born again in the waters of your Baptism. But other changes may still occur—changes in vocation, family, lifestyle. When we come face-to-face with change, we pray that God's will be done to His glory and to our good. When our plans change, it is good to remember that God's plans are far superior to ours. It is a blessing to pray, "Thy will be done." Our Lord Himself prayed such during His agonizing hours in the Garden of Gethsemane: "Father, if You are willing, take this cup from Me; yet not My will, but Yours be done" (Luke 22:42).

Because Jesus yielded to God's will, He was enabled to die for the world's sins and to overcome death and the devil. It is God's will that the world be saved and come to know the truth. We gladly carry out God's will to bring the Gospel to every nation.

PRAYER SUGGESTION

Ask God to guide you at all times but especially when you face changes.

The One Offering

The death He died, He died to sin once for all. Romans 6:10

The only book Harper Lee wrote was *To Kill a Mockingbird,* a novel set in a southern town. Margaret Mitchell authored only one novel, *Gone With the Wind.*

Jesus, the Author and Perfecter of our faith, did not write any books. He came into the world to do one important work: to offer up Himself to atone for the sins of mankind. Thus He was both the Lamb to be offered and the High Priest to do the offering.

Old Testament priests had to bring offerings mornings, evenings, and on special occasions. But Jesus brought only *one* offering for sin—Himself. We read in the epistle to the Hebrews that backsliders "are crucifying the Son of God all over again" (Hebrews 6:6). This, as the context shows, is not to be understood as though they actually nail Christ to the cross again and again. But when people who were once Christians deny Christ and reject His proffered salvation, they are, in effect, repeating His crucifixion.

Yet this fact stands: Christ's was a one-time offering. It is a misconception to say that officiants at the altar offer Christ in an "unbloody sacrifice." For one thing, it is incorrect to think of Christ's offering on the cross as bloodless. The epistle states, "Without the shedding of blood there is no forgiveness" (Hebrews 9:22). Further, it is making Holy Communion a sacrifice when it is actually a sacrament.

Jesus said, "It is finished" (John 19:30). The Greek states *tetelestai,* which says that Jesus had completely fulfilled His work of the redemption. There was not to be another crucifixion. Salvation is a "done deed." Nothing can be added to it. How thankful we are for Christ's completed work!

PRAYER SUGGESTION

Express your gratitude to the Lord Jesus for His one offering for sin.

A God Too Small

Where your treasure is, there your heart will be also. Matthew 6:21

In *The Glass Menagerie,* Tennessee Williams cast Laura Wingfield in the role of a shy, retiring young woman who found escape from reality and responsibility by listening to phonograph records and playing with her collection of glass figures. Living in a make-believe world, she confused trivia with treasures.

Just a step away from finding escape in worthless things is the preoccupation with manmade idols. Many people find refuge in various forms of idolatry: money, career, themselves. Their gods are too small and are entirely unable to help them. The psalmist declared that idols are "made by the hands of men." And "Those who make them will be like them, and so will all who trust in them" (Psalm 115:8). In the same vein the prophet Jeremiah declared, "Like a scarecrow in a melon patch, their idols cannot speak; they must be carried because they cannot walk" (Jeremiah 10:5).

In the above text Jesus speaks of fine idolatry, that is, fearing, loving, and trusting in material things and making "gods" (or life's highest good) out of them. Instead of laying up treasures in heaven, some busy themselves with the acquisition of wealth. It shows where their heart is.

Much too small is any god created by the human imagination. The true God revealed Himself in Jesus Christ for the purpose of saving sinners. "The grace of God that brings salvation has appeared to all men. It teaches us to say 'No' to ungodliness and worldly passions, and to live self-controlled, upright and godly lives in this present age, while we wait for the blessed hope—the glorious appearing of our great God and Savior, Jesus Christ who gave Himself for us to redeem us" (Titus 2:11–14).

PRAYER SUGGESTION

Pray that you may grow in the grace and knowledge of God.

God, Always the Same

I the LORD *do not change. Malachi 3:6*

"The times, they are a-changing" is an expression made popular in a Bob Dylan song that expresses some of the social and moral change experienced during the 1960s and '70s. We live in a time of change that strikes at the roots of everyday life. For example, the explosion of knowledge called "the information highway" is almost overwhelming.

"Change and decay in all around I see," said Henry Lyte in his hymn, "Abide with Me." But he goes on: "O Thou, who changest not, abide with me." This is a consoling truth. The prophet Malachi reminded the people of his time that God kept His covenant and expected the Israelites to do the same. "I the LORD do not change," he quoted God. Similarly Moses said, "Before the mountains were born or You brought forth the earth and the world, from everlasting to everlasting You are God" (Psalm 90:2).

God is unchanging in His being and in His Word. He stands by all His promises of grace and mercy. He promised the patriarchs that He would send the Messiah to deliver His people from their sins, and this promise was kept when He sent His Son, the "Woman's Seed," to crush Satan's power. Jesus Christ came at the fullness of time, born of the Virgin Mary. He was "crucified, died, and was buried." And He rose from the dead, full confirmation that God's promise was kept. Amid a changing world He "is the same yesterday and today and forever" (Hebrews 13:8).

What a great comfort to us that God is ever the same. Through the unchanging, everlasting Gospel, the power of the Holy Spirit is released to make us faithful and effective in our lives.

PRAYER SUGGESTION

Ask the Holy Spirit to keep you in the saving faith.

On Being Well-Dressed

[I want] to be found in Him, not having a righteousness of my own ... but that which is through faith in Christ. Philippians 3:9

Leo Tolstoy said this about someone who had renounced the Christian faith in favor of a philosophy: "He felt suddenly like a man who had changed his warm fur cloak for a muslin garment and, going for the first time into the frost, is immediately convinced, not by reason but by his whole nature, that he is as good as naked."

The garment that makes us well-dressed in God's sight is the robe of Christ's righteousness. Our own righteousness is comparable to "filthy rags" (Isaiah 64:6). We know Christ's righteousness was attained for us by His obedience to God's Law and by His endurance of the death penalty we deserved. Jesus earned for us a perfect righteousness, which is credited to us by faith.

One cannot endure a Russian winter if clothed in a flimsy garment. One cannot endure this life—the coldness of people's hearts, the frost of affliction, the freezing fear of death—unless we are dressed in the robe of Christ's righteousness. Wrapped up in His love, we are warm and safe, protected against life's cold climate and also from the heat of God's wrath because of sin.

St. John the Divine said that those in white robes "are they who have come out of the great tribulation; they have washed their robes and made them white in the blood of the Lamb" (Revelation 7:14). We ask ourselves today, "How well-dressed are we?"

PRAYER SUGGESTION

Ask the Savior Jesus Christ to clothe you in the robe of His righteousness.

Are We Ready?

Let no one on the roof of his house go down to take anything out of his house. Let no one in the field go back to get his cloak. Matthew 24:17–18

The firefighter's response to the alarm was immediate. He dropped everything to answer the call. And he was killed when a hand-held extinguisher exploded. Back at the station, his belongings lay where he left them, including a half-eaten sandwich.

The world was unprepared for our Lord's first coming in Bethlehem. People slept, oblivious to the fact that God had sent His Son to save them all from their sins.

In the Old Testament, the Israelites were to be ready for immediate departure from Egypt as they celebrated their first Passover. They were to eat it "on the march," as it were, "with your cloak tucked into your belt, your sandals on your feet and your staff in your hand" (Exodus 12:11).

Such spiritual sleep will also prevail at Christ's Second Coming, despite His admonition to be ready for Him when He comes again. But Christians have ample reason to be prepared.

Since our Lord has given us much to do—our daily work and our service to those who need our love, as well as our primary mission to proclaim the Gospel to all nations—we cannot sit idly by as we await His coming. Some first-century Christians, believing that the Savior would come soon, disposed of their belongings, quit working, and waited. The result was disorderly conduct, chaos even.

Readiness to receive the Lord when He comes is a matter of having our hearts and minds focused on Jesus. It is a matter of drawing near to the cross of Christ and receiving His gifts of faith and forgiveness. Let us prepare!

PRAYER SUGGESTION

Ask the Lord to keep you prepared and alert for His coming.

Dealing with Good and Evil

Do not repay evil with evil or insult with insult, but with blessing.
1 Peter 3:9

You've heard the scientific theory that for every action there is an opposite and equal reaction. This principle can be applied to daily life as well. Good or evil actions usually prompt one of four reactions.

The first kind of reaction is to repay *good with evil*, and this kind of exchange is devilish. The second reaction is to reward *evil with evil*. This the law of the jungle: an eye for an eye, a tooth for a tooth, and the like. The third is to reward *good with good*; this is humane but it isn't too difficult. People give us gifts, and we give them gifts. Friends invite us to dinner, and we return the favor. The fourth reaction is to reward *evil with good*. This is divine; this is being Christlike.

Just to say we "ought" to reward evil with good is mere moralizing. More must be added to the formula, as Peter does in the passage above. Then this: "Christ died for sins once for all, the righteous for the unrighteous, to bring you to God. He was put to death in the body but made alive by the Spirit" (1 Peter 3:18).

Christ not only gives us an example, He gives us the power to do as He has done. By His wounds we are healed from the darkness of sin and the desire for revenge. We are spiritually healed by the best medicine ever administered: the redeeming love of Christ. "[Christ] Himself bore our sin in His body on the tree, so we might die to sins and live for righteousness; by His wounds you have been healed" (1 Peter 2:24).

Yes, by His wounds we are enabled to requite evil with good.

PRAYER SUGGESTION

Ask the Lord Jesus to make you more like Him in overcoming evil with good.

One Life to Live and to Give

The good shepherd lays down His life for the sheep. John 10:11

During the Revolutionary War, an American schoolteacher, Nathan Hale, volunteered to go behind the British lines to serve the colonial army as a spy. Hale was caught, but legend has it that before he was hanged, he said, "My only regret is that I have but one life to give for my country." He stands in bold relief to another American, Benedict Arnold, who betrayed his country.

We find stories of betrayal in the Bible. In the Old Testament, Doeg betrayed David's position to King Saul. Judas Iscariot performed a similar act when he informed the spiritual leaders where Jesus could be found. The story of Jesus' betrayal into the hands of sinners stands unique among all betrayal stories, for the will of God was involved, as Jesus said: "Such things must come, but woe to the man through whom they come!" (Matthew 18:7). In other words, while Scriptures concerning Christ's death had to be fulfilled, Judas was still responsible for betraying his Master to death.

Our Lord stressed that while His death was carried out by His enemies, it was also accomplished by His own action: "No one takes [My life] from me, but I lay it down of My own accord" (John 10:18).

Because Jesus willingly gave His life, we have life. What a blessing is a redeemed life! We are enabled to live our life to the glory of God. It is improbable—but not impossible—that we may be asked to surrender life as a confessional act for our Savior. If so, we may well repeat Hale's sentiment that we regret having only one life to give. Regardless, we have our entire life to live and to give to the service of our Savior.

PRAYER SUGGESTION

Speak words of thanks for opportunities to serve the least of Christ's brethren.

Breeching the Boundary

Everyone who sins breaks the law. ... The reason the Son of God appeared was to destroy the devil's work. 1 John 3:4, 8

Prior to the Revolutionary War, there was a dispute over the boundary between Maryland and Pennsylvania. To settle it, two surveyors from England, Charles Mason and Jeremiah Dixon, were engaged to establish the line. They drew a straight line, 312 miles long, marking every mile with a limestone pillar. This boundary, the Mason-Dixon Line, later played a prominent part in U.S. history as the demarcation between free states and slave states.

Boundaries are necessary in all areas of life. A line is needed to establish what is right and wrong. God draws the line for us with the Ten Commandments, the moral law. Every departure from that line—every trespass, every transgression—is a sin. "Everyone who sins breaks this law; in fact, sin is lawlessness" (1 John 3:4). And the penalty for this sin is death (Romans 6:23).

Is there no recourse? Yes, there is, Jesus Christ came to fulfill the law in our behalf. By the shedding of His blood He atoned for all our transgressions. The boundary between us and God, created by our sin, was breeched when Jesus paid the penalty for us.

God's Mason-Dixon Line is still there to identify and condemn sinners. It is there for Christians, guiding them to righteous living in thoughts, emotions, desires, words, and deeds. Thus the Law of God is necessary as we go about our daily lives.

While we thank God for making His will known to us in the Law, we are especially thankful for the Gospel, which assures us that Christ has redeemed us from the curse of sin and death and has breeched the boundary between us and God.

PRAYER SUGGESTION

Ask the Lord to keep you from transgressing His Law and to instill a greater appreciation for the Gospel.

Performing Helpful Services

I urge you, brothers, in view of God's mercy, to offer your bodies as living sacrifices, holy and pleasing to God—this is your spiritual act of worship. Romans 12:1

In the 1880s a wealthy drug manufacturer in New York thought it would be a good idea if all the birds mentioned in Shakespeare's plays were represented in the United States. His decision brought starlings, now considered pests, to these shores.

Some services go beyond a nuisance and become a crime, as Jesus told His disciples, "A time is coming when anyone who kills you will think he is offering a service to God" (John 16:2). Saul the Pharisee thought so when he persecuted Christians. His outlook was changed when Christ appeared to him at Damascus and made him the proclaimer of salvation in Christ.

The origin of any form of service is the mercy of God. In His grace and compassion, God sent His one and only Son into the world to lay down His life for the salvation of all. Those whom the Holy Spirit has called to faith through the Gospel have a sense of commitment to Christ as a response to His service to them. They want to live under Him in His kingdom and serve Him as a form of worship by which they proclaim the worth-ship of their Lord. This is as pleasing to Him as their worship in church.

What is Christian service? Acts, words, thoughts, desires— when prompted by faith—constitute Christian service. A Christian's performance, when it is in accord with God's will and when it is to God's glory and the benefit of fellow human beings, is service in God's sight.

PRAYER SUGGESTION

Pray for strength to serve the Lord Jesus and those who are His spiritual brothers and sisters.

Reverence for Age

[The righteous] will still bear fruit in old age,
they will stay fresh and green. Psalm 92:14

When author P. H. Wodehouse died at age 93, he was working on his ninety-seventh book.

People can be active in church and community throughout their lives. They can, in the words of the Psalm, "still bear fruit." Examples from the Bible include Moses, Anna the prophetess, Simeon, Abraham, Sarah, and the apostle John, who lived to the end of the first century.

Reverence for age begins with the aged persons themselves. This is not vanity or pride, but proper regard for oneself as someone God has made, redeemed, and sanctified. The self-esteem senior citizens have is contagious. Those who stand tall before God in their golden years know that He has preserved them, that Christ Jesus has redeemed them at great cost, that the Holy Spirit makes their bodies His temple, and they will find that younger people will honor them all the more for their spirit. They will do what Moses advised: "Rise in the presence of the aged, show respect for the elderly and revere your God" (Leviticus 19:32).

God's promise to all people still stands: "Even to your old age and gray hairs I am He, I am He who will sustain you. I have made you and I will carry you; I will sustain you and I will rescue you" (Isaiah 46:4).

In the time of the fulfillment, when the Savior of the world was born, two elderly persons, Anna and Simeon, had the privilege of beholding the promised Messiah with their own eyes and touching Him with their hands. And both of them praised God and spread the good news of His birth.

PRAYER SUGGESTION

Give thanks to God for His gift of age.

Awaiting Our Permanent Home

Now we know that if the earthly tent we live in is destroyed, we have a building from God, an eternal house in heaven, not built by human hands. 2 Corinthians 5:1

When John Quincy Adams was 81, someone asked how he was. He replied, "John Quincy Adams is quite well, thank you! But the house in which he lives is becoming a bit dilapidated. I think John Quincy Adams will have to move out pretty soon; but he himself is quite well indeed."

Likewise, an aged Peter said: "I think it is right to refresh your memory as long as I live in the tent of this body, because I know that I will soon put it aside, as our Lord Jesus Christ has made clear to me" (2 Peter 1:13).

The body in which we live, like everything else in this world, is temporary. It is not our final home. We are pilgrims and sojourners on earth, doing the best we can to live to the glory of God and the good of fellow human beings.

All the while we anticipate the move we will make to the Father's house. That move is made possible for us because Jesus has gone before. He, the Son of God, came to this earth to dwell for a while, sharing our mortal life with its hardships and giving His life into death to save us. His ministry completed, He ascended to His heavenly home to prepare a place for us.

The author of the letter to the Hebrews said this about Old Testament saints: "They admitted that they were aliens and strangers on earth. People who say such things show that they are looking for a country of their own" (Hebrews 11:13–14). And we can join in the hymn: "I'm but a stranger here, Heaven is my home."

PRAYER SUGGESTION

Give thanks to the ascended Lord for having prepared a place for you in heaven.

Temptation: Cause and Conquest

"Woe to the world because of the things that cause people to sin!"
Matthew 18:7

From whom do evil temptations come? The devil is one source. He came to Eve as a serpent. When the Lord called Eve to account, she replied, "The serpent deceived me, and I ate" (Genesis 3:13). In other words "The devil made me do it."

Temptations also originate with our own *sinful nature*. Paul cautioned: "Do not let sin reign in your mortal body so that you obey its evil desires" (Romans 6:12).

Further, Jesus teaches that temptations come from the *world*, from the sinful human race as a whole. The world's moral standards are low. It is inevitable that the world will tempt people to sin.

Jesus understood the lure of the world: "Woe to the world because of the things that cause people to sin! Such things must come, but woe to the man through whom they come!" (Matthew 18:7). Our Lord is especially concerned about deceiving children and adults who are weak, saying that it would be better for such tempters if a millstone be tied around their necks and they were drowned (Luke 17:2).

Jesus, too, was subjected to temptation when He spent 40 days in the wilderness. But He conquered it by relying solely on the Word of God. The skirmish in the desert was followed by the decisive battle on the cross. By His death, Jesus redeemed us from the power of sin and Satan. Believing in Him, we can master temptation by occupying ourselves with Word and prayer, leading a life focused on Christ, and serving others by word and work.

The devil stalks us as a roaring lion does its prey. But he has lost his bite; Jesus overcame him.

PRAYER SUGGESTION

Ask for strength to overcome all temptation.

Giving Thanks to the Heavenly Father

Praise be to the God and Father of our Lord Jesus Christ, the Father of compassion and the God of all comfort. 2 Corinthians 1:3

This is a daughter's thankful tribute to her late father: "He took me to church regularly until I could drive. Then I'd drive him to church regularly. It's because of his diligence that my religion is so strong today." So said Mrs. Joseph O'Connel regarding the late Alfred Hitchcock, Hollywood movie director.

Earthly fathers who provide for their children spiritually and physically are representations of the heavenly Father. The psalmist said, "As a father has compassion on his children, so the LORD has compassion on those who fear Him" (Psalm 103:13).

Especially worth mentioning is the Father's compassion for all who are in any kind of distress. He assures them that He has not forsaken them. Although they may feel isolated in their grief, He enfolds them with His love. In Christ Jesus, His Son, He has redeemed them and made them His children. On Him they may cast all their cares, for He cares for them.

God's compassion on His children has a ripple effect: it makes them comforters of others who suffer. The apostle wrote that God "comforts us in all our troubles, so that we can comfort those in any trouble with the comfort we ourselves have received from God" (2 Corinthians 1:4).

The care and compassion of human fathers is similarly at work in families. Fathers walk in the footsteps of "the God and Father of our Lord Jesus Christ" when they show love—even tough love—to their children. This equips children to be compassionate to one another in the home. And when they become parents, they will know how to be spiritual guides to their children.

PRAYER SUGGESTION

Thank the heavenly Father for the good He does through fathers.

Love out of a Pure Heart

The goal of this command is love, which comes from a pure heart and a good conscience and a sincere faith. 1 Timothy 1:5

What happens when we love something or someone—earthly gain, pleasure, or even another person—more than God? We commit idolatry, not only breaking the First Commandment ("You shall nave no other gods before Me," Exodus 20:3), but also opening the door to sins against the other commandments.

How plainly is this fact demonstrated in the history of the Israelites in the wilderness! Instead of serving the Lord only, they sacrificed to a golden calf, sat down to eat and drink as part of the observance, and then rose up to play. The Israelites, as St. Paul explained in 1 Corinthians 10:6–8, began with idolatry and ended with gluttony, drunkenness, and sexual immorality. In brief, "The people sat down to eat and drink and got up to indulge in pagan revelry" (1 Corinthians 10:7). We see how the First Commandment is the fountainhead of the rest of the commandments. Its purpose is not fear, but love that grows out of a pure heart.

When our faith is in God and we love Him—having a clear conscience because in Christ our sins are forgiven—sins infesting our heart are purged: evil thoughts, murders, adulteries, sexual sins, stealing, lies, covetousness. These things, not the breaking of manmade rules about ceremonies and rituals, make a person morally and spiritually unclean.

God in Christ loved us, redeemed us, forgave us, cleansed us through Holy Baptism. He purified us and made us His children. And He restores us through His Word and His Holy Meal. Our response is that we are free to love God with a pure heart.

PRAYER SUGGESTION

Give thanks to God for granting you faith in Christ, enabling you to love Him without reservation.

The Power of God's Word

The Word of God is living and active. Hebrews 4:12

The Word of God, both as Law and Gospel, is powerful. As the Law, it cuts through the hardness of unbelief. As the Gospel, it is "the power of God for the salvation of everyone who believes" (Romans 1:16).

Saul the Pharisee of Tarsus had been "breathing out murderous threats against the Lord's disciples" (Acts 9:1). Near Damascus he was converted and spent the rest of his life preaching the Gospel of Christ.

Around A.D. 375 Augustine, a student in Carthage, North Africa, was living in all the sins of his time. In A.D. 387 he was baptized and became a great teacher in the church.

These people and many others were changed by the power of the Holy Spirit working through the Word of God. The above text states, "The Word of God is living and active."

God tells Jeremiah that His words are like a fire that penetrates and purges, that enlightens and warms the human heart. The Word is also like a hammer. The sinner's heart is often as hard as granite but the Word can splinter any barrier man erects against God. God wants a stony heart to become, in Ezekiel's words, "a heart of flesh" (Ezekiel 11:19). God is like a heavenly surgeon who performs heart transplants.

Both the Law and the Gospel are powerful. The Law serves as a curb, mirror, and rule. The Gospel comforts and invites. It is a balm of Gilead that soothes and heals wounded hearts. What a treasure God has given us in His Word! We do well to "hear, read, mark, learn, and inwardly digest" it, as the church collect states.

PRAYER SUGGESTION

Pray that the Holy Spirit may open your heart to the life-giving Word of God and draw you closer to Jesus, the Savior.

The Yes of Faith

John was a lamp that burned and gave light, and you chose for a time to enjoy his light. John 5:35

What is the sin that exceeds all sins? Greed and pride, envy and jealous, hatred and murder, theft and robbery—all these are great sins. But for the most part, they are the sins of human beings against other humans. These sins have social aspects.

But the greatest of all sins is unbelief, for it says no to God.

Jesus encountered the usual sins as He lived among people— the dishonesty of publicans, the immorality of harlots and those who went to them, the false witness of those who opposed Him. But the sin that grieved Him the most was the determined "no" of religious leaders who rejected His teaching and the salvation He offered. This was the ultimate sin.

It wasn't that Jesus lacked credentials. In John chapter 5 He appealed to the witness of John the Baptist and to the testimony of Moses (verses 31–47). If people accepted the word of these two, they would accept Him. Jesus spoke of the authority of the One who sent Him. He had come in the Father's name and by His authority. The three-tier testimony was evident—Moses, John, and the Father. Yet the Israelites, led by the religious authorities, said no to Jesus. It was blind, stubborn unbelief. And their unbelief was inconsistent with what was plainly evident.

But others said yes to Jesus and were blessed: "To all who received Him, to those who believed in His name, He gave the right to become children of God" (John 1:12). Christ still comes to us today in the Gospel and the sacraments. He comes with the gifts He earned on the cross: forgiveness, peace, eternal life. He asks us to speak the yes of faith.

PRAYER SUGGESTION

Thank the Lord Jesus for coming to you in His Word.

Saved to Serve

When thou art converted, strengthen the brethren. Luke 22:32 (KJV)

Some common-sense rules say that when individuals are saved, they should do the same for others. Members of the armed forces, for example, were told to dig their foxholes big enough for two. This extra effort could save someone's life. People who go hiking or diving usually go in groups of three. If one is injured, one can stay with the injured, and the third can go for help.

Something like this holds true in our spiritual lives. After a person has been converted, he is urged to help another. The "salvation foxhole" can be made big enough for one more. Peter told pious wives to try to gain their unbelieving husbands by their Christian conduct. He mentioned two of his helpers: Silas and Mark. These three would divide their pastoral work in such a way as to help others who were heavily persecuted.

Peter had learned well the lessons Jesus taught him. On the night of the betrayal, he had boasted that he would never forsake his Master; he would be willing to die with Him. He underestimated Satan. When the critical time came, Peter denied Jesus three times. After the Resurrection, Jesus noted that Peter had returned to faith, forgave him, and restored him to apostleship. But that was not the end. Peter was called to strengthen the brethren in the faith as they went forth to preach the Gospel to all people.

We who are in the faith, thanks to our Baptism and to the Gospel taught to us, now try to gain souls for Christ. The shelter we have found can be enlarged, so to speak, to accommodate one more person. We extend help to one another, just as the Lord Jesus has brought salvation to each one of us.

PRAYER SUGGESTION

Ask the heavenly Father for help that will enable you to serve one another.

The Vision of Faith

The man they called Jesus ... told me to go to Siloam and wash.
So I went and washed, and then I could see. John 9:11

Jesus healed by touching or by speaking. When He healed the centurion's servant from some distance—without ever seeing or touching—He demonstrated His power to heal without using standard means: no pills, no mud plasters.

At other times our Lord used means. He gave eyesight to a blind man by applying a mud plaster to his eyes and telling him to wash in the pool of Siloam. The healing power did not lie in the mudpack, the washing, or the water. It lay in Jesus.

Jesus can do greater works than restore physical eyesight. He imparts new life to the soul, thereby removing spiritual blindness and giving the eyes of faith. He exercises this power through the Gospel and the Sacrament of Baptism. How He does it is beyond our understanding. We can only say, as Charlotte Elliott did: "Just as I am, poor, wretched, blind; Sight, riches, healing of the mind. Yea, all I need, in Thee I find, O Lamb of God, I come, I come."

Holy Baptism washes away the filth of sin; it removes whatever it is that prevents spiritual eyesight. St. Peter told the Pentecost congregation, "Repent and be baptized, every one of you, in the name of Jesus Christ for the forgiveness of your sins" (Acts 2:38). And St. Paul wrote to Titus, "[God] saved us through the washing of rebirth and renewal by the Holy Spirit" (Titus 3:5).

Through Baptism we were given eyes to "see the kingdom of God" (John 3:3), to see Christ as our Savior from sin and death, and to see the purpose for which God has put us in this world—to see and then follow the road to eternal life.

PRAYER SUGGESTION

Ask God to give you the clear vision of faith so you may always love and trust in Him.

Little Children Worship Christ

The children shouting in the temple area,
"Hosanna to the Son of David." Matthew 21:15

A boy and his sister were arguing. When the mother asked what game they were playing, the reply was, "We are pretending to be Dad and Mom."

For better or for worse, children pick up their parents' expressions and repeat them almost verbatim. This is good, so long as the sayings are true, serve the well-being of others, and glorify God. All three criteria are met when children join their parents in worship.

So it was in Jerusalem during our Lord's last visit there. As He entered the city, the people shouted: "Hosanna to the Son of David! Blessed is He who comes in the name of the Lord! Hosanna in the highest!" (Matthew 21:9). With these words Christ's followers welcomed and worshiped Him. Later, in the temple, children took up the chant, repeating what the adults had sung outside.

"Son of David" is more than a reference to the physical descent of Jesus from King David. It is a Messianic title. The One who was to come—and did come—to save His people from their sins was frequently called by that title.

When Jesus went about His ministry, many called Him "Son of David." They were confessing their faith that Jesus of Nazareth was the promised Messiah, the Son of God, David's Son who was also David's Lord.

The Son of David is our Savior—the Savior of adults and children alike. Jesus lived on earth, died, and rose again for the salvation of all. Our children today, as did the children then, worship the Christ with their singing.

PRAYER SUGGESTION

Let your prayer be one of praise to Jesus, the Son of David, and your Savior.

On the Side of Christ

Then the man said, "Lord, I believe," and he worshiped Him.
John 9:38

The continental divide, high up in the Rocky Mountains, is a watershed. Precipitation on the eastern side of the slope drains into the Atlantic Ocean. On the western side it heads for the Pacific.

In a spiritual sense, Christ is a continental divide. Those who hear His Word divide into two sides. They are for Him or against Him. They either accept Him as the Son of God and Savior, or they reject Him. In John chapter 9 we see such a watershed.

Having given sight to a blind man, Jesus also imparted spiritual sight, that is, faith in Him as the promised Savior from sin. The now-sighted man confessed, "'Lord, I believe,' and he worshiped Him." The religious leaders, however, said no to Him. To this the Savior said, "For judgment I have come into this world, so that the blind will see and those who see will become blind" (John 9:39).

This harsh response has to be considered in the context of the total truth spoken by Jesus. He said to Nicodemus, "God did not send His Son into the world to condemn the world, but to save the world through Him" (John 3:17). The Law is applied as judgment, yes, but it shows us our need for a Savior. There is more: the Gospel of salvation through Christ. Judgment and grace are like the two sides of the same coin. Every decision against Christ entails divine judgment on oneself.

The Lord Jesus has opened our spiritual eyes and given us faith. We confess with the once blind man: "We believe!" The flow of our lives is toward the great ocean of eternal life with Him. Thank God for that!

PRAYER SUGGESTION

In your prayer, acknowledge your need for that sight of faith and thank Jesus for granting it to you.

Christ, the Rose of Sharon

The desert and the parched land will be glad; and the wilderness will rejoice and blossom. Isaiah 35:1

The Song of Songs is a simile for the love Christ has for His bride, the church. He is the Rose of Sharon, and when He, the promised Messiah, came into the world, He established there a heavenly kingdom and offered forgiveness of sins. His Gospel transformed the wilderness of sin and death into a fertile land that blossoms. Paul also spoke of Christ and the church as the Bridegroom and the bride, pleading for husbands and wives to follow the example of Christ, who in love gave Himself up for the salvation of the church.

Jesus Christ as the Rose of Sharon distinguishes Himself from mankind. People are like flowers in that they live and bloom for a while then fade away. Job said, "Man born of a woman is of a few days and full of trouble. He springs up like a flower and withers away" (Job 14:1–2).

Jesus Christ died for the sins of the world, rose from the dead, and ascended into heaven, where He prepares a place for us in the Father's house. How thankful we are! In a hymn we sing, "You are my heart's most beauteous Flower." In another hymn we call Him "the Flower of heaven." He is the eternal Rose of Sharon that never dies or fades away. In Him we have "an inheritance that can never perish, spoil or fade—kept in heaven for you, who through faith are shielded by God's power until the coming of the salvation that is ready to be revealed in the last time" (1 Peter 1:4–5). "Fair are the meadows, fair are the woodlands, Robed in flowers of blooming spring; Jesus is fairer, Jesus is purer; He makes our sorrowing spirit sing."

PRAYER SUGGESTION

Thank the Lord Jesus for attaining eternal life for you in heaven.

Everlasting Life

Some of the Sadducees, who say there is no resurrection,
came to Jesus with a question. Luke 20:27

The Sadducees were rivals of the Pharisees. Distinctive beliefs of this rather vocal group were their denial of the existence of angels or spirits and their rejection of the resurrection of the dead. They were greatly influenced by Greek philosophy.

On Jesus' last visit to Jerusalem, the Sadducees came to Him and tried to trick Him into a denial of the afterlife. After our Lord had silenced the Pharisees, the Sadducees hoped to gain points on them by putting Jesus to shame. They told Him the well-known story of the seven brothers who had married the same woman successively—each after an older brother had died. (A levirate marriage law, Deuteronomy 25:5–10, directed a dead man's brother to marry the widow.) Their trick question was: "At the resurrection, whose wife will she be, since the seven were married to her?"

The Savior's reply was simple and straightforward: in the resurrection those who dwell in the presence of God will neither marry nor be given in marriage. As we are told in other passages from Scripture, in heaven all believers will have glorified bodies. St. Paul in 1 Corinthians 15 calls them spiritual bodies. They have a real existence, but it is spiritual and not like it was on earth.

Exactly what a glorified body is like is not fully known. We get some idea when we consider Jesus' body after His resurrection (Philippians 3:21). Our Savior often spoke of a very real life beyond the grave. It is to be a life in His Father's house of "many rooms," a never-ending life to be spent with Him. Earthy concerns are obsolete. Of this Jesus assures us in Scripture. Need we ask more?

PRAYER SUGGESTION

Give thanks to the Savior for silencing the enemies of His Word and for assuring us of life in the world to come.

Where Is He Today?

He [Jesus] thus revealed His glory,
and His disciples put their faith in Him. John 2:11

Many people, influenced by science and the shortcomings of the human intellect, look for tangible evidence of the Christian faith. They want to see, hear, touch, and taste for themselves. Some say they would believe Christ and His teachings if they see Him for themselves.

Obviously this is not possible. Yes, our Savior is with us, for He said, "I am with you always, to the very end of the age" (Matthew 28:20). But Jesus is no longer *bodily* present. Jesus now sits at God's right hand.

Yet His presence with us is, in a way, more compelling. Our Lord comes to us today in a more powerful and effective manner than bodily presence. How so?

He is present in Word and sacraments. When the Gospel of our salvation is proclaimed, we hear the very Word that He Himself proclaimed. When somebody speaks to us one-on-one and tells us what Jesus said and did, it is as though we hear Jesus say the words Himself. Along with that Word are the physical elements of water in Baptism and bread and wine in Holy Communion. When these elements are present with the Word of God, we are in personal fellowship with Him. He is in us and we are in Him.

Therefore, we are free to lay aside the burden of our doubts and hear what Jesus says: "If anyone chooses to do God's will, he will find out whether My teaching comes from God or whether I speak on My own" (John 7:17).

PRAYER SUGGESTION

Ask the Lord to let the Holy Spirit bear the testimony of faith in you.

"Project Jonah"

As Jonah was three days and three nights in the belly of a huge fish, so the Son of Man will be three days and three nights in the heart of the earth. Matthew 12:40

It is common to hear about programs to save whales. This is meet and right. We need to be good stewardship of the earth God gives us. A reversal of terms has occured. It was once a large fish that saved a man. Now man is working to save sea creatures.

Jesus promoted a spiritual "Project Jonah." When contemporaries demanded a tangible sign that He had come from God, He replied, "None will be given... except the sign of the prophet of Jonah" (Matthew 12:39). Then followed the above text. Our Lord wanted people to draw a lesson from Jonah and to apply it to Him.

When the religious authorities wanted proof that Jesus came from God, He responded, "A wicked and adulterous generation asks for a miraculous sign!" (Matthew 12:39). There was no need for a new sign because plenty of old ones were available. Jesus explained the parallelism: Jonah's three-day stay in the fish foretold His three-day stay in the grave and His resurrection.

Skeptics still demand a sign that Jesus is God's true Son. But there is still no need. Jesus' death, burial, and resurrection are sufficient proof that He came from God and is the world's Savior. Paul wrote, "What I received I passed on to you as of first importance: that Christ died for our sins according to the Scriptures, that He was buried, that He was raised on the third day according to the Scriptures" (1 Corinthians 15:3-4).

"Project Jonah" leads to "Project Jesus." Christ's Word and His work in our hearts is all the proof we need.

PRAYER SUGGESTION

Thank the heavenly Father for sending His Son, our Savior Jesus Christ, to be His spokesman in all things pertaining to our salvation.

The Greening of a Christian

Whoever is thirsty, let him come; and whoever wishes,
let him take the free gift of the water of life. Revelation 22:17

Futurists predict a bright tomorrow for this country, sometimes calling it the "greening of America." Sometimes they hit, sometimes they miss. Prosperity is hard to predict.

The Bible speaks of greening in another sense. The psalmist prayed, "Restore our fortunes, O LORD, like streams in the Negev" (Psalm 126:4). What a difference water makes! Irrigation changes wastelands into productive fields.

An even greater change occurs when "the water of life" enters the desert of a soul that thirsts for God. The living water our Savior offers in the Gospel of salvation is this: forgiveness of sins, peace with God, a new purpose in life, and eternal life. When this Water refreshes the individual, a new life begins immediately. This is the greening of a Christian.

Christians use the opportunities in everyday life to grow in grace and to be fruitful in every good work. Faithful stewards, they develop and apply the talents God has entrusted to them. In the footsteps of their Lord, they grow great in humble service. As Christ's witnesses they repeat His invitation: "Whoever is thirsty, let him come, and whoever wishes, let him take the free gift of the water of life." Those who come will be refreshed and become "green," becoming fruitful in all good works.

The water of life that Christ supplies is not metered. He never sends you a spiritual water bill. It costs nothing to drink and to grow into a greening Christian. So if you are thirsty, drink!

PRAYER SUGGESTION

Thank God for having opened for you a fountain flowing with fresh water—the Word of Christ.

Mountaintop Events

Before the mountains were born or You brought forth the earth and the world, from everlasting to everlasting, You are God. Psalm 90:2

When Moses pronounced his last blessing on the children of Israel before going to Mount Nebo to die, he desired good things for them: "the choicest gifts of the ancient mountains and the fruitfulness of the everlasting hills" (Deuteronomy 33:15).

Mountains are often mentioned in the Bible. God gave the Ten Commandments on Mount Sinai. The temple on Mount Moriah bespoke His presence among His people. And Jerusalem, the holy city, was built on Mount Zion.

As the New Testament opens, we read about the significance of mountains in redemptive history. On "a very high mountain" (Matthew 4:8) Jesus was tempted by the devil, and there He overcame him, foreshadowing the time when He would utterly crush his power by His death on Mount Calvary.

Before ascending what a hymn calls "Calvary's mournful mountain," Jesus took Peter, James, and John up a high mountain to reveal His glory in the Transfiguration. This event also foreshadowed His ascension into heaven from the Mount of Olives.

The story of salvation in Christ unfolded on many mountaintops. Our joyful response is to praise God for His saving deeds. "We sing th' almighty power of God, Who bade the mountains rise, Who spread the flowing seas abroad, And built the lofty skies."

PRAYER SUGGESTION

Thank God for His grace in Christ as revealed on mountaintops.

The Cedars of Lebanon

The trees of the LORD are well watered,
the cedars of Lebanon that He planted. Psalm 104:16

The cedars of Lebanon are frequently mentioned in the Bible. They were prized for their scented wood that was used for temples and royal palaces. The cedars King Hiram sent were welcomed by King Solomon for the building of the temple. The Bible calls Solomon's palace "The House of the Forest of Lebanon."

Jesus as a carpenter likely was acquainted with cedar. He would have seen the cedars on Mount Lebanon while on His journeys. He was also aware that before His time the prophet Elijah stayed with a Phoenician widow during the great drought in the land of Israel, calling attention to the fact that Elijah was sent there to teach the Gentiles the ways and Word of the true God.

A spokesman far greater than Elijah was to seek refuge in the Tyre and Sidon region: Jesus. He and His disciples went there for a little vacation. But He didn't find the sought-for rest; a native woman recognized Him and sought His help for a demon-possessed daughter. The disciples urged Jesus to send her away, but He used the situation to teach an important lesson on the power of a persistent faith.

At another time Jesus came close to the north country to reveal His glory to Peter, James, and John on a mountain, probably Mount Hermon. Peter wrote years later: "We ourselves heard His voice that came from heaven when we were with Him on the sacred mountain" (2 Peter 1:18). There Jesus revealed His glory, and from that height He could behold the glory of God's handiwork in nature: "The trees of the LORD ... the cedars of Lebanon."

PRAYER SUGGESTION

Praise God for His wonderful works, especially for sending His own beloved Son to give His life for us.

The Joy of Discovery

Philip found Nathanael and told him, "We have found the one Moses wrote about ... Jesus of Nazareth." John 1:45

This portion of gospel introduces a series of discoveries with the phrase "we have found." The participants, along with believers past and present, had been looking for the Messiah.

First we see Andrew searching for his brother, Simon, and exclaiming, "We have found the Messiah" (John 1:41). Andrew did more than merely tell Simon—he brought him to Jesus. Next we see Philip breaking the good news of the discovery to Nathanael. Nathanael was skeptical, perhaps expecting the Messiah to emerge from Jerusalem, not from Nazareth. But his skepticism gives way, and he exclaimed to Jesus, "Rabbi, You are the Son of God; You are the King of Israel" (John 1:49).

Each, in turn—Andrew, Philip, Nathanael—experienced the thrill of a great discovery. They found the Messiah, who had been promised by Moses and the prophets. They found Him whom John the Baptist, just the day before, had called "the Lamb of God, who takes away the sin of the world!" (John 1:29).

And so it has been through the ages. People have searched, people have discovered. Christianity has always been a matter of great personal discovery, a matter of finding Christ, a matter of finding Him *for themselves*. They have come to see Him as the Son of God, the promised Deliverer. There is not only great excitement in this discovery, but also great comfort and assurance. This is how Horatius Bonar puts it: "I heard the voice of Jesus say, 'Come unto Me and rest; Lay down, thou weary one, lay down Thy head upon My breast.' I came to Jesus as I was, Weary and worn and sad: I found in Him a resting place. And He has made me glad."

PRAYER SUGGESTION

Express your personal thankfulness to Jesus for His presence in your life as Savior.

Gifted Daughters, a Blessing

We reached Caesarea and stayed at the house of Philip the evangelist, one of the Seven. He had four unmarried daughters who prophesied. Acts. 21:8–9

In the book of Acts we read about Philip, one of seven deacons in the Jerusalem church. A true evangelist, Philip explained the Messianic prophecy of Isaiah to the Ethiopian he met along the road. Philip was active in Samaria. And he eventually settled in Caesarea, where Paul and his party, bound for Jerusalem, stayed in his house while their ship was being readied.

Of interest is the family fact that Philip had four unmarried daughters. From the Holy Spirit, the daughters had received the gift of prophesy, that of not only *fore*telling but also *forth*telling God's counsel of salvation as revealed in Holy Scripture. They expounded the Word of God, as the prophet Joel had foretold, "Your sons and daughters will prophesy" (Joel 2:28).

Philip's home was likely the scene of frequent spirited discussions. We are not specifically told how Philip's daughters used their gift of prophecy to edify the church. Undoubtedly they "forthtold" the Word of God to children, brought the comfort of God's Word to the sick, and were of service to the elderly. We can surmise that they were of help to their father in his evangelism work.

Young people today are God's gift to the Christian church. What a blessing they become when they lay their personal gifts and talents at the foot of Christ's cross and serve Him in their special ways!

PRAYER SUGGESTION

Thank the Lord Jesus for endowing young people with the gifts they need to serve Him.

The Lord of Life

You will not abandon me to the grave,
nor will You let your holy One see decay. Psalm 16:10

There is only one whose body did not see corruption in the tomb. He is Jesus Christ. Corruption of the body is the result of sin. Jesus, the holy One, committed no sin. "He committed no sin, and no deceit was found in His mouth" (1 Peter 2:22). Our Lord could challenge His opponents, "Can any of you prove Me guilty of sin?" (John 8:46). None could. The decay of sin could not touch Him.

Jesus' time in the tomb is a fact of considerable importance. His burial in Joseph's garden was a fact stressed by early Christians. In fact, it was one of three great truths imparted to Saul the Pharisee after His conversion. St. Paul wrote, "What I received I passed on to you as of first importance: that Christ died for our sins according to the Scriptures, that He was buried, that He was raised on the third day according to the Scriptures" (1 Corinthians 15:3–4).

We know why the burial of Christ is important. It came in fulfillment of the Holy Scriptures, as Psalm 16, the Easter psalm, states. Further, it was necessary to dispel any claim that Jesus was only seemingly dead or subject to suspended animation. No, He was truly dead. It was not enough for Him as the would-be Savior to be crucified, to suffer greatly, to be in a swoon. Only by dying the death, which the first Adam deserved, could He be the Second Adam, the Lord of life.

PRAYER SUGGESTION

Finish this prayer, "Lord Jesus, You became the Lord of my life when You ..."

Liberty, Not License

Where the Spirit of the Lord is, there is freedom. 2 Corinthians 3:17

In the summer of 1893, after viewing "spacious skies" and "amber waves of grain," Katherine Lee Bates wrote the song, "America, the Beautiful."

Would this patriotic poetess be disappointed today about the building up of the landscape or the settling of soot on America's "alabaster cities"? Would she be more concerned about the crime than the grime in these cities? Would she worry about the what's-in-it-for-me attitude that sometimes replaces the sacrifices of pioneers for the sake of the public good? Perhaps she anticipated this. Having praised the early pilgrims' quest for freedom, she told America: "Confirm thy soul in self-control The liberty in law."

Many privileges we enjoy as citizens have their underpinnings in the Christian religion. Freedom is one. When people realize and enjoy the freedom Jesus Christ won for them—freedom from sin, death, and the devil—they are in a position to espouse civil liberties as well. The freedom in our civil lives is precious, it needs to be exercised and defended. Freedom of speech, as has been said many times, does not entitle anyone to enter a crowded theater and shout "Fire!" when there is no fire.

"Where the Spirit of the Lord is, there is freedom" (2 Corinthians 3:17). Our salvation does not lie in doing the works of the Law, it results from faith in the perfect obedience and atonement of Jesus Christ. Indeed, "The law was given through Moses; grace and truth came through Jesus Christ" (John 1:17). This is the Gospel, and in lands where it is believed and applied, civil liberty can flourish.

PRAYER SUGGESTION

Pray that freedom may be properly appreciated and practiced in the land.

Intact Liberty

Consecrate the fiftieth year and proclaim liberty throughout the land to all its inhabitants. Leviticus 25:10

On July 4, 1776, the bell in Independence Hall in Philadelphia was rung to proclaim the independence of the United States of America. The text from the book of Leviticus was inscribed on it.

The liberty proclaimed to the Israelites was mostly an economic one. It provided that every fiftieth year, land was to revert to the original owner to strengthen the family. In that year there was to be no sowing or reaping. The people lived off their reserves.

The Declaration of Independence was a political document with a somewhat religious orientation. It declared that all people were "endowed by their Creator with certain unalienable rights," including life, liberty, and the pursuit of happiness.

Liberty and freedom are still in our vocabulary. Citizens have the duty and privilege to uphold the principles articulated in the Declaration of Independence. Civic freedom needs to be preserved.

The Declaration of Independence was not conceived in a vacuum. It was profoundly influenced by the tenets of the Christian faith. "It is for freedom that Christ has set us free. Stand firm, then, and do not let yourselves be burdened again by a yoke of slavery" (Galatians 5:1). Jesus Christ rendered full obedience to the demands of God's Law and freed us from observances of the Sabbath, circumcision, dietary laws, and the like. Our Savior bore the penalty for all our sins and disobediences. We are free to serve the living God, thanks to faith in the merit of Christ. We must not bargain our Christian freedom away but stand firm on it.

PRAYER SUGGESTION

Give thanks to God for the freedom we enjoy as citizens.

The Church Is Multinational

"Go and make disciples of all nations, baptizing them in the name of the Father and of the Son and of the Holy Spirit." Matthew 28:19

If you attended a patriotic occasion yesterday, you may have heard a plea for national unity. The Pledge of Allegiance to the U.S. flag holds to the tenets of one nation, one constitution, one flag.

In recent years efforts have been made to introduce multinational concepts in public education and to recognize the multicultural fabric of our society. When it comes to Christianity, there is no question about it being multinational and multilingual. Jesus commanded His apostles to make disciples of all nations. The church on Pentecost began as multilingual, for the people said that, "each of us hears them in his own native language" (Acts 2:8). In one of his visions St. John the Divine wrote this: "Then I saw another angel flying in midair, and he had the eternal gospel to proclaim to those who live on the earth—to every nation, tribe, language and people" (Revelation 14:6).

As present-day disciples, representatives go forth from Christendom to publish the glad tidings of peace and forgiveness in Christ Jesus. Bible translators work to bring the same Word of God to many different people. Think how the apostle Paul, for example, traveled all over the Roman Empire to establish the Christian church. In the presence of God, ethnic, racial, and national differences don't count. The apostle wrote, "Here there is no Greek or Jew, circumcised or uncircumcised, barbarian, Scythian, slave or free, but Christ is all, and is in all" (Colossians 3:11).

Christianity in pagan lands brings many byproducts. Christianity succeeds at uniting nations where others fail.

PRAYER SUGGESTION

Ask the Lord to prosper the work of His church everywhere in the world.

No Difference

There is no difference, for all have sinned and fall short of the glory of God, and are justified freely by His grace through the redemption that came by Christ Jesus. Romans 3:22–24

In the old song "The Robin and Chicken," two birds discover their differences. They don't look alike. The robin thinks it strange that the chicken can't sing. The chicken thinks it strange that the robin can't crow. The song concludes, "Each thought the other knew nothing at all."

We readily see personal and group differences in our society. The so-called melting pot does not blend traits to the point that people lose their identity. The analogy of a mosaic might be more appropriate, for the individual pieces remain intact as they form a comprehensive picture.

Despite these differences, people are the same when considered from a spiritual perspective. First, sin is universal. "All have sinned and fall short of the glory of God." People cannot adequately glorify and please God.

Thanks to God, there is no difference in a second spiritual respect either. All people are included under God's grace. All "are justified freely by His grace through the redemption that came by Christ Jesus." This doesn't mean that all will be saved and go to heaven. It means that Jesus Christ, by the shedding of His blood, paid the ransom for all. Those who by Holy Spirit-given faith accept God's gift of salvation are declared just and righteous.

So, we let differences enrich our life together while we affirm the common denominators: All people are sinners and for all there is redemption by the cleansing blood of Christ.

PRAYER SUGGESTION

Tell God you are grateful for putting all your sins on Jesus and declaring you righteous.

If at First You Don't Succeed ...

Let us not become weary in doing good, for at the proper time we will reap a harvest if we do not give up. Galatians 6:9

The devil and his agents saw to it that Paul encountered roadblocks at every turn. But his zeal to preach the Gospel of Jesus Christ, crucified and raised from the dead, never flagged.

Paul exhorts his readers to stand firm in the saving faith, to grow constantly in the holiness of life, to grow and to sow life in the Holy Spirit to obtain faith's harvest: life everlasting. Steadfastness of purpose was certainly revealed in Paul's apostleship. Persistence was also to characterize a Christian's caring and sharing for others. "Let us not become weary in doing good" (Galatians 6:9), he encouraged.

We do well to adhere to our spiritual purposes, repeating our efforts as necessary—six times, seven times, and more. What does our Lord Jesus want us to do when an offending brother or sister appears to spurn our admonitions? Give up? By no means! Read in Matthew 18:15–17 what the next steps are to be. What shall we do when our prayers, especially our intercessions, appear to go unanswered? Jesus tells us to be constant in prayer—be like the widow who kept on going to a judge until she got justice. What are we to do when our children seem slow in learning or even refuse to heed our counsel? We keep on doing what is for us a duty and a privilege.

Good closing words, "As we have opportunity, let us do good to all people, especially to those who belong to the family of believers" (Galatians 6:10).

PRAYER SUGGESTION

Ask the Holy Spirit to grant you steadfastness of faith and persistence in doing good for Jesus' sake.

The People Were Impressed

The people were amazed at His teaching,
because He taught them as one who had authority. Mark 1:22

The comment came early in Jesus' ministry. Having called His disciples, Jesus entered the city of Capernaum where He would make His headquarters. He entered the synagogue on the Sabbath and began to teach. This was in accordance with Jewish custom, which permitted a layman, usually an elder, to comment publicly on the Scripture reading for the day.

But there was something different about Jesus' comments. He taught as one having authority, as one who knew what He was talking about. The scribes, or Bible scholars, of that time were different. There was something unique about the manner and message of Jesus. Here was no droning about the cut-and-dried traditions of the elders, no sing-song delivery of pious platitudes. No, here was a dynamic Man with a message, a Man who spoke authoritatively. Small wonder that the hearers were amazed!

The Greek word used here for authority—*exousia*—is synonymous with power. It is the same word Jesus used when commissioning the apostles: "All authority in heaven and on earth has been given to Me" (Matthew 28:18). Although in the state of humiliation, Jesus spoke with perfect knowledge of the Father's will. No one else, not an apostle, high priest, or Pharisee, could teach as Jesus did.

It is important to remember this. Jesus was not merely one teacher among many—like Buddha, Confucius, or Mohammed. Jesus was then and is now divin, the Son of the Highest. When He speaks in His Word, it behooves us to listen, to believe, to obey.

PRAYER SUGGESTION

Pray these words: "Lord, open now my heart to hear, And through Your Word to me draw near."

We May Move Away, but Love Abides

Now these three remain: faith, hope and love.
But the greatest of these is love. 1 Corinthians 13:13

Saying farewell is a part of life. Although it is sometimes painful, expressing feelings of love can take the sadness out of parting. The song "How Can I Leave Thee?" suggests that the person going away may take the little blue flower, the forget-me-not, and "wear it upon thy heart." He concedes, "Flowret and hope may die, yet love with us shall stay."

St. Paul did better. If our sentiments at parting time are rooted in the love of Jesus Christ, we retain faith and hope too. In his wonderful chapter, 1 Corinthians 13, the apostle gives love "top billing." It abides because faith and hope, its source, abide. Love continues long after the more flashy spiritual gifts—speaking in tongues, prophecy, and insights into mysteries—have run their course.

The love we have for one another stems from the love of God in Christ Jesus, His Son. To the Ephesians, Paul wrote, "I pray that you, being rooted and established in love, may have power, together with all saints, to grasp how wide and long and high and deep is the love of Christ, and to know this love that surpasses knowledge" (Ephesians 3:17–19).

God first loved us. In this love He gave His one and only Son into death on a cross—and then called Him out of the tomb—so we might experience what life is like in relation to Him and in relation to one another. Divine love, unlike the blue forget-me-nots of which the poet speaks, never fades. Based on such a love, our love for one another likewise abides, even when the years and miles separate us.

PRAYER SUGGESTION

In your prayer re-dedicate yourself to the faithful exercise of Christian love because of the greatness of Christ's love.

Songs Old and New

Sing psalms, hymns and spiritual songs with gratitude in your hearts to God. Colossians 3:16

The author of "I Cannot Sing the Old Song" said she avoids the old tunes because "Their melodies would waken old sorrows from their sleep. … For visions come again Of golden dreams departed And years of weary pain." But she holds onto the hope of a better time when "my voice may know the old songs For all eternity."

If we hesitate to sing old songs, we can try new ones bringing joy and hope. The truth conveyed is the important thing, not whether the songs are old or new.

Besides the psalms, many spiritual hymns and songs are available as the vehicles of divine wisdom from the Word of God by which we teach and admonish one another. They are expressions of "gratitude in your hearts to God." Such gratitude stems from having received the forgiveness of our heavenly Father on account of Jesus Christ, His Son.

God's people in Babylon were reluctant to comply with the request of their captors that they "sing us one of the songs of Zion" (Psalm 137:3). They replied, when in sorrow they had hung their harps on the willows, "How can we sing the songs of the Lord in a foreign land?" (Revelation 5:9). It would provoke bitter tears of remembrance.

We take inspiration from saints in heaven who "sang a new song" to Him: "You were slain, and with Your blood You purchased men for God from every tribe and language and people and nation. You have made them to be a kingdom and priests to serve our God" (Revelation 5:9–10).

PRAYER SUGGESTION

Take a hymn of praise from your hymnal and use it as the basis for your prayer.

Different Gifts

We have different gifts, according to the grace given us. Romans 12:6

John Henry Newman wrote "Lead Kindly Light" while the ship on which he was sailing was becalmed at sea. Having passed through a time of conflict, he needed quietness to gather his thoughts. Conversely, John B. Dykes composed the music while walking briskly through one of the busiest streets of London.

It is true that no two persons are exactly alike in their endowments and dispositions. Diverse, too, are life's experiences through which we pass. Through education, the distinctive gifts are developed. Learning comes through experiences in everyday life. In making the most of our learning experiences, formal and informal, we become better instruments in God's hands for performing His work and will.

The natural and spiritual gifts God imparts show divine forethought. Instead of making all of us alike, He provided for a variety of gifts so His people may serve in a multiplicity of ways, thus fulfilling the manifold needs in Christ's body, the church.

In His great wisdom and love, God showed further forethought in granting the greatest gift of all: the saving faith in the redeeming merit of Jesus Christ. The Holy Spirit generates faith through the Gospel and the sacraments. He effects a great change in the person converted, not only imparting new spiritual gifts but also the willingness to use them. As a new creation in Christ, we say yes to God's mercy, offering ourselves in body and mind for "spiritual worship" (Romans 12:1). We gladly engage in it, for we are "transformed by the renewing of your mind" (Romans 12:2).

PRAYER SUGGESTION

Ask the Holy Spirit to help you discover His gifts to you and teach you how to use them.

Keep Blooming!

Even to your old age and gray hairs I am He,
I am He who will sustain you. Isaiah 46:4

The summer passes quickly. Somewhere in the outdoor world will be "the last rose of summer, left blooming alone." What if you are—or you think you are—that human rose?

Here you are by yourself. The temptation is great to withdraw from the arena of life and to retreat deeper into yourself. But that would not be good, not for yourself or those still near you.

One great truth is that you are not really alone. There are people around you, where you live, work, and shop. There are friends in your church worshiping and working with you. Above all, God is with you in His gracious presence, and the Lord Jesus keeps His promise: "Surely I am with you always" (Matthew 28:20). God's promise to His people of long ago is the same to us today: "I have made you and I will carry you; I will sustain you and I will rescue you" (Isaiah 46:4).

As His child, you can live in daily communion with Him through Word and prayer. You are created in His image, redeemed through Jesus Christ, and sanctified by the Holy Spirit.

To be a rose in God's flower garden means you are a *blooming* rose, that is, a person still bringing forth the fruits of faith to God's glory and fulfillment of human needs. Your words of encouragement, your pleasant smile, your greeting by cards or telephone— these are activities that make you bloom.

This is God's promise: "The righteous will flourish. ... They will still bear fruit in old age, they will stay fresh and green" (Psalm 92:12, 14).

PRAYER SUGGESTION

Ask God, for Jesus' sake, to make you a rose that blooms.

Unity in Christ

You are no longer foreigners and aliens,
but fellow citizens with God's people. Ephesians 2:19

How can people of various ethnic backgrounds live and work peacefully together? The maple leaf, Canada's emblem, entwines three other emblems: thistle, shamrock, and rose. The people who came to Canada from the three countries symbolized—Scotland, Ireland, and England—find unity under the symbol of the maple leaf. Of course, people from many other lands have found a home in Canada, adding distinctive strengths to the country. The maple leaf entwines them all.

In first-century times, tensions developed in the church as Jewish people and Gentiles converted to Christianity. The Gentiles were of many backgrounds: Greek, Roman, Scythian, and others. How could the two major groups find unity in the church? Many coming out of Judaism thought the Old Testament rites of circumcision, Sabbath observances, dietary rules, and so forth should be continued. The Gentile converts were of a different opinion.

We note how the apostle Paul dealt with the problem. He led his readers in Ephesus to the foot of Christ's cross. From the accursed tree of the cross he plucked a leaf "for the healing of the nations" (Revelation 22:2). Christ died for the sins of all, thus bringing peace and opening the door to full and equal membership in God's household. He writes that Christ "Himself is our peace, who has made the two one ... by abolishing in His flesh the law with its commandments and regulations. His purpose was to create in Himself one new man out of the two, thus making peace, and in this one body to reconcile both of them to God through the cross" (Ephesians 2:14–16).

PRAYER SUGGESTION

Ask Christ Jesus to bless you and fellow Christians with His peace.

The Chariot Swung High

Suddenly a chariot of fire and horses of fire appeared ...
and Elijah went up to heaven in a whirlwind. 2 Kings 2:11

The verse for today is the inspiration for the song, "Swing Low, Sweet Chariot." The singer requests that the chariot sweep him up and take him to heaven. His most joyful experience was "The brightest day that ever I saw [was] when Jesus washed my sins away." He is ready for even brighter days in heaven.

Elijah likewise was eager for his heavenly homecoming. As Elijah and Elisha passed through several towns, companies of prophets told Elisha: "Do you know that the LORD is going to take your master from you today?" (2 Kings 2:3). He said he did, and he was determined to stay with his teacher to the end.

Elijah and Moses are in heaven in both soul and body. They appeared in glorified bodies and spoke with Jesus on the mount of transfiguration. Moses represented the Law and Elijah the prophets. The reading above describes Elijah's ascent to heaven, and as for Moses we read in Jude 9 that the archangel Michael carried his body to heaven.

On the Last Day, Jesus will come again in glory to take all His people bodily into eternal life. An entourage of angels "will gather His elect from the four winds, and from one end of the heavens to the other" (Matthew 24:31). Included are all who had their sins washed away by Jesus. It is a double cleansing—by the purifying blood of Jesus and the water of Baptism.

As we await that day, we remain steadfast in the faith that the chariot will come for us too.

PRAYER SUGGESTION

Ask the Lord Jesus to help prepare you for the day when He will come again to take you to heaven.

Pleading for a Tree

"'Sir,' the man replied, 'leave it alone for one more year. ... If it bears fruit next year, fine! If not, then cut it down.'" Luke 13:8–9

Many people have favorite trees. They hate to see them cut down to clear the land for highways or housing developments. Over the centuries, poems and songs have been written to express this sentiment.

The tree in Jesus' parable was a fig tree a man planted in his vineyard. When it didn't bear fruit, he told the caretaker to cut it down. But the latter pleaded for the tree. He said he would dig around it and fertilize it. Given more time and care, it might become productive.

In the words preceding the parable, Jesus urged His hearers to repent. This would imply that they believe in Him as their Savior and bear fruit. John the Baptist had spoken along the same lines, that people "produce fruit in keeping with repentance" (Matthew 3:8). The ax, he said, was already at the root of the trees. But John also preached the Gospel, pointing to Jesus as the Lamb of God bearing the sin of the world.

The Lord Jesus is the caretaker who pleads for us. His intercession would be that the heavenly Father would give spiritual backsliders another chance. He would send them the Holy Spirit to work on their hearts through the Gospel.

Christ's intercession—"Spare that tree!"—is the continuing part of His high-priestly office. His sacrifice for us on the cross is forever finished. It was, in the expression of the writer to the Hebrews, "once for all." But in heaven Jesus continues to plead for us. We are thankful for this, asking Him in the lines of a hymn: "In the hour of trial, Jesus, plead for me."

PRAYER SUGGESTION

Express your gratitude to Jesus for interceding for you before the Father.

The Helping Hand of God

When You open Your hand, they are satisfied with good things.
Psalm 104:28

How are we to understand the expression "hand of God"?

"Hand of God" is a figurative expression, an accommodation to our limited understanding. In today's verse it stands for God's care for people and animals, as a rule through the laws of nature but sometimes through direct intervention.

Sometimes the hand of God is raised in righteous wrath. The enemies of God are not always aware of His power as typified by His right hand. They should be, for the hand that made the universe can just as easily destroy it. Believers need also be aware of God's right hand. We are reminded to humble ourselves "under God's mighty hand" (1 Peter 5:6) so He will exalt us in due time. All the while God's hand is especially a providing and protecting one, as the apostle continued, "Cast all your anxiety on Him because He cares for you" (1 Peter 5:7).

The helping hand of God was also very active to effect our spiritual salvation. From His own right hand God sent His Son to be our Savior from sin, death, and the devil. Born of the Virgin Mary, this true Son of the Father laid down His life for us. Having completed His redeeming work, He rose from the dead, ascended into heaven, and sits at the right hand of God. There He intercedes for us, and from thence He will come to judge the living and the dead.

Jesus promised to make room for us in the Father's house in heaven. There, as the psalmist declared, "You will fill me with joy in Your presence, with eternal pleasures at Your right hand" (Psalm 16:11).

PRAYER SUGGESTION

Give thanks to God for all His blessings, especially for His grace in Christ Jesus, our Lord.

Christ's Presence with Us

"Surely I am with you always, to the very end of the age."
Matthew 28:20

The presence of family members turn a house into a home when love prevails. A vacation becomes much more enjoyable when another person is along to admire the scenery. A church group comes to life when someone is there with constructive thoughts matched by enthusiasm.

Christ's presence made a great difference to His disciples. His presence with them in the storm-tossed boat gave them assurance. How faith-strengthening it was to hear His sermons, see His miracles, and witness His love when healing the sick! So close was the relationship that St. John could say in retrospect that their ears had heard, their eyes seen, and their hands touched the eternal Son of God. When Christ appeared to the disciples after His resurrection, their fears subsided and faith returned, for they "were overjoyed when they saw the Lord" (John 20:20).

So it is with us. Our Lord brings life and light into the gloom. His presence turns our desert into a paradise. He brings many blessings, assuring us that by His death He imparts life. To the desperate He holds out hope. To the ill He gives "sight, riches, healing of the mind." To those mourning He repeats what He once said to Mary and Martha: "I am the Resurrection and the Life" (John 11:25). He rejoices with those who rejoice, telling them of the even greater joy of eternal life.

We will never have heaven on earth, but we have Him who gained it for us. His promise stands: "Where two or three come together in My name, there am I with them" (Matthew 18:20).

PRAYER SUGGESTION

Give thanks to the Lord Jesus for bringing joy into your life.

A Joyful Homecoming

He got up and went to his father. Luke 15:20

Some sons and daughters leave home in a huff, thinking they can roam amid pleasures and palaces in a glamorous world. By comparison, life at home seems dull, repressive. So with hardly a good-bye they leave. Fortunate are those who gain perspective while at large. Seeing the error of their ways, they come home to their heavenly Father in repentance and faith. They are at peace with their parents also.

Luke chapter 15 is like a lost-and-found column. Jesus tells in three parables how a lost sheep, a lost coin, and a lost son were found. He stresses that in all three instances great joy attended the restoration of the lost. People on earth rejoiced while in heaven the angels celebrated the events. In the parable of the prodigal son, the father said to the reluctant older brother, "This brother of yours was dead and is alive again; he was lost and is found" (Luke 15:32). It was a joyful homecoming for the father and the returning son.

Jesus describes the heavenly Father as always willing to welcome back His sons and daughters who have strayed. When they speak the hard words with sincere intent: "We have sinned," He forgives them and takes them back into His family. The Father does this because He gave up His divine Son to atone for all their sins and to bring them peace. He is the one who tells the parables: Jesus Christ, who suffered, died on a cross, and rose again to effect the salvation of all. For us the door to our heavenly Father's "home sweet home" is open.

PRAYER SUGGESTION

Give thanks to the Father in heaven for having made us His beloved children through the merit of Jesus Christ, His Son.

He Returned to Return Thanks

He threw himself at Jesus' feet and thanked Him—and he was a Samaritan. Luke 17:16

The man had come to Jesus with an urgent request, this man with leprosy. "Jesus, Master, have pity on us!" (Luke 17:13). Short and to the point, this prayer was a plea for unearned mercy, an outright appeal to divine grace. Jesus answered in His own way and time. The miraculous cure came while they were en route to the priests for a health inspection. "And as they went, they were cleansed" (Luke 17:14).

The first leg of the prayer journey was now over. But what about a return trip to make the petition-thanksgiving cycle complete? Only one man—one of ten and a Samaritan at that—was up to it. With his thanksgiving our Lord was well pleased: "Rise and go; your faith has made you well" (Luke 17:19).

Turning back to give thanks may seem like going in a direction we don't want to go. The other ex-lepers followed their natural impulses, hurrying forward to the enjoyments of a healthful life. However, true spiritual progression always entails going God's way, even when it means a detour. We go God's way when we retrace our steps to thank Christ by word and deed for His mercy.

The thanksgiving journey, from the human side, can be a lonely one. You may have to walk alone and unaccompanied. But it is a pilgrimage that the love of Christ equips us to make. We remember how Jesus walked the lonesome road to Calvary's cross to redeem us from the leprosy of sin. He walked the way of sorrows because love for us urged Him on. For the joy that was set before Him He endured the cross. Christ's love and mercy for us prompt us to give thanks.

PRAYER SUGGESTION

Express your gratitude to Jesus for your healing from the leprosy of sin.

Hearts Aglow with Love

"As I have loved you, so you must love one another." John 13:34

The Heidelberg Catechism, written in 1562, says "The chief end of man is to glorify God and enjoy Him forever."

Who can glorify God and enjoy Him unless that person, first of all, loves Him? And how do we love God with all our heart, soul, and mind, which, according to Jesus, is "the first and greatest commandment" (Matthew 22:38)?

Love begins with God, who first loved us. So great was His love that He gave His own beloved Son to lay down His life for the salvation of all sinners. The Son, a full participant in this love divine, declares, "I have loved you." He wants us to love one another in like manner. But how is this possible?

By the hand of faith we accept the salvation God's love offers. Having accepted it, we are moved and enabled, thanks to the work of the Holy Spirit in our hearts, to love God with all the body, mind, and spirit.

One part of love for God is love for the neighbor. Since as Christians we love God, we will love also our brothers and sisters in Christ. This is love in action, in the words of Paul: "as we have opportunity, let us do good to all people, especially to those who belong to the family of believers" (Galatians 6:10).

Such love casts out fear, suspicion, selfishness, for it needs the whole heart for itself. St. Augustine said of early Christians, "That they might not be frozen with fear, they burned with the fire of love." Noticing this, their pagan neighbors exclaimed, "How they love one another!"

Are we on fire with a love like this?

PRAYER SUGGESTION

Add your prayer to these hymn lines: "Oh, may my love to Thee Pure, warm, and changeless be, A living fire."

The Faith of Our Forefathers

In You our fathers put their trust; they trusted and You delivered them. Psalm 22:4

"O God, beneath Thy guiding hand Our exiled fathers crossed the sea; And when they trod the wintry strand, With prayer and psalm they worshiped Thee."

This song is a tribute to the Pilgrim fathers and mothers who settled in Massachusetts in 1620. We owe much to these and other pioneers who brought their Christian religion to the New World.

To have respect for those who have gone before us—and gratitude toward God for what He accomplished through them—is an extension of the commandment to honor father and mother. The psalmist, in great suffering, found comfort in God's faithfulness to the patriarchs who trusted in Him and was convinced that God would extend that same faithfulness to him.

In his song of praise, Zechariah celebrated the birth of John the Baptist, his son, recalling how God "show[ed] mercy to our fathers" (Luke 1:72) by fulfilling His covenant. It enabled later generations to "serve Him without fear in holiness and righteousness before Him all our days" (Luke 1:74–75). John fulfilled God's plan by proclaiming Jesus as the Messiah, the Lamb of God who takes away the world's sin.

We still share every promise God made to the generations before us. We worship God "with prayer and psalm." The same God who guided and sustained our Christian ancestors' promises to be with us. With David, we can joyfully "Cast your cares on the LORD and He will sustain you; He will never let the righteous fall" (Psalm 55:22).

PRAYER SUGGESTION

Ask the Holy Spirit to strengthen you spiritually so you can follow in the footsteps of your Christian ancestors.

Jesus, Our Prayer Instructor

"This, then, is how you should pray:
'Our Father in heaven, ...'" Matthew 6:9

In His Sermon on the Mount, Jesus covered many subjects pertaining to spiritual life. Prayer was one.

First, Jesus denounced the customs of the Pharisees, who made pretence of piety as they went through the motions of praying in the synagogues and on street corners. They concentrated on posture and other details, making prayer a public exhibition. But they were hypocrites. Jesus described their hypocrisy—how they, among other things, "for a show make lengthy prayers" (Matthew 12:40).

Jesus was not condemning public prayer, but He did condemn using prayer as a cover-up. He went on to say how prayer to the heavenly Father has the promise of a divine answer. A sure way to keep our minds on our petitions is to speak to God in our private rooms, with the doors shut to keep out distractions.

Jesus gave another example of inappropriate prayer—that of the pagans who make "many words" (Matthew 6:70), as though this helps gain divine attention. It is not necessary to be loquacious, for the heavenly Father knows what is in our hearts even when we express it in short, broken prayers and in sighs.

How are we to pray? Jesus gave us a model prayer. It has a well-balanced structure: an introduction, seven petitions (three for spiritual blessing, one for temporal blessings, and three for averting evil), and a closing doxology. We do well to model the Lord's Prayer when we pray.

Jesus wants us to pray with confidence and in His name. This is important, for He, by His redeeming work, reconciled us to God and made our prayers acceptable.

PRAYER SUGGESTION

Pray now in Jesus' name, stating your needs and giving thanks.

The Forgiving Heart

When you stand praying, if you hold anything against anyone, forgive him. Mark 11:25

In the prayer Jesus taught us, the Lord's Prayer, the Fifth Petition asks, "Forgive us our debts, as we also have forgiven our debtors." We can pray this petition sincerely only if we have a forgiving heart toward others.

To be forgiving is often difficult. This fact is depicted in Harold Bell Wright's *The Shepherd of the Hills.* In it, the character Old Matt is bitter because his daughter died in childbirth. He blames the father of the child, who is the son of "the shepherd of the hills." Old Matt eventually forgives him—that is, when he dies from a robber's bullet. It shouldn't take an event like this to become forgiving.

What does it take? Forgiving proceeds from a changed heart, and that change is effected by the power of the Word of God. That Word speaks to us in God's law, convicting and convincing us that we ourselves are sinners. But to really enable us to be forgiving we need the Gospel, which is the Good News that in Christ God has forgiven us our many debts and trespasses. Nowhere in the Bible is this truth stated more clearly than in Paul's second letter to the Corinthians: "If anyone is in Christ, he is a new creation. ... God was reconciling the world to Himself in Christ, not counting men's sins against them. ... God made Him who had no sin to be sin for us" (2 Corinthians 5:17–21).

When this truth of the Gospel is taken to heart, we become forgiving toward those who sinned against us.

PRAYER SUGGESTION

Ask God, for Jesus' sake, to forgive you even as you forgive others.

Poverty and Plenty

At [the rich man's] gate was laid a beggar named Lazarus. Luke 16:20

Being rich is not in itself sinful. Abraham in the Old Testament was wealthy but had God's endorsement as the "father of believers." He was a generous man who, for example, sent his private army of 318 men to rescue Lot and other people from marauders. Those who, like Abraham, are rich ought to use their wealth to the glory of God and the well-being of the unfortunate.

To make His point, Jesus cited an extreme example of poverty: Lazarus, a beggar covered with sores, having dogs as comrades, living off crumbs from the rich man's table. As it is no vice to be rich, so it is no virtue to be poor.

Both plenty and poverty have built-in hazards, prompting the writer of Proverbs to say, "Give me neither poverty nor riches" (30:8). The rich are apt to forget God and give their heart to Mammon. The poor are tempted to steal and to become demanding.

The point in Jesus' parable is that God's Word—Jesus refers to it as Moses and the prophets—teaches us that there is life in the hereafter, either in heaven or in hell. Salvation comes to those who have faith, a "faith expressing itself through love" (Galatians 5:6). This saving faith looks to Jesus, who became the Author and Perfecter of it by going to Calvary's cross to redeem us and to open the doors of heaven to us. Believing in Him, we are "rich toward God" (Luke 12:21).

PRAYER SUGGESTION

Count your blessings, thanking God for them.

Raising the Roof to Get to Jesus

They made an opening in the roof above Jesus and ... lowered the mat the paralyzed man was lying on. Mark 2:4

Jesus had returned to His headquarters in Capernaum after an extended absence, and the news soon got around. In a short time a crowd had gathered where He was staying. In fact, there was no more sitting or standing room. Jesus took this opportunity to preach the Word of God to the crowd.

Four men approached the house carrying a paralytic man. When they saw that they could not enter because of the crowded doorways, they climbed a stairway on the side of the house, removed some tiles from the roof, and lowered the paralyzed friend down in front of Jesus.

When our Lord saw the faith of the four men and of the paralytic, He was moved to compassion and said to the sick man, "Son, your sins are forgiven." This caused some teachers of the law to take exception. "This is blasphemy! Who can forgive sins but God alone?"

Jesus said to them, "Which is easier: to say to a paralytic, 'Your sins are forgiven,' or to say, 'Get up, take your mat, and walk'?" To show that one is as easy as the other for the Son of God, Jesus did both. He forgave his sins and cured him of his paralysis.

In contrast to the quibbling scribes, the faith of the four friends stands out. In their love and concern they took extraordinary measures to bring the paralytic to Jesus: they raised the roof. Likewise, when our faith in Jesus enables us to trust in the forgiveness of sins, which He earned for us as the Lamb of God, it prompts us to act in love for those in distress. It may call for deeds of an unusual kind.

PRAYER SUGGESTION

Thank the Lord Jesus, your dearest Friend, for His forgiveness and for prompting friends to help you.

Marks of Honor

I bear on my body the marks [stigmata] of Jesus. Galatians 6:17

The Greek word *stigma* (plural: *stigmata*) means a mark of disgrace or reproach. Certainly the red symbol of sin that marked Hester Prynne in Nathaniel Hawthorne's novel, *The Scarlet Letter,* was a stigma.

The Lord Jesus bore stigmata on His hands, feet, and side when He returned from the grave. They were proof that He had been crucified. His enemies would regard them as tokens of disgrace, for only the most despised criminals were crucified.

Thomas expressed his disbelief in Christ's resurrection. He declared, "Unless I see the nail marks in His hands and put my finger where the nails were, and put my hand into His side, I will not believe it" (John 20:25). A week later Jesus again appeared to the assembled disciples and paid special attention to Thomas. Thomas did not have to take the touch test. He saw Jesus, heard His invitation, and confessed, "My Lord and my God" (John 20:28). He did not have to inspect the stigmata to believe, and that is the way it should be.

St. Paul suffered much for Jesus—beatings, stonings, and the like, which left their marks on his body. Jesus had stigmata verifying the true death He suffered as our Savior. The apostle's marks could not merit his salvation. However, since he experienced great cruelty as a witness for Jesus, he considered his scars stigmata for Jesus. He considered it an honor.

Our Lord's nail marks are precious to us, for they are credentials of His true identity as our Savior.

PRAYER SUGGESTION

Thank the Lord Jesus for the healing that is yours through His wounds.

We Pray to Jesus, the Healer

The people brought to Jesus all who had various kinds of sickness, and laying His hands on each one, He healed them. Luke 4:40

The school nurse had just completed her health talk. "Tell me, David," she said to a bright-eyed seven-year-old, "what is the first thing we do when we catch a cold?"

David rose to his feet and replied in a confident tone, "We pray to Jesus." That wasn't the answer the nurse expected, but before she knew it, she heard herself say, "Yes, David, we pray to Jesus."

In a time when science has made incredible advances, we are tempted to put our faith in human ingenuity and forget the love and power of God. We are tempted to forget that Jesus Christ is truly the Healer of souls and bodies.

The people of Capernaum who brought their sick to Jesus were undoubtedly acquainted with the psalmist's words, "Praise the LORD, O my soul; all my inmost being, praise His holy name. Praise the LORD, O my soul, and forget not all His benefits—who forgives all your sins and heals all your diseases" (Psalm 103:1–3). God does this for the sake of Jesus, who bore all our sins and griefs.

Do we consciously and confidently come to God in prayer with all our ills? Do we ask Him to extend His healing hand to us, stand by us, restore our ailing bodies and minds to health? And having been restored to health through the wonders of modern medicine, do we give Him the glory? Do we humbly acknowledge that it is He "who redeems your life from the pit and crowns you with love and compassion" (Psalm 103:4)? May God grant that we do.

PRAYER SUGGESTION

Turn the opening verses of Psalm 103 into your own words of prayer.

What the Heavens Declare

What is man that You are mindful of him? Psalm 8:4

In the poem "Stars of the Summer Night," Henry W. Longfellow gazes into "yon azure deeps" and contemplates how the stars and moon hide their "golden light" so his beloved can sleep.

The psalmist also looked into the sky. He set his thoughts on the Creator who reveals His glory in the heavens and beyond. The universe, he said, is "the work of Your fingers" (Psalm 8:3). Larger than we can comprehend, it is nevertheless delicately made. Moreover, sun and moon stay in perfect rhythm to keep time and to give light, as Genesis reveals: "Let them serve as signs to mark seasons and days and years, and let them be lights in the expanse of the sky to give light on the earth" (Genesis 1:14–15).

In this magnificent universe, one little creature is the object of God's special love. God bestowed a great distinction on the human being in making him the caretaker of "all flocks and herds, and the beasts of the field, the birds of the air, and the fish of the sea" (Psalm 8:7–8).

But God did more. He thought so highly of mankind that He caused His own Son to become one of us. In order to lift up the sinful human race, the Son of God lowered Himself to servant-hood and took our place. Jesus Christ, the Son of Man, entered the state of humiliation, becoming obedient to death, even death on a cross. What a miracle of divine love, exceeding even the miracle of creation!

Beyond the stars and moon of a summer night, we see a reflection of the glory of God, who sent His Son to bring us back into His family.

PRAYER SUGGESTION

Praise God for His mercy in making you His son or daughter through Jesus Christ, His Son.

Jesus Was Willing

A man with leprosy came to Him and begged Him on his knees,
"If You are willing, You can make me clean." Mark 1:40

Scripture tells that Jesus is able "to sympathize with our weaknesses" (Hebrews 4:15). So it was on this occasion. Jesus, filled with compassion, extended His hand and touched the patient, something most people wouldn't do for fear of catching this dreaded sickness. Jesus responded with, "I am willing ... Be clean." Immediately the man was healed.

We notice that he did not in any way reveal a show of right. He was not demanding. He cast himself on the mercy of Jesus. In our prayer instruction we learned about a distinction we make when asking for divine blessings. When we ask for spiritual blessing—those pertaining to the welfare of the soul—we pray without distinction, without saying, "Lord, if You will," or "If it is good for me," for we know that God wants it and we need it. When we pray for temporal blessings, including bodily health, we pray conditionally. That is what this man did: "If You are willing."

We can learn a lot from this man's prayer. In days of sickness, adversity, poverty, unemployment, we do well to fall down before our Lord and say, "If You are willing." Jesus Himself prayed this way: "My Father, if it is possible, may this cup be taken from Me. Yet not as I will, but as You will" (Matthew 26:39).

Our Lord knows what is best for us. We can confidently leave the final decision in His hands and pray accordingly.

PRAYER SUGGESTION

Ask the Holy Spirit to teach you in accordance with God's will and with Jesus' love.

Prayer, an Incense Offering

May my prayer be set before You like incense; may the lifting up of my hands be like the evening sacrifice. Psalm 141:2

"Thou, whose all pervading eye Naught escapes, without, within, Pardon each infirmity, Open fault and secret sin." These words are from "Softly New the Light of Day." In it, the author asks Jesus to "look with pitying eye" on his failings, for He has known "all of man's infirmity."

Whether we pray in the evening when the sun has set or when the morning light is breaking, we regard our prayers as offerings to God, as David thought of his prayers. In the holy place of the Old Testament temple was a golden altar on which incense was offered. It was at such an altar that the priest Zechariah was officiating when an angel appeared to him, telling him that he would have a son to be named John who would prepare the way for the Messiah.

As burning incense gives off a pleasant aroma, so our prayers please God as they come before Him. This is so when we approach God humbly, confessing our sins and asking for pardon. When we pray in firm confidence and in Jesus' name, we can be assured that our petitions will receive a sympathetic reception. The Lord Jesus, now enthroned in heaven, was once with us here on earth. He understands our infirmities, for He Himself endured suffering and was in all respects tempted like we are.

For Jesus' sake as the Lamb of God that once bore the sins and griefs of us all, the Father in heaven will forgive our "open fault and secret sin," as the poet declared. "Let us then approach the throne of grace with confidence" (Hebrews 4:16).

PRAYER SUGGESTION

Let your prayer be one of thanksgiving for God's love to you in Jesus Christ.

Speaking and Hearing

Samuel said, "Speak, for Your servant is listening." 1 Samuel 3:10

What wonderful gifts of God are our abilities to speak and to hear! They make communication possible. Thoughts and sentiments can be conveyed.

People who are unable to hear compensate by depending on other senses. They can see a friendly smile, feel a loving embrace, smell dinner being cooked. This, too, is effective communicating.

Speaking has its place in the exercise of our Christian faith. God's Old Testament people heard His voice. Such a person was Samuel, a spiritual trainee in God's house under Eli. One night God called his name to convey an important message about the forthcoming doom of Eli's family. When God called him yet again, Samuel replied, "Speak, for Your servant is listening."

God speaks to us in His Word, telling us of His love in Christ Jesus, sent to redeem us. In whatever form this Word comes to us —Scripture readings, sermons, hymns—in it God speaks. And we speak to God in prayer and to one another. "Let the Word of Christ dwell in you richly as you teach and admonish one another with all wisdom, and as you sing psalms, hymns and spiritual songs with gratitude in your hearts to God" (Colossians 3:16).

The correlation of speaking is hearing, and it too plays a part in our Christian lives. Jesus said, "Blessed rather are those who hear the Word of God and obey it" (Luke 11:28). On entering God's house—and as we go about our daily duties—we say with Samuel, "Speak, for Your servant is listening."

"Lord, open Thou my heart to hear And by Thy Word to me draw near."

PRAYER SUGGESTION

Tell God that you are willing to listen when He speaks to you.

A Change in Vocation

"Come, follow Me," Jesus said, "and I will make you fishers of men."
Matthew 4:19

It is not unusual for people to make dramatic career changes. For example, Zane Grey, the author of Western novels, had a degree in dentistry.

The Bible tells of individuals whom God called from secular work into a spiritual vocation. First Kings tells about Elisha, who seemed to be a prosperous farmer when God called him to be a prophet. Elisha was the successor of Elijah, rendering outstanding service as a man of God. Along the same lines, God called Amos, a shepherd and a caretaker of sycamore-fig trees, to be a prophet.

As the New Testament era dawned with the coming of Jesus as the Messiah, we read of great changes in the lives of people who came under His ministry. Our Lord needed apostles to carry on His work. Jesus recruited fishermen, among others. Walking along the shore of the Sea of Galilee one day, He called Peter, Andrew, James, and John to follow Him and to become "fishers of men."

The Lord continues to reach out to people in their vocation to become full-time workers in His church. He wants them to use their talents and special skills to become messengers of the Good News. They are to proclaim the same truth the apostle Peter so eloquently preached on Pentecost: Jesus was nailed to a cross, "but God raised Him from the dead. ... Repent and be baptized, every one of you, in the name of Jesus Christ for the forgiveness of your sins" (Acts 2:24, 38). The fact that there are such recruits shows that the Holy Spirit is at work among us.

PRAYER SUGGESTION

Ask the Lord of the harvest to send workers into the harvest fields.

The Unending Life

In Him was life, and that life was the light of men. John 1:4

Our Lord spoke often on life, notably on how full life in Him, who is Life Personified, is to be attained. Jesus declares, "I have come that [My sheep] may have life, and have it to the full" (John 10:10). This abundant life, as the Good Shepherd makes clear, culminates in eternal life. Jesus explains how life to the full was gained: the Good Shepherd laid down His life for them on Calvary's cross. Believers in this life have a foretaste, for they know the blessedness of communion with Jesus.

Many events in the life and ministry of Jesus have full, unending life as their theme. In the wilderness He fed the multitude miraculously with bread and fish. In the synagogue in Capernaum, emphasizing that people do not live by earthly bread alone, He continued the discussion of the higher life He gives to those who believe in Him as the One whom God sent for the salvation of all people.

Everyone who believes in Jesus Christ "has eternal life" here and now (John 3:36). What is more, He said He would raise up departed believers on the Last Day. Then begins the enjoyment of everlasting life, life in its fullness.

By what means is this life imparted? By means of God's Word to be sure. And by means of the Sacraments the Lord instituted—Baptism and Communion—to generate, strengthen, and preserve faith in the remission of sins and the life unending.

What a joy and comfort it is to be alive in Christ!

PRAYER SUGGESTION

Ask the Lord Jesus to come into your heart to give you full, unending life.

The Call to Steadfast Faith

Let us run with perseverance the race marked out for us. Hebrews 12:1

Every year thousands participate in the Boston Marathon. But by the time runners reach Heartbreak Hill the ranks have thinned.

Christianity is like a marathon, like a long-distance endurance test. In order to give a good account of ourselves in this continuing race, we need to keep in mind what is involved. To be in proper shape, we need training; we need to "throw off everything that hinders and the sin that so easily entangles" (Hebrews 12:1). We get rid of the weight of evil by confessing our pet sins and then forsaking them. Bad habits can be overcome.

Further, the race of faith calls for perseverance, patience, and steady performance, for it is not a quick 100-yard dash but a life-long marathon. Only by steadfastness of purpose can we run our race to the finish.

The strength to stay in the race comes from fixing "our eyes on Jesus, the Author and Perfecter of our faith, who for the joy set before Him endured the cross" (Hebrews 12:2). In our stead He completed His race to the finish line, to Calvary. He endured in His course, ignoring the shame, for He kept in mind that it was for our salvation. Amid physical pain He felt the joy set before Him— the joy of knowing that He was redeeming sinful mankind.

When we trust in Christ Jesus, we are given strength to finish the race. No Heartbreak Hill can keep us from advancing toward our heavenly goal.

PRAYER SUGGESTION

Look up the hymn "My Faith Looks Up to Thee" and repeat its truths in your own words.

The Power of God's Word

The Word of God is living and active. Hebrews 4:12

Some people regard words as useless. They say, "Talk is cheap." In some situations this may be true.

Yet words can be powerful. A kind word or two can encourage the disheartened. Words like "I will" can establish a legal, binding relationship, such as a marriage. A few words from an authority figure can send another on an important mission. The centurion said, "I tell this one, 'Go,' and he goes; and that one, 'Come,' and he comes. I say to my servant, 'Do this,' and he does it" (Matthew 8:9).

How much greater is the power of the words of God! The psalmist declares, "By the Word of the LORD were the heavens made, their starry host by the breath of His mouth" (Psalms 33:6).

God speaks to us through Holy Scripture. His Law is sharp, like a two-edged sword. It penetrates obdurate hearts, convicting people of their sins. The Gospel, too, is powerful and effective. Paul called it "the power of God for the salvation of everyone who believes" (Romans 1:16). Further, God has spoken most eloquently through His Son, the personal Word. Of Him the Bible bears witness, and He bore witness to "what was written" (Acts 13:29).

Our Lord declares, "The words I have spoken to you are spirit and they are life" (John 6:63). The Gospel is still today the power that changes hearts. The Gospel makes those who believe in Christ "a new creation" (2 Corinthians 5:17).

What a power it is!

PRAYER SUGGESTION

Pray that the Word of God may strengthen your faith in Christ and make you fruitful in all good works.

The River of Salvation

Then the angel showed me the river of the water of life, as clear as crystal, flowing from the throne of God and of the Lamb. Revelation 22:1

One could wish we had more rivers like the one Robert Burns extols in "Flow Gently, Sweet Afton": "Thy crystal stream, Afton, how lovely it glides."

Spiritually speaking, there is a river like the Afton. The psalmist said, "There is a river whose streams make glad the city of God" (Psalm 46:4).

God's grace in Christ Jesus is like a clear, refreshing stream that never runs dry. It is abundant. "From the fullness of His grace we have all received one blessing after another" (John 1:16), and "Where sin increased, grace increased all the more" (Romans 5:20). This forgiving grace, said Paul, comes through Jesus Christ, who carried the world's sin to Calvary's cross.

The riverbed contains the water and causes it to flow. The river of God's grace is contained in and comes to us through the means of grace, Word and Sacrament.

St. John the Divine saw the church of Christ in its final perfection in heaven. What a vision he had! A river, as clear as crystal, flows from God's throne and the exalted Lamb, continuing "down the middle of the great street of the city" (Revelation 22:2). The Tree of Life flourishes on its bank, yielding abundant fruit. Someday we will be there to enjoy eternal life. Until then, we have a foretaste of heaven as the Gospel of forgiveness in Christ is proclaimed to us.

PRAYER SUGGESTION

Ask the Lord of the church to keep the river of salvation flowing through the world.

Good Came Out of Evil

Joseph said to them [his brothers] ... "You intended to harm me, but God intended it for good to accomplish what is now being done, the saving of many lives." Genesis 50:19–20

An unusual monument stands in Enterprise, Alabama. It pays tribute to the boll weevil, the enemy of cotton crops, for causing the farmers there to turn to a more prosperous crop: peanuts. Sometimes it takes an evil to direct our efforts to something good.

The sons of Jacob clearly had evil in mind when they sold their brother Joseph into slavery. They wanted him out of the way, stopping short of outright murder. But God turned an evil intent into a good outcome. Joseph, as Egypt's prime minister, made provision for a coming famine by storing up food supplies.

This is a great mystery. When God intervenes to make evil serve His purpose, He still holds the doers responsible for their sins. He does not regard the good ending as justifying the means. Judas Iscariot did evil when he betrayed Jesus. God turned this great misdeed into a steppingstone to the great event: the death of Jesus for the salvation of all.

After Stephen was murdered, a great persecution was touched off and many Christians left Jerusalem. Good came out of this, for wherever the refugees went, they spread the Gospel. After Saul, a consenting witness of Stephen's martyrdom, became a Christian apostle, he experienced many setbacks. But they all turned out to the advantage of Christianity.

God can cause good to come out of evil in our lives as well. We can safely and confidently entrust all of life's events to our heavenly Father, who in Christ Jesus has made us His children.

PRAYER SUGGESTION

Ask God, for Jesus' sake, to turn your hurts into healing events.

Christ, Seated at God's Right Hand

That power is like the working of His mighty strength, which He exerted in Christ when He raised Him from the dead and seated Him at His right hand in the heavenly realms. Ephesians 1:19–20

In the front of the St. Louis Art Museum is a statue of the city's namesake: King Louis IX, leader of the Seventh Crusade. It has been the victim of vandals: the seven-foot sword, a symbol of his power, held by the king has been stolen three times.

A living king, not just a stone king, can also be stripped of his power symbolically. But there is one King who will never be robbed of His power. He is Jesus Christ, to whom is given all power in heaven and on earth.

While He was on earth the Son of God laid aside His divine majesty. He came as the Servant, to serve and to give His life as a ransom for all mankind. "Being found in appearance as a man, He humbled Himself and became obedient to death—even death on a cross" (Philippians 2:8).

When our Lord fulfilled His mission, the Father raised Him from the dead, seating Him at His right hand in heaven. God exalted Him "far above all rule and authority, power and dominion, and every title that can be given, not only in the present age but also in the one to come" (Ephesians 1:21). On the Last Day, the King of kings will return to judge the living and the dead.

The power of Christ is complete and permanent. It covers earth and heaven, time and eternity. His sword and crown, in a spiritual sense, are His permanent possessions. We share in everything that is Christ's. He tells us "Who there My cross has shared, Finds here a crown prepared."

PRAYER SUGGESTION

Give thanks to Christ Jesus, your King, and renew your promise to serve Him in His kingdom.

Traveling Light

Calling the Twelve to Him, He sent them out two by two. Mark 6:7

Summer is the time many people take vacations. As they do, they typically take along appropriate clothes and plenty of money.

Jesus was not on vacation as He traveled through Galilee. He was working, proclaiming repentance and the presence of God's kingdom. All the while He was preparing those who traveled with Him to do the same. On two occasions He sent out His workers two by two (Luke 10:1 and Mark 6:7). For these journeys they were instructed to take along nothing except a staff—no bread, no bag, no money. They were to trust that God would provide food and lodging through the people who accepted their message.

After Pentecost the apostles again went out on a mission, a permanent one. Again these messengers of Christ traveled light. They were not promised a fixed income. Peter remarked that he had no silver or gold; he had something better to offer—healing of body and soul. The Twelve were well supplied with the Gospel and with power to heal the sick and exorcise demons. They called on sinners to repent and to believe in the risen Savior.

Every Christian does well to travel light, unencumbered by cares, pleasures, and greed. For Christians, life's journey is a mission trip, for we are Christ's witnesses in the world. The necessities of life—food, clothing, and shelter—are sufficient for contentment. If God gives us more—well-appointed homes, two or more automobiles, enjoyable vacations—we have all the more reason to be thankful and to practice wise stewardship.

PRAYER SUGGESTION

Express your gratitude to God for all His blessings, especially for the gift of Christ's Gospel to share with fellow travelers on life's road.

Jesus, Our Advocate

We have one who speaks to the Father in our defense—Jesus Christ, the Righteous One. 1 John 2:1

It is an interesting fact that two St. Louisans, Eugene Field and Dred Scott, are linked in history. Field's son, an attorney, represented Scott—a slave—in federal court when he sued for his freedom. The case was dismissed on grounds that Scott was not a citizen and could not sue.

God the Father appointed His Son to be our advocate, for we were enslaved in sin. Jesus' on-going plea for us is effective. First, He sacrificed Himself for us on the altar of the cross, making atonement for all our sins and gaining our freedom once for all. The Resurrection gave proof of this.

Jesus actively continues to make intercession for us. He pleads our case, speaking to the Father in our behalf. Even when our faith grows weak and we stumble and fall, He implores the heavenly Father for mercy and patience. "He is the atoning sacrifice for our sins, and not only for ours but also for the sins of the whole world" (1 John 2:2). Indeed, "The blood of Jesus, His Son, purifies us from all sin" (1 John 1:7). Jesus not only brought a sacrifice— He *is*, to this day, the atoning sacrifice.

Scott's attorney was not successful in gaining his freedom. But Jesus, our advocate, gained our spiritual freedom. Now we can say with Paul, "Who is he that condemns? Christ Jesus, who died— more than that, who was raised to life—is at the right hand of God and is also interceding for us" (Romans 8:34).

PRAYER SUGGESTION

Ask the Lord Jesus to continue to pray for you, especially in times of temptation.

Three Great Truths

Jesus answered, "I am the Way and the Truth and the Life.
No one comes to the Father except through Me. John 14:6

Bo Giertz, a bishop of Gothenburg, Sweden, declared these to be the three great lies: there is no God, there is no devil, and everyone can be saved in his own way.

We can be sure that the author of these untruths is the devil himself. He is pleased when people discredit his own presence and power. He wants them to reject God's salvation.

Scripture affirms three great truths in opposition. Our Lord assures us that God not only exists but that He is our heavenly Father. He is a God of love, "As a father has compassion on his children, so the LORD has compassion on those who fear Him" (Psalm 103:13).

The counterpart of the second great lie is this statement of Jesus, "[the devil] was a murderer from the beginning, not holding to the truth, for there is no truth in him. When he lies, he speaks his native language, for he is a liar and the father of lies" (John 8:44). Jesus Himself was Satan's target when he tempted Jesus in the wilderness.

Third, how are we saved? How do we get to heaven? Jesus said, "through Me." This is to say, by faith in His redeeming merit. People's own ways of saving themselves are ruled out. On this Holy Scripture is clear: "It is by grace you have been saved, through faith—and this not from yourselves, it is the gift of God—not by works, so that no one can boast" (Ephesians 2:8–9).

It comes down to this: Whom are we going to believe—Satan, the father of lies, or Jesus, who is the Truth?

PRAYER SUGGESTION

Pray that the Holy Spirit, through Word and Sacrament, may keep you steadfast in faith.

God Is for Us

If God is for us, who can be against us? Romans 8:31

One child paraphrased today's verse this way: "If God isn't for us, we are up against it." This isn't exactly what the text says, but the reply contains a truth that the Bible teaches in many places.

God is against sin, especially the master sin of unbelief. God is against the unbeliever. The risen Christ declares, "Whoever believes and is baptized will be saved, but whoever does not believe will be condemned" (Mark 16:16). God's condemning judgment against the unbeliever is a dire sentence, as the writer of the Hebrews epistle has written, "It is a dreadful thing to fall into the hands of the living God" (Hebrews 10:31).

But the blessed truth is that God accepts us as His children for the sake of Jesus Christ. "He who did not spare His own Son, but gave Him up for us all—how will He not also, along with Him, graciously give us all things? Who will bring any charge against those whom God has chosen? It is God who justifies" (Romans 8:32–33). Those whom God has declared just by faith cannot be condemned—not by Satan, not by the hostile world, not by the human conscience.

Since God is for us, He blesses us with His gifts: mercy, grace, salvation, and eternal life. He makes us more than conquerors in life's conflicts. He keeps and guards us so "neither death nor life, neither angels nor demons, neither the present nor the future, nor any powers, neither height nor depth, nor anything else in all creation, will be able to separate us from the love of God that is in Christ Jesus our Lord" (Romans 8:38–39).

It is a wonderful thing that God is for us!

PRAYER SUGGESTION

Praise God for His saving grace for you in Christ Jesus.

Total Commitment

Jesus replied: "Love the Lord your God with all your heart and with all your soul and with all your mind." Matthew 22:37

Some churches and social agencies sponsor halfway houses where released prisoners can transition to community life. Such places may be called Dismas Houses, after the crucified thief who repented and received Paradise.

It is quite proper in some instances to go halfway. If we are going on a long trip, it is feasible to stay overnight in a "halfway house," or motel, and complete the journey the next day. People coming out of hospitals may stay for a while in convalescence centers before returning home. These are types of halfway houses.

How about personal Christianity—is it sufficient to go halfway, taking up permanent residence, as it were, in halfway houses? Is God satisfied if we offer Him only half of our hearts? Can we restrict our love to God, serving Him only on Sundays in church, but not on weekdays? Can we divide our affections, loving only our friends but not our enemies?

Jesus calls for total commitment to the God of our salvation. He commands us to love the Father—and Him only—with all our hearts, souls, and minds. Add to that also our bodies, as St. Paul said, "Offer your bodies as living sacrifices, holy and pleasing to God—this is your spiritual act of worship" (Romans 12:1).

Our Savior, having come into the world to redeem us, did not live in a halfway house. He was one for the road, including the final road, that took Him to Calvary's cross. His was a total commitment in our behalf. From Him comes the power and willingness to serve Him and others gladly.

PRAYER SUGGESTION

Pray for total commitment to Christ Jesus, the Savior of us all.

God Provides for Us

"Consider the ravens: They do not sow or reap, they have no store-room or barn; yet God feeds them." Luke 12:24

The story of St. Francis of Assisi feeding the birds is familiar. For another man of God, Elijah, the role was reversed: the birds fed him. "I have ordered the ravens to feed you there" (1 Kings 17:4).

Jesus mentions ravens in today's text where He teaches that God provides for His creatures, especially for man. Job asked, "Who provides food for the raven when its young cry out to God and wander about for lack of food?" (Job 38:41). The psalmist gave the answer: "He [the LORD] provides food for the cattle and for the young ravens when they call" (Psalm 147:9). Jesus elaborates on this theme as He teaches how God in His providence takes care of us.

The truth of God's care needs emphasis. When people turn from their Provider to gods of their own creation or choice, they in effect declare that God is dead. Earthly goods—food, clothing, transportation, a home, money in the bank—are necessities. It is our attitude toward them that matters. It is one thing to use them as means to an end and another to make status symbols of them. Mammon is a deceitful god. He promises much, but he pays off with anxiety.

How different is life under our living, loving, and all-knowing Father above! Jesus tells us that God knows our needs and will provide. God is our Father, and we are His children by Baptism into faith in Jesus Christ. Brought under God's grace, we are free to seek first His kingdom and righteousness, convinced that all needed earthly and bodily blessings will be ours as well.

PRAYER SUGGESTION

Base your prayer on this petition in the Lord's Prayer: "Give us this day our daily bread."

God's Handwriting in the Sky

I have set My rainbow in the clouds, and it will be the sign of the covenant between Me and the earth. Genesis 9:13

The clouds, it can be said, join all creation in conveying the truths of God's power, wisdom, and love. After the Flood, God sent a rainbow as a sign of His covenant to never again destroy the earth by water.

Clouds and rainbows remind us of another of God's promises. When there is not enough water, clouds bespeak God's blessing of rain. Jesus said, "When you see a cloud rising in the west, immediately you say, 'It's going to rain,' and it does" (Luke 12:54).

Clouds drifting are fitting vehicles for the King of heaven and earth to ride in majesty. The prophet declared, "See, the LORD rides on a swift cloud" (Isaiah 19:1), with the psalmist adding, "O LORD my God, You are very great. ... He makes the clouds His chariot and rides on the wings of the wind" (Psalm 104:1–3).

Daniel saw in a vision how someone like the Son of Man was "coming with the clouds of heaven" (Daniel 7:13). This Messianic prophecy was fulfilled in the life of Jesus Christ. One instance comes especially to mind: When He was transfigured on the holy mountain, there "a bright cloud enveloped them, and a voice from the cloud said, 'This is My Son, whom I love; with Him I am well pleased'" (Matthew 17:5).

When Jesus had fulfilled His ministry on earth, He ascended into heaven. As the disciples looked on, "a cloud hid Him from their sight" (Acts 1:9). What God reveals of Himself in the clouds He declares very plainly in His Word that bears witness to Christ, our Savior.

PRAYER SUGGESTION

Give thanks to God for sending us His Son to be our Savior and for clearly revealing Him to us.

When Is a Good Work Well Done?

"Whatever you did for one of the least of these brothers of Mine, you did for Me." Matthew 25:40

A theologian has pointed out that a Christian's works should not only be good but also well done. When is a work "well done"? "Whatever your hand finds to do, do it with all your might" (Ecclesiastes 9:10). In other words, we ought to devote ourselves fully to the tasks we undertake in faith. Half-measures or the mere doing of a thing for the sake of doing it, thinking it therefore merits God's favor, is not a good deed well done.

Today's text points out that a good work is well done when the object of our love is the same as its subject: Jesus Christ. When our love of Jesus prompts us to serve, when it is the Lord whom we are serving, our deeds are both good and well done.

The Bible gives many examples of such deeds. For instance, Tabitha sewed garments for the poor, fulfilling Jesus' words when He said, "I needed clothes and you clothed Me" (Matthew 25:36). The apostles, assisted by many unsung converts, proclaimed Christ's Gospel to the world, assured of Christ's presence in their midst and desirous to do it for Him. Paul declared, "Christ's love compels us because we are convinced that One died for all—and therefore all died" (2 Corinthians 5:14). In love, Christ laid down His life for the salvation of us all.

Faith in Christ enables us to do good works and do them well.

PRAYER SUGGESTION

Ask the Holy Spirit to increase your love for Christ and to help you, in that love, to do good works well.

Be What You Are!

Do not think of yourself more highly than you ought, but rather think of yourself with sober judgment. Romans 12:3

When people misrepresent themselves, it is usually as being better than what they are. Having the proper self-image and self-regard is difficult. This is so even for Christians who are blessed with "the measure of faith" (Romans 12:3). The Old Adam lives in them even after their coming to faith. Sometimes he gains the upper hand. An out-of-proportion ego takes over, causing people to think more highly of themselves than they ought. When this becomes a permanent self-conception, faith perishes and, along with it, the fruits of faith: humility, good judgment, love of the neighbor, and reverent love for God. Into that spiritual vacuum rushes pride in its many forms.

We can visualize ourselves in light of both the Law and the Gospel. When we look at ourselves through the lens of God's Law, we see ourselves as "poor, miserable sinners" according to the church's confession.

But we must not stop with the Law. In the light of the Gospel a different self-image appears. There we see ourselves as God's redeemed people. This is true; God thought so highly of us that He gave His beloved Son, our Lord and Savior Jesus Christ, to redeem us and to present us to the heavenly Father as His children. This is what we have become and what we are: God's precious people. As such we now evaluate ourselves.

The Holy Spirit working in us enables us to feel good about ourselves. There is no need to pretend to be what we are not. As Christians we are on the top rung as we scale "Jacob's ladder" to heaven.

PRAYER SUGGESTION

Praise God for what you have become, thanks to Christ's mediation.

How Great Is Christ's Love!

I pray that you ... may have power ... to grasp how wide and long and high and deep is the love of Christ. Ephesians 3:17–18

Things have dimensions. We may know the size of a room, a house, a church. Noah's ark was 450 feet long, 75 feet wide, and 45 feet high. Solomon's temple proper was 90 x 30 x 45 feet. How about the love of God in Christ—can it be measured?

What does the Gospel tell us about the *breadth* of divine love? Our Lord Himself replies: "God so loved the world that He gave His one and only Son, that whoever believes in Him shall not perish but have eternal life" (John 3:16). God's love includes all people. It is worldwide.

The Bible reveals the *length* of Christ's love: the entire distance—at the end, walking to Calvary's cross. No one can have greater love than that. It is long-suffering, unending, unfailing.

The third dimension of Christ's love is its *height*. To a Christian, a towering mountain speaks not only of God's power and majesty but also of His love. Its highest peak points to the sky as if to say, "As high as the heavens are above the earth, so great is His love for those who fear Him" (Psalm 103:11).

There is nothing shallow or superficial about the love of Christ, for it has great *depth*. While we all were yet sinners, Christ died for us. This is reaching down to the bottom of the barrel. His love is deep like the sea, deep as a well that never runs dry.

Christ wants us all to know this love.

PRAYER SUGGESTION

Pray that you may grow in the understanding of Christ's love.

Where Is Your True Self?

"Where your treasure is, there your heart will be also." Luke 12:34

When English physicist Michael Faraday was a boy, he stuck his head through a fence and wondered where his true self was—on one side of the fence where his head was or the other with the rest of his body.

Jesus wants us to know where our true self is. It is where the heart is. People can be bodily present in one place while their heart is elsewhere. Individuals have been uprooted from their homes and sold into slavery. Wars have displaced many. In their hearts, these people are where they formerly lived.

Christians need to ask themselves where their hearts are. If preoccupied with earthly wealth, they will devote themselves to its acquisition. This fact is clearly demonstrated in the life of Judas Iscariot. Physically, he was in the company of the Master and the other disciples, but his true self had another master: greed, aided and abetted by Satan.

Many give themselves over to worry about things as though they had no heavenly Father to provide for them. Such worry, in many cases, can be traced to high regard for worldly goods.

To get back into focus, Jesus Christ is our treasure, our highest good. He is that because He is our one and only Savior. In Him is life, for now and for eternity. He fulfilled God's law by His perfect obedience. He died in our behalf and rose again to secure the forgiveness of our sins, bringing us peace with God and peace of conscience. He means more to us than all the gold and silver, all the dollars and diamonds, all the pesos and pearls in the world.

Jesus is our treasure, and our heart is with Him.

PRAYER SUGGESTION

Tell God in prayer that you want to give yourself over to Christ and His kingdom.

Our Debt Is Canceled

"A man who owed him ten thousand talents was brought to him."
Matthew 18:24

A trusted—but untrustworthy—employee at the University of Missouri embezzled $667,000. After serving his prison sentence, he began to pay back $50 a month. At that rate, restitution would be made by the year 2973.

Jesus taught us to pray, "Forgive us our debts." Because we are sinners, we are all debtors before God. What is our possibility of repaying our debt? It doesn't exist. Jesus makes this clear in His parable of a man who owed his master 10,000 talents—about a million dollars. He begged for the opportunity and time to repay the debt, although repayment was impossible. The master took pity on him and canceled the debt. The terrible thing this man then did was to shake down someone else for a relatively paltry debt.

The point Jesus makes is that we have good reason to forgive those who trespass against us, for their sins against us are minor when compared to our sins before God. Our debts are enormous and we can do nothing to make amends.

God was indeed merciful. He made us His forgiven children. "When the kindness and love of God our Savior appeared, He saved us ... because of His mercy. He saved us through the washing of rebirth and renewal of the Holy Spirit, whom He poured out on us generously through Jesus Christ our Savior" (Titus 3:4–6). Our debt under the Law was erased when Jesus made restitution on the cross. God did more when He gave us His Holy Spirit through Baptism to grant us faith in God's gift of salvation.

Thank God, our debt is canceled and we are free to serve Him in gratitude.

PRAYER SUGGESTION

Express your gratitude to the triune God for your salvation.

Having Christ's Attitude

Your attitude should be the same as that of Christ Jesus.
Philippians 2:5

A guest in a luxury hotel was angry. Someone in the room next to hers was incessantly practicing on the piano. She complained to the manager, who told her the person next door was the great pianist and Polish statesman, Paderewski. What a difference it made to know this! Proud to be staying next door to the celebrity, the lady invited her friends to come to her room to hear Paderewski play.

St. Paul would urge us to have the attitude of Christ Jesus because it was at no time puffed up with pride. Our Lord towers above all the great people of this world, not due to His human accomplishments but because He in His very nature is God. It was not as a potentate from heaven that He came into this world. He "made Himself nothing, taking the very nature of a servant" (Philippians 2:7). He came to serve in humility and to give His life as a ransom for all.

Blessed are we to have Him as our Friend! From Him we learn to avoid all forms of egotism and vanity. The Holy Spirit, sent by Christ, works the saving faith in us, granting us the attitude that our Savior had.

Having the attitude of Christ qualifies us to be His witnesses in any situation in life, planned and impromptu. The opportunities to bear witness to Christ come in many ways. "Always be prepared to give an answer to everyone who asks you to give the reason for the hope that you have" (1 Peter 3:15).

PRAYER SUGGESTION

Pray that Christ may make you aware of opportunities to speak for Him.

Finding Christ, Our Highest Good

These are the Scriptures that testify about Me. John 5:39

People who visit the Baseball Hall of Fame in Cooperstown, New York, find a bonus in other historic sites in the area. Nearby are the Farmers' Museum, the homes of famous persons, and the U.S. Military Academy.

In the Bible we read of people who found something more rewarding than what they were looking for. A Samaritan woman went to Jacob's well for water but found Jesus, who offered her living water. On the shore of the Galilean sea some men were getting ready to catch fish, but before the day was over, they were following Jesus to become fishers of men.

Some people today turn to the Bible to verify a point in history or to savor the language. In doing this, they may come upon something far more essential: the great truth of salvation in Jesus Christ.

God does indeed move in mysterious ways His wonders to perform. He let Saul the Pharisee travel to Damascus to arrest Christians. Instead Saul was called by Christ and became His apostle.

The Holy Scriptures offer rich rewards to all who read them with open, honest minds. But the greatest good is Jesus Christ. He Himself declared that the Scriptures testify of Him. Their testimony is that Jesus of Nazareth is the promised Messiah, that He was crucified to make atonement for the sins of the world, that He rose from the dead to put the seal of certainty on His Word and work. We can rejoice that we are free to look for Him every day in the Bible.

PRAYER SUGGESTION

Thank the Lord Jesus for revealing Himself in the Bible as your Savior.

Interrupted Vacations

Leaving that place, Jesus withdrew to the region of Tyre and Sidon.
Matthew 15:21

In 1921, while vacationing with his family, Franklin D. Roosevelt contracted polio. He recovered enough to continue a political career all the way to the White House.

Things sometimes interfere with our plans. Consider Jesus' life and ministry. As was their practice, Jesus and His disciples rested after strenuous work and travel. At one point He sought seclusion by going to the region of Tyre and Sidon. But His vacation was interrupted when a Canaanite woman earnestly and persistently sought His help for her demon-possessed daughter. Jesus granted her request, praising her faith.

We often experience interruptions in our rest periods. Perhaps someone in great need requests our help. What will we do? It may not be convenient or interfere with our plans when someone knocks on our door and wants assistance. Our love to the neighbor, which is of one piece with our love of Christ, will not let us say no. Like our Lord Himself, as is the case of the Canaanite mother, we will render whatever service we can.

Jesus did more than set an example. He is our Savior, the true Son of God who became human so He could serve and give His life as a ransom for all. Our faith in Him prompts and enables us to sacrifice for the good of others, even if it interrupts our rest and relaxation.

PRAYER SUGGESTION

Ask the Lord to help you make the right decisions when emergencies arise.

Christ Gathers His Flock

You were like sheep going astray, but now you have returned to the Shepherd and Overseer of your souls. 1 Peter 2:25

Sheep figured prominently in Jesus' life from the beginning. He was born in Bethlehem, in the house of David, where David was a shepherd. Sheep were present when news of the Savior's birth was announced to the shepherds. And as Jesus traveled during His life and ministry, He often saw flocks of sheep.

The Old Testament Scriptures often refer to sheep and shepherds: "The LORD is my Shepherd" (Psalm 23). "We are His people, the sheep of His pasture" (Psalm 100:3), "He tends His flock like a shepherd" (Isaiah 40:11). When John the Baptist called Jesus "the Lamb of God" (John 1:29), he used a Messianic term: "He was led like a lamb to the slaughter" (Isaiah 53:7).

Jesus expressly states, "I am the good shepherd; I know My sheep and My sheep know Me" (John 10:14–15).

When something happens to the shepherd, the sheep feel alone and abandoned. "I will strike the shepherd, and the sheep of the flock will be scattered" (Matthew 26:31). On the night of Jesus' arrest, the disciples were indeed scattered. But the risen Christ assembled them again. He commissioned them to gather people from all nations and make them members of Christ's flock through the Gospel and Holy Baptism.

The people whom Peter addressed in his first letter had been scattered because of persecution, but faith in Jesus Christ held them together. And among us Christ is still the common bond. He suffered and died for all. As Peter concluded, "I have written to you briefly, encouraging you and testifying that this is the true grace of God. Stand fast in it" (1 Peter 5:12).

PRAYER SUGGESTION

Ask the Good Shepherd to keep you close to Him and to His flock.

God Made Us His House

We are [God's] house, if we hold on to our courage and the hope of which we boast. Hebrews 3:6

American author Washington Irving bought a small, run-down farmhouse and turned it into a beautiful home called Sunnyside. Located in the historic Hudson Valley in New York, it is still a showplace.

It took a lot of doing for God to make us His house. By nature we were sinful, deficient in every respect—comparable to the dingy farmhouse Irving bought. But God turned us into a beautiful house for Himself. He was moved to compassion by our helpless and hopeless condition. He ordained that His Son should become a man in order to be the Cornerstone of His spiritual house. Jesus Christ, God's Son, gave His life on the cross and rose again to be our Savior. As Head of the holy Christian church, the communion of saints, He made us His house and lives in us through the Gospel.

In his Sunnyside home, Irving did his work as an author. Likewise God is at work in us by His Spirit to make us a better, more beautiful house. It is an ongoing development, as St. Paul told the Philippians, "It is God who works in you to will and to act according to His good purpose" (Philippians 2:13).

Since we are God's refurbished house, we reflect this fact in the kind of earthly homes we establish. Our home can become a source of blessing to us and to others. In it we can practice Christian hospitality as early Christians did. Philemon, Cornelius, Lydia, Aquila, and Priscilla, and many others opened their homes for worship services. Like them, we can ask: How can we use our homes to glorify God and to serve people about us?

PRAYER SUGGESTION

Thank God for your home, asking His guidance for its proper use.

Applying the Test

Test the spirits to see whether they are from God. 1 John 4:1

A humorist offered this witticism: "There are so many changes in religion today that someone's thinking of putting out a Bible in loose-leaf."

There is some truth in this, for some religious leaders are really trying to change things around. What changes do they advocate? Some call the miracle accounts myths. Others say the apostles' teachings were meant for only their time. Old heresies are repeated but offered as something new—the denial of the deity of Jesus Christ along with denying His virgin birth, His physical resurrection, or His promise of the Second Coming. Religion is in a state of flux because many people fail to "test the spirits," to check out their teachings. This is not an unreasonable request. Testing is done in many areas of life. Children in school are tested. Job applicants are tested. Automobiles are tested.

In today's text John suggests that Christians determine for themselves whether religionists wanting our attention "are from God." How can this be determined? By comparing their teachings with Holy Scripture. Christians in Berea, who received the message of Paul and Silas "with great eagerness," "examined the Scriptures every day to see if what Paul said was true" (Acts 17:11).

We are interested in whether a religious teacher is rightly proclaiming the way of salvation through faith in Christ, who died for our sins and rose again. This truth is permanent; no "loose-leaf Bible" can ever declare otherwise.

PRAYER SUGGESTION

Pray that the Holy Spirit lead you into all truth as you read the Bible.

Our Lord's Outdoor Ministry

[Jesus] sat down and taught the people from the boat. Luke 5:3

The Holy Land teemed with excitement because of Jesus' ministry. Cities and towns emptied out as people took to the road to see and hear the Lord wherever He could be found: on the seashore, in the wilderness, on a mountainside and other outdoor places. Our Lord, of course, taught also in synagogues and temple courts (Mark 12:37).

Jesus dealt with people where they lived and where they came to Him. Peter, who accompanied Jesus during His ministry, said "You know what has happened throughout Judea, beginning in Galilee after the baptism that John preached—how God anointed Jesus of Nazareth with the Holy Spirit and power, and how He went around doing good and healing all who were under the power of the devil, because God was with Him" (Acts 10:37–38).

Wherever Jesus preached, indoors or out, He proclaimed the coming of the kingdom of God. He called for repentance and faith in the forgiveness of sins. He told Nicodemus about the great love of God for the world's sinners, prompting Him to send His only-begotten Son that people, believing in Him, might have eternal life. Jesus summed up His redemptive ministry in these words, "The Son of Man did not come to be served, but to serve, and to give His life as a ransom for many" (Matthew 20:28).

We can learn from Jesus to practice our Christianity outdoors while at work or on vacation.

PRAYER SUGGESTION

Pray for a faith that exercises itself in love wherever you are.

The Equipment We Need

Take the helmet of salvation and the sword of the Spirit, which is the Word of God. Ephesians 6:17

At the United States Military Academy at West Point is a collection of small offensive weapons used in warfare through the ages—everything from clubs and swords to automatic rifles. They give proof of mankind's deep involvement in fighting.

In Paul's time, the Roman army was a dominant presence. He himself was a man of peace, with no intention to spread the Gospel by force. He proclaimed peace with God through Jesus Christ and peace with fellow men as a result. This peace could be attained and retained only by the use of spiritual weapons, since the devil and his evil angels were spiritual. To make his point, the apostle used language people could understand. As Jesus often did, Paul drew on everyday life to communicate a message.

Paul compared Christians in a hostile world to a soldier equipped for war. For protection he needed "the whole armor of God." This armor included a belt, which is the truth of God's Word, and "the breastplate of righteousness," which is the righteousness of Christ, imparted to us by faith. Other needed items were shoes, a shield, and the "helmet of salvation."

Paul included only one offensive weapon: "the sword of the Spirit, which is the Word of God." Why a sword? It has the power to penetrate to the heart. Peter preached the Law, with the result that his hearers were "cut to the heart" (Acts 2:37). Then He consoled them by speaking of Christ's redemption, offering them forgiveness.

The modern world has changed its weapons of warfare, but Satan has not changed. Against him we can prevail only by using the Word of God.

PRAYER SUGGESTION

Thank God for having equipped you with the Gospel of Jesus Christ.

The Two Go Together

We are heirs—heirs of God and co-heirs with Christ, if indeed we share in His sufferings in order that we may also share in His glory. Romans 8:17

Mohandas Gandhi, India's nationalist leader and social reformer, had a list of what he called "deadly sins": Wealth without work, pleasure without conscience, knowledge without character, commerce without morality, science without humanity, worship without sacrifice, and politics without principle. He believed that certain things could not be separated.

For Christians, there are also certain things that cannot be separated. Some gladly accept honor and privilege at Christ's hand but then refuse to suffer with Him when challenged to do so by a hostile world. Is it possible to be that one-sided?

The apostle said we are God's children not by birth but by adoption. We became God's family when we were baptized into the faith that Jesus Christ, having died for all sinners, reconciled us to the heavenly Father. "God made Him who had no sin to be sin for us, so that in Him we might become the righteousness of God" (2 Corinthians 5:21).

Since we are God's children, it follows that we are also the "heirs of God and co-heirs with Christ." While we can do nothing to gain the inheritance of eternal life, we can do ever so much to lose it. We cannot separate our roles as God's honored and privileged children and as disciples to follow Jesus through thick and thin.

So we say, "Lord, I can't have it both ways: accept eternal life but refuse the cross. I thankfully accept the inheritance, and I will gladly suffer with You should this become necessary."

PRAYER SUGGESTION

Say to the Lord Jesus that you will follow Him, even if you must travel on a road of hardships.

We Don't Know the Day

"No one knows about that day or hour, not even the angels in heaven, nor the Son, but only the Father." Matthew 24:36

George Orwell fought in the Spanish Civil War on the side of the communists. He learned, through bitter experience, that the latter were totalitarians opposed to personal freedom. He wrote *1984* as a prediction that communists, led by Big Brother, would be in total control. Obviously, Orwell was wrong.

Even the wisest people can make mistakes when predicting the future. Consider those who have set dates for Jesus' Second Coming, but the Last Day has not yet come. Even Jesus, the Son of God, does not know when it will be.

What we do know is that Jesus *will* come again. His second coming will differ from His first in that then He came in deep humility to serve and to die for all sinners. When He returns, He will come in glory to judge.

Our Lord plainly reveals that He will come again but not *when* it will be. The day and hour, even the decade and century, have not been announced. So it behooves us to be prepared by continuing strong in the faith, by watching and praying, by drawing comfort from the promise of His coming.

How do we await our Lord's coming? We do so not in fear but with joyful expectation, as Jesus said we should do when we see the signs of the times, "When these things begin to take place, stand up and lift up your heads, because your redemption is drawing near. … When you see these things happening, you know that the kingdom of God is near" (Luke 21:28, 31).

PRAYER SUGGESTION

Ask the Lord Jesus to grant you readiness for His coming.

The Role of a Christian Mother

I have been reminded of your sincere faith, which first lived in your grandmother Lois and in your mother Eunice. 2 Timothy 1:5

In her book *First Ladies,* Margaret Truman, the daughter of President Harry Truman, wrote that her mother set the standard for first ladies to act naturally in a world of unnatural expectations. It was a good tribute.

Timothy, whose father was a Greek pagan, was blessed with a pious mother, Eunice, and grandmother, Lois, who possessed a "sincere faith." Timothy himself had such a faith.

True faith is not an accident, not the product of man's own doing. How did Timothy's faith come about? "How from infancy you have known the holy Scriptures, which are able to make you wise for salvation through faith in Christ Jesus" (2 Timothy 3:15). The Bible not only testifies to Christ as the Messiah, who bore the punishment for the sins of the world, and also as the source of faith in Him as the Savior. Through Word and Sacraments, the Holy Spirit creates and sustains the saving faith.

Eunice, assisted by Lois, played an important role in teaching God's Word to her son. She selected simple truths from the writings of Moses, the prophets, and the psalmists and taught them to Timothy. She taught him how these truths applied to Christian life. And she taught him how to pray. Undoubtedly she took him to worship services in God's house. Since the father was an unbeliever, it fell to mother to do the spiritual nurturing.

What a model for mothers today! They also can teach God's Word to their children, teaching them to say and sing: "Jesus loves me, this I know, For the Bible tells me so."

PRAYER SUGGESTION

Pray that mothers today may lead their children to Christ, as did Eunice.

Women as Citizens

There is no authority except that which God has established.
Romans 13:1

The nineteenth amendment is very brief: "The right of citizens of the United States to vote shall not be denied or abridged by the United States or by any state on account of sex." The right to vote added an important dimension to women's citizenship. Christian women could regard their franchise as not only adding to their responsibilities but also as opening a new door to service.

The responsibilities are implicit in what Holy Scripture teaches about government and citizenship. Stressed are the duties to obey the powers that be, to pay taxes, and to accord respect and honor to whom this is due. "Give to Caesar what is Caesar's, and to God what is God's" (Matthew 2:21).

The right to vote, since it involves public life, brings opportunities for greater service to one's country and to all its inhabitants. Christian women follow the prompting of their faith as they render public service. They influence community life, government, education, and industry.

Christian women appreciate, above all, their role as servants of Jesus Christ in home and church. Paul's writings about spiritual citizenship apply to everyone: "You are no longer foreigners and aliens, but fellow citizens with God's people and members of God's household, built on the foundation of the apostles and prophets, with Christ Jesus Himself as the chief cornerstone" (Ephesians 2:19–20).

PRAYER SUGGESTION

Give thanks to God for stable government and for all cooperating citizens.

Piety with Wisdom

"The master commended the dishonest manager because he had acted shrewdly." Luke 16:8

Jesus spoke in a parable about a dishonest but clever steward. The man told his master's debtors to falsify their bills. The one owing for 800 gallons of olive oil was told to reduce the figure to 400. Another debtor was directed to shrink his obligation for 1,000 bushels of wheat to 800. The crooked manager counted favor with the debtors in the hope that some day, when he was fired, they would take him into their homes for free room and board.

What did Jesus teach? Certainly He did not advocate dishonesty. He advocated wisdom. He said, "The people of this world are more shrewd in dealing with their own kind than are the people of the light" (Luke 16:8). He went on to say that Christians should so deal with their worldly goods—giving liberally for missions, for example—that they lay up for themselves treasures in heaven. Of course, they are saved by God's grace alone. But theirs is a faith that works by love. Christ Jesus died for their salvation. In thankfulness they practice a stewardship that reflects both piety and wisdom.

It is clear from the Bible that some "people of light" lacked wisdom. Peter was not wise in overstating his loyalty the night Jesus was betrayed. He went back on his word. The mother of James and John was not wise in requesting places of honor for her sons in Jesus' kingdom. For that she was chastised. The disciples were not wise to try to keep people away from Jesus. For that they were admonished.

These happenings are recorded in Holy Scripture for our learning. Christ wants His followers to blend piety with wisdom.

PRAYER SUGGESTION

Ask the Lord Jesus to grant you true wisdom through His Word and Spirit.

Whose Word Is It?

When you received the Word of God, which you heard from us, you accepted it not as the word of men, but as it actually is, the Word of God. 1 Thessalonians 2:13

Either of two things may occur when a man preaches from the Bible: Some may regard the message as being of human origin and some may accept it as the Word of God.

Sometimes a speaker may claim his teaching is from God when it is nothing but his own word. Such was the case with the Pharisees: "Their teachings are but rules taught by men" (Matthew 15:9). They tried to equate man-made mandates and traditions with God's Law and thus sought to give them divine status.

The reverse can also happen: to give God's commandments man-made status, that is, regard them as social mores that can be considered outdated. In our anti-authority age, this is perhaps the most likely of the two responses. This is breaking the first commandment and creating false gods: ego, money, pleasure, or whatever is considered life's highest good. God says, "You shall not murder" (Exodus 20:13), but many think they have the right to murder unborn infants. God's "You shall not commit adultery" (Exodus 20:14) is ignored by those who engage in sexual activity outside of marriage.

How can we tell whether a religious teaching is from God or from man? The only sure guide is Holy Scripture. It sets the standard by which anyone's teaching is to be judged. More than that, we study the Scripture to make us wise "for salvation through faith in Christ Jesus" (2 Timothy 3:15). Salvation earned for us by the Savior is the central message of the Bible.

PRAYER SUGGESTION

Ask the Holy Spirit to strengthen your conviction that God speaks to you in His Word.

The Right Way

"I am the way and the truth and the life. No one comes to the Father except through Me." John 14:6

In 1938 Douglas Corrigan was scheduled to fly from New York to Long Beach, California. Instead he flew across the Atlantic to Dublin, Ireland, claiming a faulty compass. It earned him the nickname "Wrong Way Corrigan."

There are many wrong-way people in the world. The first ones to get their directions mixed up were Adam and Eve. Yielding to Satan's temptation, they disobeyed a clear commandment of God and became subject to the consequences. All their descendants go the same wrong way. They would be lost except for the grace of God. He sent His Son to walk the way of the cross for us all. They who believe in Him have eternal life. Not only does Jesus show us the way to the Father—He *is* the Way.

Jesus declared Himself as the Way as He prepared His disciples for His departure from them through death and His return to the Father. He said, "You know the way to the place where I am going" (John 14:4). When Thomas asked Him to show the way, Jesus said, "I am the Way."

Jesus is the only Way to the Father. He is the One God sent to be our Redeemer. He gave His life as a ransom for sinners, was buried, and rose again, exactly as the Scriptures said He would.

Jesus is the only Way to heaven because He is "the Resurrection and the Life" (John 11:25). Spiritual life comes from Him, and with it eternal life.

Thanks to Jesus, we are not wrong-way Christians. Believing in Him, we are on the right course.

PRAYER SUGGESTION

Give thanks to the heavenly Father for having sent us His Son as the Savior.

God, Three in One

Holy, holy, holy is the LORD Almighty. Isaiah 6:3

In a small town in Nebraska, in an earlier age of the automobile, was a garage with a gasoline pump in front. Three men were in charge: a father, his son, and a bookkeeper. When customers drove up for gasoline, they would honk the horn. One of the three would come out to the pump to serve the customer. The three, representing one firm, were equal in the service they rendered.

This three-in-one human relationship is a weak illustration of the triune God—three distinct persons in one undivided being.

The God in whom we believe has revealed Himself as Father, Son, and Holy Spirit. Into His name we were baptized, as Jesus directed. At His own baptism the triune God was revealed. The Father spoke from heaven, the Son stood in the water, and the Holy Spirit descended on Him in the form of a dove. The apostles taught that God is triune: "May the grace of the Lord Jesus Christ, and the love of God, and the fellowship of the Holy Spirit be with you all" (2 Corinthians 13:14). And intimations of the Trinity are found in the Old Testament.

The triune God is the God of our salvation. God as a whole was active. Briefly put, the Father *thought* (planned) it, the Son *wrought* by His death and resurrection, and the Holy Spirit *brought* it to us through the Gospel. Our minds cannot grasp the mystery of the Trinity, but in our hearts we believe in Him. With St. Paul we can exclaim, "Oh, the depth of the riches of the wisdom and knowledge of God! How unsearchable His judgments, and His paths beyond tracing out!" (Romans 11:33).

PRAYER SUGGESTION

Praise the triune God for having revealed Himself in Holy Scripture.

A Daughter Restored

Her parents were astonished. Luke 8:56

It is interesting to note that several well-known authors were the daughters of clergymen. They are Jane Austen *(Pride and Prejudice),* and the Bronte sisters, Charlotte *(Jane Eyre)* and Emily *(Wuthering Heights).*

The Bible says children are a "reward from Him" (Psalm 127:3), a gift from God. Another psalm makes this plain: "Our sons in their youth will be like well-nurtured plants, and our daughters will be like pillars" (Psalm 144:12). The New Testament honors daughters and sons as equal partners in salvation: "There is neither ... male nor female, for you are all one in Christ Jesus ... and heirs according to the promise" (Galatians 3:28–29).

The daughter of Jairus was especially precious to him and his wife because she was their "only daughter" (Luke 8:42). Jairus, as ruler of the synagogue, presided over worship services (comparable to the clergymen with gifted daughters above.) The father was not proud. He fell down at Jesus' feet and pleaded for his dying daughter.

Our Lord responded to the father's pleas. En route to Jairus's home He healed an ailing woman. His announcement that the girl was not dead but asleep provoked laughter from the professional mourners—a good indication that she was dead. But Jesus' almighty word, *Talitha, cumi* ("My child, get up!" [Luke 8:54]), brought her back to life. At Jesus' miracle the parents were rightfully, and thankfully, astonished. They experienced firsthand that the Son of God has power over death.

By Himself rising from the dead, Jesus gave evidence that He had fulfilled His mission: to redeem us from sin and death.

PRAYER SUGGESTION

Ask Jesus to be your Lord in life and in death.

Honest Work

"My Father is always at His work to this very day, and I, too, am working." John 5:17

Honest work brings rewards beyond money: satisfaction, contentment, peace of mind. A disturbing number of people choose to miss these rewards when they try to acquire wealth through games of chance. While it is true that some people win at gambling, such winnings are absent to the vast majority. Common results of gambling include the growth of greed, covetousness, and even addiction.

But back to those who do an honest day's work: mechanics, carpenters, teachers, nurses, doctors, homemakers, accountants, and others. All honest work is honorable. All who run an honest business or are employed in the same can not only look the whole world in the face, they can lift up their hearts and minds to God, thanking Him for the gifts of health and ability to work.

Jesus, our Lord and Savior, was a worker. He said, "As long as it is day, we must do the work of Him who sent Me. Night is coming, when no one can work" (John 9:4). He kept busy, preaching, teaching, and healing. But He did more: He gave His life for us amid great suffering. The prophet Isaiah spoke of the "travail of His soul." "Travail," says the dictionary, is very hard work. But our Lord did not skip the ultimate cost of finishing the work His Father had given Him to do in our behalf.

Let us remember this! When our work becomes difficult and discouraging, as it sometimes will, we can look to Jesus, the Author and Finisher of our faith, for vigor and vision.

PRAYER SUGGESTION

Give thanks to God for enabling you to earn your daily bread and to have something extra to share with others.

Questions the Bible Answers

The jailer ... asked, "Sirs, what must I do to be saved?" They replied, "Believe in the Lord Jesus, and you will be saved." Acts 16:29–31

Is the Bible a reference book? No and yes.

No, the Bible does not answer many questions: How old is the world? Can angels dance on the point of a needle? When will Jesus return in glory?

And, yes, the Bible answers important and pertinent questions. Did God make the world? Is Jesus both true man and true God? Can people get to heaven by being good and doing good?

When the jailer in Philippi asked about the way of salvation, Paul and Silas answered, "Believe in the Lord Jesus, and you will be saved." This is the most important answer all of Holy Scripture gives. God gave us His Word to testify Jesus Christ, the Savior, to make us "wise for salvation through faith in Christ Jesus" (2 Timothy 3:15). Jesus came into the world to give His life as a ransom for sinners. All who believe in Him have forgiveness and the promise of life eternal.

In brief, the Bible has answers that pertain to our salvation. It touches on other subjects—history, languages, human behavior, science—but these are not its main purpose, of course. Yet when it speaks, it always speaks the truth. God gave us His Word, both Law and Gospel, to show us the need for the Savior and to lead us to Him.

PRAYER SUGGESTION

Ask the Holy Spirit to open your understanding of the Scriptures and to lead you to Christ.

God's Call to Faith

[God] has saved us and called us to a holy life—not because of anything we have done but because of His own purpose and grace. This grace was given us in Christ Jesus before the beginning of time.
2 Timothy 1:9

When President Warren G. Harding died in 1923, Vice President Calvin Coolidge was fishing on a lake in Vermont. His father, a justice of the peace, swore him in as president in the lamplight of a farmhouse.

The call to an important mission can come at unexpected times and places. The prominent English writer C. S. Lewis confessed that God brought him into His service while he was "kicking and screaming." Saul the Pharisee was on a trip to arrest Christians in Damascus when he was converted.

The most unexpected conversions took place on Mount Calvary when Jesus was crucified. A thief repented and turned to Jesus for salvation. The Roman centurion in charge of the crucifixion confessed, "Surely this man was the Son of God!" (Mark 15:39).

The Holy Spirit, through the Gospel, continues to call people to saving faith in Jesus Christ when, humanly speaking, one would not expect it. It can occur while they are traveling, vacationing, working, resting, or experiencing setbacks in life. Things they once learned were recalled. Perhaps at a critical time a Christian witnessed to them about Jesus.

Whatever the circumstance, God extends the call by "His own purpose and grace," convincing those called that Jesus Christ has taken all their sins on Himself and gained eternal life for them.

PRAYER SUGGESTION

Pray that God may open your heart to a more complete understanding of His grace in Christ.

Life with Wisdom

Wisdom has built her house; she has hewn out its seven pillars.
Proverbs 9:1

An oft-visited street in New Orleans is called Felicity. Other cities have similarly named streets. Regrettably, it doesn't follow that people living on so-named streets find happiness.

God wants people to find felicity where they live. How do they do that? The writer of the book of Proverbs suggests that one way to find it is through wisdom. Much more than learning, wisdom is marked by good judgment, good character, faith, and piety. Wisdom begins with the fear of the Lord. God is honored when our daily conduct is based on "the Holy Scriptures, which are able to make [us] wise for salvation through faith in Christ Jesus" (2 Timothy 3:15). Christian living is prompted by love for God.

Christian life based on God's Word can be compared to a solidly built house buttressed by seven pillars, which, according to Isaiah 11:2, are comparable to the seven gifts of the Spirit, namely, the Spirit plus wisdom, understanding, counsel, power, knowledge, and the fear of God.

Jesus said a wise builder constructs his house on a rock foundation. Everyone who hears Christ's words and puts them into practice is like a wise builder. The words of Jesus are powerful because they are backed up by His works, His perfect obedience of God's law and His suffering and death on the cross for us. Faith in Him brings felicity that is stronger than any adversity.

We sing, "Oh, blest that house, it prospers well! In peace and joy the parents dwell. And in their children's lives is shown, How richly God can bless His own."

PRAYER SUGGESTION

Ask God to guide you through His Word to find happiness in Christ.

Befriending Strangers

Keep on loving each other as brothers.
Do not forget to entertain strangers. Hebrews 13:1–2

We go to church to worship God, together with other believers. There, we have the opportunity to show love to brothers and sisters in the faith and to welcome strangers. A cheerful greeting can open the door to personal mission work.

It is easy, of course, to speak to fellow church members, but Jesus tells us we can do more. "If you greet only your brothers, what are you doing more than others? Do not even pagans do that?" (Matthew 5:47). We can befriend strangers, which our Lord regards as a service to Him.

The Bible refers often to strangers, many of whom were uprooted from their homes by religious persecution. John wrote, "Dear friend, you are faithful in what you are doing for the brothers, even though they are strangers to you" (3 John 1:5). The writer of Hebrews adds that "some people have entertained angels without knowing it" (13:2), a reference to Abraham showing hospitality to visitors who were angels.

As Christians, we can use our homes to good ends. If we meet a newcomer at church, we can invite him or her to our home for a visit. Christian hospitality can do wonders. It benefits both the host and the guest.

The words of Jesus are still true today: "I was a stranger and you invited Me in" (Matthew 25:35). Acts of hospitality are the fruits of faith in Jesus Christ, who walked the way of the cross to befriend us with the forgiveness of sins and to make us God's children and the heirs of eternal life in the Father's heavenly home.

PRAYER SUGGESTION

Ask the Lord Jesus to give you a generous heart toward strangers.

Fruit-Bearing Christians

"If a man remains in Me and I in him, he will bear much fruit."
John 15:5

The word "polycarpic" is of Greek origin and describes a plant bearing fruit on a perennial basis. The term is suggestive of Polycarp, a pupil of the apostle John, who was spiritually fruitful during his long life. Polycarp was martyred for Christ in A.D. 166. Brought into a stadium for execution before spectators, he could have kept his life had he professed loyalty to Caesar instead of Christ. But he refused, testifying that he had served his Lord for 86 years—from the time of his infant Baptism—and that he would not deny Him in old age.

God's people, however long they live, are called to be "polycarpic," that is, fruit-bearing in keeping with their abilities and opportunities. The psalmist said, "They will still bear fruit in old age, they will stay fresh and green, proclaiming, 'The LORD is upright'" (Psalm 92:14–15). They recognize that God is working in and through them.

Jesus said much the same in His discourse on the vine and its branches. He who remains in Him, and He in him, will bear much fruit. This union comes about when the Holy Spirit brings people to the saving faith through the Gospel and through the water of Holy Baptism. It is nurtured through diligent use of the means of grace: God's Word and the sacrament of Holy Communion. The faith thus engendered relies totally on the redeeming merit of Jesus Christ, who is the Vine supporting the branches.

What a joy it is for our Savior when we are spiritually productive! It tells Him that He did not suffer and die in vain but that His labors of body and soul are still producing fruit.

PRAYER SUGGESTION

Ask God for vision and vitality to be a fruit-bearing Christian.

Receiving and Sharing the Water of Life

As the deer pants for streams of water, so my soul pants for You,
O God. Psalm 42:1

Animals need water. An elephant can drink up to 80 gallons a day while a camel can go for days without water.

Humans need water too—natural water for their bodies and spiritual water for their souls. God's Word is likened to refreshing water of which all are invited to drink. "Come, all you who are thirsty, come to the waters" (Isaiah 55:1). St. John closed Revelation with the invitation, "Whoever is thirsty, let him come; and whoever wishes, let him take the free gift of the water of life" (22:17).

Jacob's well at the village of Sychar was the setting for Jesus' words to the Samaritan woman, "Whoever drinks the water I give him will never thirst. Indeed, the water I give him will become in him a spring of water welling up to eternal life" (John 4:14).

We know how the Gospel, which Jesus proclaimed and of which He is the content, refreshes our souls. His words are "spirit and they are life" (John 6:63). They convey the promise of forgiveness of sins, peace with God, and eternal life.

What is more precious than the refreshment the Word of God offers! It quenches our soul's thirst and makes us, fountains flowing with blessings to the good of others. When we, having received the cup of salvation, pass it on and invite others to drink, we are using the only means—the Gospel of Jesus Christ—to turn the deserts of this world into refreshing oases.

The history of mission, from apostolic times until now, bears out how Christ's Gospel refreshes heathen lands spiritually and socially.

PRAYER SUGGESTION

Pray that your thirsty soul may be refreshed through receiving the Gospel of Jesus Christ.

Weekday Christianity

Sing to the LORD, praise His name; proclaim His salvation day after day. Psalm 96:2

Consider this statement culled from a church-related periodical: "It is in our ordinary lives that we exemplify our values and teach them to others." This statement calls for Christian living on a daily basis.

Old Testament believers exemplified their faith by worshiping in God's house on the Sabbath. Their prayers and praise were pleasing to God, as is our church worship on Sundays. David declared, and we join him in his resolve, "I will declare Your name to my brothers; in the congregation I will praise You" (Psalm 22:22).

But we profess our faith and show it in Christian living on weekdays as well. Our day-to-day living is for the most part ordinary. We follow a routine of work and rest. But our days become extraordinary when we worship God in our home devotions and practice Christian living. When we do this, we proclaim the salvation God has prepared for us all.

God hears our daily praise and thanksgiving, but He isn't the only one. People around us see and hear it too. By our Christian example, we "teach others." We bear witness to our Savior Jesus Christ, who in love gave His life for all people, even for those who do not yet realize it. God appoints us to "show and tell" what He has done in Christ for the salvation of all.

"You are a chosen people, a royal priesthood, a holy nation, a people belonging to God, that you may declare the praises of Him who has called you out of darkness into His wonderful light" (1 Peter 2:9). We are God's privileged people who praise Him both on Sundays and on weekdays.

PRAYER SUGGESTION

Pray for strength to glorify God in your life every day.

Persistence in Prayer

Will not God bring about justice for His chosen ones, who cry out to Him day and night? Luke 18:7

An 8-foot iron bar weighing 1,500 pounds was suspended from a chain. Hanging next to it was a cork on a silk thread. After the swinging cork had struck the bar for half an hour, the bar began to move. This is an illustration of the power of persistence.

Jesus teaches us to be persistent in prayer. He tells of a widow who went to a judge many times for justice. The judge ignored her until finally he granted her request so he would have peace. Jesus draws the application: Christians are to be steadfast in their prayers to God.

Scripture bids us to pray diligently. "Be joyful in hope, patient in affliction, faithful in prayer" (Romans 12:12). Again, "Pray continually; give thanks in all circumstances, for this is God's will for you in Christ Jesus" (1 Thessalonians 5:17–18).

What does it mean to pray without ceasing? Some groups take this to mean that God wants perpetual prayer—prayer marathons, so to speak. So all day and all night long, people take turns to pray continually. Is this what God wants us to do? Obviously not, for He has given us work to do. He wants us to have rest periods as well. To pray unceasingly means to be diligent in prayer. Morning prayers, evening prayers, table prayers, and prayers in special circumstances add up to the diligence God wants.

Many are the inducements for praying faithfully, especially the invitation of Christ to come to Him with our burdens, lay them on Him, and find rest for our souls. Our Lord does indeed provide for our needs, for He Himself is our Rest, our Peace.

PRAYER SUGGESTION

Tell Jesus that you are taking to heart His invitation to pray diligently.

Just Retribution

"A gallows seventy-five feet high stands by Haman's house. He had it made for Mordecai. ..." The King said, "Hang him on it!" Esther 7:9

A German proverb says he who digs a hole for another may himself fall into it. This possibility became a reality for Haman, prime minister under King Xerxes of the Persian Empire. Haman had come to hate Mordecai, a rival at the royal court and foster father of Esther, the future queen. His hatred of Mordecai, a Jew, grew to include all Jewish people. Haman plotted to destroy them all and to have Mordecai hanged. But God intervened, a deliverance still observed with the festival of Purim. For his treachery, Haman was hanged on gallows prepared for another.

The book of Esther gives honor and praise to God for preserving His people in a foreign land. The promised Messiah was to be born from those who escaped Babylonian captivity to settle in the Holy Land. This book also shows the faith of Esther (also known as Hadassah) amid the whims of Xerxes. God is mightier than any human potentate. The writer of Proverbs said, "The king's heart is in the hand of the LORD" (21:1).

This Old Testament book teaches also that the sin of hatred will not go unpunished. History alone has made this abundantly clear. Those who want to destroy God's people are candidates for the same kind of destruction. Jesus said, "All who draw the sword will die by the sword" (Matthew 26:52).

Not hatred but love—to God and to others—is to mark our daily lives. We are enabled to love because God first loved us. To prove that love, God sent His own Son to atone for our sins and to prepare the way for us to follow Him to eternal life.

PRAYER SUGGESTION

Ask God for an outpouring of love into your heart for others.

God's Surpassing Wisdom

It is by grace you have been saved. Ephesians 2:8

On January 8, 1935, twin sons were born in Tupelo, Mississippi. The first, Jesse Aaron, was stillborn. The other, Elvis Aaron, lived and went on to become a prominent entertainer. Why the one and not the other? Some things in life are hard, if not impossible, to understand.

Jesus said that at His Second Coming two men will be working in a field. One will be taken but not the other. Why the difference? The answer from Holy Scripture is: one was a believer in Christ and the other was not.

But a problem is involved here. God's Word teaches that none can believe in Christ unless the Holy Spirit works faith through the Gospel. Further, "Those God foreknew He also predestined to be conformed to the likeness of His Son, ... and those predestined, He also called; those He called, He also justified; those He justified, He also glorified" (Romans 8:29–30).

Here is a matter that passes our understanding. It has to do with the relationship between God's universal grace—the fact that God wants all people to be saved (1 Timothy 2:4)—and salvation by God's grace alone. If God predestines and gives the power to believe, why does He not do this to all? Perhaps in eternity we will understand.

In the meantime we faithfully adhere to the truths of salvation God has revealed in His Word. We all are sinners, incapable of self-salvation. To save us, God sent His Son to redeem us, and He continues to send the Holy Spirit to create and confirm faith in us. How thankful we are that the work God has performed in us and through us proclaims it to others!

PRAYER SUGGESTION

Pray that God may complete the work He has begun in you.

It Is Always Daytime

"Whoever lives by the truth comes into the light, so that it may be seen plainly that what he has done has been done through God." John 3:21

Edgar Allan Poe was given to strange ways. One of them was his preference for darkness. During the day he would draw the shades to block the sun.

The world lies in the darkness of sin and unbelief. For instance, some evildoers love shadows that cover their misdeeds. While honest people sleep, they ply their wicked trades.

Jesus came to be the Light of the world. He spoke the truth of God's Word as it sheds light on sinfulness and the truth of God's grace. In His nighttime conversation with Nicodemus, our Lord spoke what is known as the Gospel in a nutshell: "God so loved the world that He gave His one and only Son" (John 3:16). God gave His Son to be the Second Adam, to be obedient where the first Adam was disobedient and to make full restitution for all disobedience.

All we have to do is have faith in Christ as the one and only Savior. Faith brings forgiveness, peace with God, light to guide us day to day, and everlasting life. Now all God's people can stand in the light of God's Word. Believers have nothing to hide; there is no need to be secretive, no need to sit in darkness while it is day.

For Christians, it is always daytime. "The hour has come for you to wake up from your slumber, because our salvation is nearer now than when we first believed" (Romans 13:11). It is time to let our light shine to the glory of God.

PRAYER SUGGESTION

Ask God to let you bask in the sunshine of His love in Christ.

God: the World's Landlord

The earth is the LORD's, and everything in it, the world,
and all who live in it. Psalm 24:1

Take a walk in any park or undeveloped area and you will see litter. Forest fires are often the result of campfires or cigarettes. Overdevelopment and waste disposal have destroyed much of the world's natural environment.

God desires that we be faithful and thoughtful stewards of His creation. The earth and everything in it—air, water, flora, and fauna—are His. The whole universe, in fact, belongs to God. And He has made provision for its preservation by giving sunshine and rain, the power of reproduction, and other interacting forces. The divine Creator is also the supreme Artist, the painter of scenes on earth and in the sky, the sculptor of rock formations and delicate flowers.

Also belonging to God as His precious possessions are the people inhabiting the earth. Christians especially can understand and fulfill their roles as stewards. They cultivate the ground to grow food, realizing that daily bread and all blessings are God's gift, for His is the seed, the soil, the sunshine, the moisture. From Him come wisdom, strength, and good health to work.

Christians recognize God's ownership of them as His people. He has not only made them but has also redeemed them. "You are not your own. You were bought at a price" (1 Corinthians 6:19–20). St. Peter told us what that price was: "the precious blood of Christ, a lamb without blemish or defect" (1 Peter 1:19).

God is our Landlord; we are mere renters, tenants, stewards. Our permanent home is heaven, prepared for us by Jesus Christ.

PRAYER SUGGESTION

Ask God to keep you mindful of the role He wants you to fill as Christ's redeemed.

Hatred and Murder: the Only Cure

Love does no harm to its neighbor.
Therefore love is the fulfillment of the law. Romans 13:10

Killing is an old sin. Cain, the first son, slew his brother out of jealousy. Not many generations later, Lamech boasted, "I have killed a man" (Genesis 4:23). Nowadays our prisons are well populated by convicted murderers. Human nature has not changed through the centuries. It is still true what Jesus said: "Out of the heart come evil thoughts, murder..." (Matthew 15:19). Usually this is the order: first evil thoughts, hatred, jealousy, then murder.

There is only one way to overcome hatred and what it can lead to, and that is to become a new person in Christ, to be clothed with Him and to have Him in the heart by faith in His saving merit. Faith begets love for the neighbor, even for one who sins against us.

No one exemplifies this change of heart more than Paul. As Saul the Pharisee, he was "breathing out murderous threats against the Lord's disciples" (Acts 9:1). He took to the road to do more of this in Damascus. But en route Jesus confronted him. With this conversion came a new heart. As an apostle, he knew and proclaimed the love of Christ that "surpasses knowledge" (Ephesians 3:19). This love comes about in Paul's readers when Christ dwells in their "hearts through faith" (Ephesians 3:17). Paul, once filled with murderous hate, gave us that most beautiful chapter on Christian love—1 Corinthians 13. He declared that love "always protects, always trusts, always hopes, always perseveres" (1 Corinthians 13:7).

This continues to be what true love does in us and through us.

PRAYER SUGGESTION

Pray that love for Christ and for His people may always be uppermost in your heart.

Strength Amid Weakness

When I am weak, then I am strong. 2 Corinthians 12:10

Some men boast about their physical strength. For instance, the song "John Henry" is about a steel-driving man of prodigious strength. And strength contests and competitions are popular the world over.

There is another kind of strength, not physical but mental and spiritual. Paul possessed this kind of strength. For some time he suffered from a "thorn in [his] flesh" (2 Corinthians 12:7), probably some kind of sickness or physical ailment. He prayed for its removal, hoping to regain his strength. The Lord, as is often the case, answered the prayers with something better than what the apostle had requested: "My grace is sufficient for you, for My power is made perfect in weakness" (2 Corinthians 12:9). This answer gave promise of God's help amid human weakness. It prompted Paul to declare this paradox, "When I am weak, then I am strong." This strength came from God.

By faith, many Christians have experienced this to be true. Hebrews chapter 11 is a detailed report on what God's people accomplished because they trusted in God. Despite human weaknesses, they prevailed in very difficult circumstances.

God's strength is still ours. In fact, the more we let God take over when we have problems, the more we succeed. When it comes to salvation, we depend entirely God. Christ Jesus, God's Son, took the full load of our sin and grief upon Himself so we might be redeemed and be endowed with new life.

St. Paul's words are an appropriate theme for our lives: When we rely on Christ, we are truly strong.

PRAYER SUGGESTION

Ask God to grant you strength when you are weak.

Supervising God's Creation

Rule over the fish of the sea and the birds of the air and over every living creature that moves on the ground. Genesis 1:28

Many of God's creatures are endangered because their habitats and food sources are destroyed. At the time of creation, God gave Adam and Eve and their descendants the responsibility to supervise what God had made. This assignment was made difficult when, because of sin, the ground was cursed. This curse went far. Fruitful gardens and fields became deserts. Good plants became noxious weeds. Many wild animals became ferocious. And man himself became a plunderer.

Nevertheless, God's commission to our first parents is still in effect. We, their descendants, are still to exercise a wise dominion over all of nature. This is to be done not only for human welfare but also to the glory of the Creator. St. Paul declared, "Since the creation of the world God's invisible qualities—His eternal power and divine nature—have been clearly seen, being understood from what has been made" (Romans 1:20). In other words, we are to let God's creation bear witness to all people that God exists. God teaches us through His creation. As the psalmist said, He "satisfies your desires with good things so that your youth is renewed like the eagle's" (103:5).

Beyond good stewardship of our natural resources, God calls us to an even greater responsibility and privilege, that is, to be witnesses to all the world concerning His saving love in Christ Jesus, His Son and our only Savior. What a joy and privilege!

PRAYER SUGGESTION

Pray to God for wisdom to maintain a good environment where you live.

Our Worst Enemy Is Overcome

The great dragon was hurled down—that ancient serpent called the devil, or Satan, who leads the whole world astray. Revelation 12:9

Many people have an aversion to snakes. But snakes are not our worst enemy.

There is a serpent of dragon-like proportion and power against whom we have to be on constant guard. It is the devil and his evil spirits who, because of disobedience and false pride, were cast out of heaven. Satan is doomed to spend eternity in hell. For a while, though, until the Last Day, he has a degree of freedom to move about in our world.

The devil struck first in the Garden of Eden. An avowed enemy of God, he could not avenge himself on the Lord. So Satan turned to Adam and Eve, the crown of creation whom God had made in His own image. Taking the form of a serpent, he literally talked them into sin.

He hasn't quit yet: "the whole world is under the control of the evil one" (1 John 5:19). The fallen world is given over to all the fruits of the flesh: "sexual immorality, impurity and debauchery; idolatry and witchcraft; hatred, discord, jealousy, fits of rage, selfish ambition, dissensions, factions and envy; drunkenness, orgies, and the like" (Galatians 5:19–21). All the while Satan tempts people to the greatest sin of all—unbelief.

Although God's people need to be alert, they need not fear Satan. That "ancient serpent" tried to tempt Jesus to disobedience and unbelief in the wilderness. But he failed. Jesus overcame him once for all on Calvary's cross. Because of Jesus' triumph, we are victorious over sin, death, and the devil as well. Praise be to God!

PRAYER SUGGESTION

Pray that the wicked foe may have no power over you and that Christ may rule in your heart.

Making the Right Choice

*"What good is it for a man to gain the whole world,
yet forfeit his soul?" Mark 8:36*

Sometimes choice means the loss of life, as in the case of the captain of the *Titanic*. When alerted to the threat of icebergs, he chose to follow the wishes of the ship's owners to try to set a speed record.

Jesus spoke of another choice involving life. What if someone could gain the whole world but in so doing lost his life, even his soul? The Lord asks, "What good is it? ... What can a man give in exchange for his soul?" (Mark 8:36–37). The obvious answer is: nothing. The context of these remarks shows that Jesus was comparing life under Him as a disciple, with the sacrifices this involved, to a life devoted to selfish pursuits. The choice for the latter would result in total loss. On the Last Day, Christ will deny such a person a place in heaven.

How different it is when Christ is acknowledged as Lord and Savior! He enriches us with the greatest treasure—salvation He earned for us by His death as the sacrificial Lamb of God.

In the light of Christ's love for us, and by the strength of faith the Holy Spirit gives in Baptism and sustains in Communion, we can make the right choices. We can say, "As for me and my household, we will serve the LORD" (Joshua 24:15).

Other choices are then made—what vocation to follow, where to live, what schools to attend, where to seek recreation, who our friends will be, and who our spouse might be. Always we will ask the foremost question: How can I best serve my Lord?

PRAYER SUGGESTION

Ask the Lord Jesus to guide you when you have an important choice to make.

Influencing Others for Good

"I have set you an example that you should do as I have done for you." John 13:15

In Shakespeare's *Othello,* Iago goads Othello into a murderous fury. The Bible also tells of instances when people provoked others to sin and, in so doing, shared their guilt. The writer of Proverbs stated, "The accomplice of a thief is his own enemy" (29:24).

Sometimes people are misled by those whom they respect. All Christians need to be on their guard, lest by careless words or actions they mislead children or those weak in faith into sin. Jesus has sharp things to say to those who cause "one of these little ones who believe in Me to sin" (Matthew 18:6). Who would want to cause a weak brother or sister to sin (1 Corinthians 8:11)?

How good it is, on the other hand, when Christians help someone grow in faith and understanding, as when parents bring up their children "in the training and instruction of the Lord" (Ephesians 6:4). Such instruction is often given by example; attitudes are caught rather than taught.

We can also influence weak and wavering adults by what we say and do—and by what we *are.* Consider Aquila and Priscilla, a Christian couple assisting the apostle Paul. In Ephesus they were of help to Apollos, a promising evangelist who was not clear on all things. We read, "When Priscilla and Aquila heard him, they invited him to their home and explained to him the way of God more adequately" (Acts 18:26).

Jesus set the example of serving others, but He did more than that. In giving His life for us, He redeemed us and made us willing servants.

PRAYER SUGGESTION

Pray that the Holy Spirit helps you set a good example for others.

God at Work through the Word

The seed sprouts and grows, ... first the stalk, then the head, then the full kernel in the head. Mark 4:27–28

The seeds contain enormous power. Sown into the ground, these little "workers" take off their jackets and get busy. New plants emerge and mature. People can prepare the soil, fertilize it, irrigate, and sow the seeds. But that is all they can do. They cannot put the germinating power into the seed itself.

That is the way it is with the Word of God, the Gospel of Jesus Christ. As Christians we proclaim it in our neighborhoods and to the world at large. We prepare ourselves, speak words people can understand, use the media at our disposal, and the like.

But there is a limit to what we can do. When it comes to producing results in people—creating the saving, heart-changing faith—we can do nothing at all. "No man can redeem the life of another or give to God a ransom for him" (Psalm 49:7). We are powerless to redeem another from sin, and we are powerless to implant the faith that brings such redemption. God the Holy Spirit does it all through the Word and the Sacraments. The Gospel has wonderful power "for the salvation of everyone who believes" (Romans 1:16). It creates new life in Christ, sustains the growing faith, and causes it to bear fruit in the believer.

The Word is effective because it transmits divine power—the power of God the Father, who made us; the power of God the Son, who redeemed us; the power of God the Holy Spirit, who brings us to faith. The triune God effects our salvation.

PRAYER SUGGESTION

Pray that God may preserve and prosper you in your faith in Jesus.

Steadfastness amid Suffering

You have heard of Job's perseverance and have seen what the Lord finally brought about. James 5:11

It is hard to imagine how Job, a pious man, could endure the staggering losses he suffered. Lost were his oxen, sheep, camels, family, and health. How did Job react? He said, "The LORD gave and the LORD has taken away; may the name of the LORD be praised" (Job 1:21).

In his New Testament epistle, James underscored the faith of Job, stressing his perseverance and his patience amid suffering. Job remained steadfast even when his own wife suggested that he "curse God and die" (Job 2:9). His friends were of no help to him, for they argued from various viewpoints that Job was being punished for his sins. In the end, God showed His grace. His compassion and mercy were revealed when He restored Job to his former status.

Job is an example to us. His unwavering faith led him to celebrate Easter and the Resurrection long before Jesus Christ came into the world, for he confessed, "I know that my Redeemer lives, and that in the end He will stand upon the earth. And after my skin has been destroyed, yet in my flesh I will see God; I myself will see Him with my own eyes—I, and not another" (Job 19:25–27).

The book of Job was written for our learning, as Paul wrote, "Everything that was written in the past was written to teach us, so that through endurance and the encouragement of the Scriptures we might have hope" (Romans 15:4). The blessing the apostle then expressed is ours also: "May the God who gives endurance and encouragement give you a spirit of unity among yourselves as you follow Christ Jesus" (Romans 15:5).

PRAYER SUGGESTION

Ask God, for Jesus' sake, to grant you steadfast faith amid suffering.

Are Marriages Made in Heaven?

They called Rebekah and asked her, "Will you go with this man?"
"I will go," she said. Genesis 24:58

You have heard it said that marriages, like other social contracts, stem entirely from human contacts and rest on mutual agreement. Consequently, they can be terminated by the persons involved. Some want to leave God out of their marriage entirely.

On a wider scale, the guidance of God is recognized. History, many say, is "His story." They agree that God has a hand in world events and the affairs of society. They agree that God keeps the sparrow from falling, for that is what Jesus said. William Cullen Bryant said eloquently to the waterfowl that God "guides through the boundless sky thy certain flight." Joyce Kilmer's line in his poem "Trees" states that "only God can make a tree." Many would add that God, as Creator and Preserver, makes the fragile violets, the lilies of the field, the green meadows. But He has nothing to do with the making of a marriage?

Many agree with the Lord's words to Jeremiah that a human being is no accident, that God decided Jeremiah should come into this world to hold a holy office before he was ever conceived and born. But God has no part in guiding people, a man and a woman, to a marriage out of which they were born?

Our Lord leads us in the right direction. He, conceived by the Holy Spirit and born of the Virgin Mary, declares, "What God has joined together, let man not separate" (Matthew 19:6). God guides us, urging us to do His will. Husbands and wives, loving and serving one another, are a portrait of Christ loving the church and giving up His life for her. No marriage so honored is accidental.

PRAYER SUGGESTION

Pray that God, for Jesus' sake, may help us to always regard marriage as honorable.

Unbelief, a Stopper

Jesus could there do no might works. ... He marveled because of their unbelief. Mark 5:5–6 KJV

When celebrities come home, their communities often welcome and honor them. Not so with Nazareth and Jesus. The residents there would not allow Him to do mighty works there. Why was that?

As God the Son, Jesus was certainly able to do anything He wanted, anywhere and any time. He could heal the sick, raise the dead, still a storm. Had He so desired and had there been a reason, He could have moved mountains. Why could He not do mighty works in Nazareth?

The reason for shutting the door to Jesus was unbelief. His fellow townspeople refused to accept Him as the Messiah. They went so far as to try to throw Him off a cliff in order to kill Him.

There is no greater barrier to the work of Jesus Christ than unbelief. This resistance is exercised not only in big cities and small towns. When a person says no to the Savior and the good He wants to do in the heart, he or she has, so to speak, tied His hands. Persistent, stubborn unbelief stops the Lord. Why doesn't He use His power to compel a person to believe? The Lord does not proceed this way. He will not violate people by overpowering them and forcing them to believe. Such spiritual force-feeding would not be nourishing.

Jesus Christ works by love. He witnesses to the love of God that does not abandon sinners but pleads with them to accept Him in faith and thus obtain the salvation He procured. When He comes to us, He does not break down the front door; He knocks. He wants to come in and share with us the gifts He brings.

PRAYER SUGGESTION

Say thanks to the Lord Jesus for appealing to you with His saving love.

The Guardian Angels

[God] will command His angels concerning you to guard you in all your ways. Psalm 91:11

Much has been said and written about angels. There are books, songs, movies, and Web sites.

The perils facing us make the ministry of angels very necessary. They guard us also against the devil. In Martin Luther's prayers for morning and evening we pray to God: "Let Your holy angel be with me that the wicked foe may have no power over me."

When the psalmist declares that angels attend us in all our ways, the understanding is that we have their coverage as we discharge our God-pleasing, Christian vocation. The promise does not extend to activities that are sinful or that put God to the test. When Satan tempted Jesus to leap from the highest point of the temple, he quoted this psalm but left out important words. Our Lord refused to yield to this temptation, for He knew the omitted phrase "in all your ways" did not assure Him of angelic protection for so foolish an act.

The function of angels is threefold: to praise God, to carry out His commands, and to serve mankind. The holy angels, confirmed in their bliss, show great interest in what God has done in Christ for our salvation. "Angels long to look into these things" (1 Peter 1:12). We can imagine them gazing into the mystery of God's love for sinners. Theirs was the joyful mission of announcing the Savior's birth and His resurrection. At today's festival of St. Michael and All Angels, we thank God for sending us His ministering spirits.

PRAYER SUGGESTION

Pray that God may send His holy angels to watch over you.

Jesus: the Way to Heaven

"You know the way to the place where I am going. ... I am the Way and the Truth and the Life." John 14:4, 6

When President Thomas Jefferson commissioned Meriwether Lewis and William Clark to explore the Louisiana Purchase, the only direction he could give them was to follow the Missouri River. Otherwise the way was unknown.

Concerning life's journey from earth to heaven, Jesus said to His disciples, "You know the way." They knew it because He had told them, "God so loved the world that He gave His one and only Son, that whoever believes in Him shall not perish but have eternal life" (John 3:16).

Not everything on life's way is so clear. The journey can be excitingly exploratory, but for the most part, it is a day-to-day routine. Nor do we know how long the trip will take. "The length of our days is 70 years—or 80, if we have the strength" (Psalm 90:10).

But on one important point we have clarity: We know where we are going and we know the way. In today's reading Jesus prepares His disciples for His departure. He is returning to the heavenly Father, but they will travel on to be His witnesses in the world. For them, too, there will be a heavenly homecoming. He tells them He is going ahead to arrange for accommodations in the Father's house. "You know the way to the place where I am going." When Thomas asked, "'Lord, we don't know where You are going, so how can we know the way?' Jesus answered, 'I am the Way'" (John 14:5–6).

Jesus is the one and only Son of the Father, and the one and only Way to Him. He reconciled us to God by bearing our sins to Calvary's cross and leaving them there.

PRAYER SUGGESTION

Ask for the Holy Spirit's guidance as you travel toward your heavenly destination.

Grace and Truth in Christ

The Word became flesh and made His dwelling among us ... full of grace and truth. John 1:14

With scientific discoveries turning up so many facts and with the Internet giving access to the information, one might think that truth abounds. But this is not necessarily so, for there is a difference between factual data and truth. Truth goes beyond facts.

Mark Twain said, "Truth is such a precious article that we should all economize in its use." He implied that it is too valuable to toss about carelessly.

In the realm of spiritual beliefs, truth is even more precious. God reveals His truth abundantly in His Word and He broadcasts it in the Gospel of Jesus Christ. But people are preoccupied with self-centered pursuits. They have not tuned in. Both their reception and perception leave much to be desired.

Because this has been true since the fall into sin, God sent His truth to earth in the person of Jesus Christ. Because Jesus was the bearer of the message of God's grace, He was called the Word. In Him "love and faithfulness meet together; righteousness and peace kiss each other" (Psalm 85:10). In Christ, God's grace is revealed, for the truth is that He, by fulfilling all righteousness for us and enduring death, has made our peace with God.

When He stood before Pontius Pilate, Jesus declared that He came into the world to bear witness to the truth. And He tells us, "If you hold to My teaching, you are really My disciples. Then you will know the truth, and the truth will set you free" (John 8:31–32). Jesus not only speaks the truth; He is truth personified. We can be sure of that!

PRAYER SUGGESTION

Pray that the Holy Spirit may lead you deeper into the truth concerning God's forgiving grace in Christ, His Son.

The Power of Baptism

This water [of the Flood] symbolizes baptism that now saves you also. 1 Peter 3:21

In 1993, the overflowing waters of the Mississippi and Missouri rivers were called "a 500-year flood." The flood devastated whatever lay in the way—homes, towns, and businesses—and left behind a mess of smelly mud and muck.

By comparison, more ravaging was the Flood of Noah's time. Except for eight persons in the ark, it wiped out the human race. Peter referred to the Flood as he made a point in the verse for today. As the water bore up the ark in which Noah's family was saved so "Baptism ... now saves you."

Of course, we know that water from a river or from a faucet does not have the power to wash away sins and bring salvation. The power is in Christ's Word, both in His *command* to baptize (Matthew 28:19) and in the *promise* He speaks that saves and brings forgiveness (Acts 2:38).

Christ's Word in Holy Baptism is backed by His sin-atoning work. "Christ died for sins once for all, the righteous for the unrighteous, to bring you to God" (1 Peter 3:18). By virtue of His all-sufficient atonement, as verified by His resurrection, Baptism saves because it creates and confirms faith in the merit of Jesus Christ as Savior.

The water of Baptism and the Word of God do wonders. Sin is like a rampaging flood that destroys, but Baptism saves. In the newness of life in Christ, it strengthens, upholds, and equips all the members of the family for a life of service. The water of Baptism cleans up the messes that floods of sin create.

PRAYER SUGGESTION

Ask for the help of the Holy Spirit to keep the power of Baptism working in you and through you.

Who Is the Greatest?

"If anyone wants to be first, he must be the very last, and the servant of all." Mark 9:35

Jesus and the disciples He recruited as witnesses in the world constituted a walking "seminary." The enrollees often had group meetings, and they had discussions that were, at times, quite heated. On one such occasion Jesus asked what they had discussed. They hesitated to answer for they had been arguing about who was the greatest.

Jesus sat down to set the Twelve straight: "If anyone wants to be first, he must be the very last." The Master did not stop with words. He gave the group an object lesson in humility. He placed a child in their midst, a child who personified the kind of unfeigned faith and love that should mark every disciple, young or old.

Because such a child represents discipleship, Jesus went on to say, "Whoever welcomes one of these little children in My name welcomes Me; and whoever welcomes Me does not welcome Me but the One who sent Me" (Mark 9:37).

The person who has a childlike—not childish—faith is a true representative of Christ. Such a person even is a witness of the Savior by what he is, speaks, and does. Not only such witnessing disciples but also those in need are Christ's representatives, for He said of the good we do for "one of the least of these brothers of mine," we do for Him (Matthew 25:40).

There is a dual message here: be humble like a child and serve Christ by serving those in need. This we gladly do on both counts, for Christ was humble and in love gave His life for us all.

PRAYER SUGGESTION

Tell the Lord Jesus that you want to be a serving disciple of His.

With Jesus on the Sea of Life

The disciples went down and woke Him, saying "Master, Master, we're going to drown!" Luke 8:24

Shortly after a storm wrecked the vessel of a prominent Englishman in what was later called the Bermuda Triangle, Shakespeare wrote his play *The Tempest.* In the epilog, the character Prospero declares, "my ending is despair, Unless it be relieved by prayer. Which pierces so, that it assaults Mercy itself, and frees all faults."

Caught in a strong squall on the Sea of Galilee was a boat carrying Jesus and His disciples. When the storm reached such strength that the disciples, some of them experienced boatmen, felt they needed Jesus, they pleaded for His help, doing so with such urgency that they assaulted the mercy and might of the Master. They woke Jesus and He stilled the storm. The disciples were amazed at His power over the elements.

Jesus can—and does—still the storms arising in the human soul. Sin and the fear of death are like strong winds and waves disturbing our inner calm. Then along comes the devil to arouse doubt about God's promise to guard and guide us on life's voyage. Our faith can easily fail us when we need it the most.

Like the disciples, we can confidently approach the Lord with our prayers, for He is our Savior from sin, the Sovereign of life. Faith in Him assures us of His mercy and frees us from all faults.

The encouragement stated in Hebrews 4:16 is most appropriate: "Let us then approach the throne of grace with confidence, so that we may receive mercy and find grace to help us in our time of need."

PRAYER SUGGESTION

Ask the Lord Jesus to calm whatever inner and outer storms blow in your life.

A Time of Silence

Jesus withdrew from that place. Many followed Him, and He healed all their sick, warning them not to tell who He was. Matthew 12:15–16

A pastor and his wife took their grandson to a church where a simple marriage ceremony was to be performed. When the organ started playing, the boy whispered, "They shouldn't play music. Isn't this a quiet wedding?"

Jesus seemingly opted for a quiet wedding when at Cana He at first refused to do a startling miracle to provide wine. He said, "My time has not yet come" (John 2:4). On other occasions Jesus would quietly and patiently bide His time. God's plan of salvation could not be hurried. "There is a time for everything, and a season for every activity under heaven" (Ecclesiastes 3:1).

In a Galilean synagogue Jesus healed a man's crippled hand. His enemies objected to this because it was done on the Sabbath. When healing the sick, He ordered them not to reveal that He was the promised Messiah.

The quiet procedure of Jesus, so different from the publicity-seeking actions of many would-be reformers and crusaders, prompted St. Matthew to apply to Jesus the Messianic prophecy of Isaiah, "He will not quarrel or cry out; no one will hear His voice in the streets ... till He leads justice to victory" (Matthew 12:19–20). The Messiah is presented as the Servant who without self-promotion and fanfare, quietly, gently, and tenderly did His work of healing the sick and nurturing faith.

At Jesus' baptism the Holy Spirit came on Him, marking the beginning of a quietly effective ministry that still blesses us. Jesus got things done without a lot of noise. Are we like that?

PRAYER SUGGESTION

Base your prayer on these words of Jesus: "Learn from Me, for I am gentle and humble at heart" (Matthew 11:29).

On Staying Connected

"I am the Vine; you are the branches. If a man remains in Me and I in him, he will bear much fruit." John 15:5

Printing presses, computers, vacuum cleaners, clocks—machinery and appliances stop working when they are disconnected from their power source.

Human beings are not machines, of course, but our activities and personal growth falter when we become detached from society. We begin to live in a world of our own and risk becoming unproductive.

In our spiritual lives, we need to be connected to the higher power—God—to be effective in glorifying Him and serving others. Jesus uses the illustration of a vine and its branches. He identifies Himself as the vine and His followers as the branches. Jesus says, "No branch can bear fruit by itself; it must remain in the vine. Neither can you bear fruit unless you remain in Me" (John 15:4). We need to be connected to the power source—Jesus Christ—if there are to be the sweet grapes of words and works of love.

We were grafted to Christ in Holy Baptism. By the power of the Holy Spirit, we were born again and given faith. Faith is the critical connection. By faith we receive the blessings Jesus procured for us on the cross: forgiveness and the gift of a productive life. The result is that we are willing and able to bear fruit.

Train out of service? Household appliance dead? Branch not bearing fruit? Spiritually barren life producing grapes of wrath and the fruits of futility? Check your connection to Christ. Turn to the Word and the Sacraments. Then Christ's power will flow in you and through you again.

PRAYER SUGGESTION

Pray that the Holy Spirit may strengthen your faith connecting you with Christ.

The Power of Love

"Greater love has no one than this, that he lay down his life for his friends." John 15:13

The owner of a bakery in a Chicago suburb believed his customers needed bread for their souls as well as their bodies. So he hung a sign in his shop that read, "Christ died, that's history. Christ died for me, that's salvation."

Jesus, the Bread of Life, gained salvation for all when in love He became an atoning sacrifice on the cross. He called His disciples His friends, telling them that love prompted Him to lay down His life for them. What's more, His redeeming, life-giving love extends to all mankind, including His enemies. "When we were God's enemies, we were reconciled to Him through the death of His Son" (Romans 5:10).

The saving love of God in Christ, when accepted in faith, prompts and empowers us to love God and other people. Human love cannot function as God desires until, by faith, we "plug into" the power of Christ's love.

Christian love not only has a sublime source, it also has a sublime standard. How much did Jesus love us? So much He gave His life for us. This is the new measure for Christian love. Believers seek to love one another *as Christ has loved them*. What is new about this? The Old Testament Scriptures said, "Love your neighbor as yourself" (Leviticus 19:18). Jesus teaches, "Love each other as I have loved you" (John 15:12).

"Oh, the height of Jesus' love! Higher than the heavens above, Deeper than the depth of sea, Lasting as eternity. Love that found me—wondrous thought! Found me when I sought Him not."

PRAYER SUGGESTION

Thank your Savior for His love and ask Him to help you to extend it to others.

Well-Dressed with Humility

All of you, clothe yourselves with humility toward one another.
1 Peter 5:5

Humility is hard to define and even harder to live. To be humble does not mean to be like Uriah Heep in Dickens's *David Copperfield*, with his clammy handshake and with his line, "I am a very 'umble person." Nor does it require that we think of ourselves as ants or worms. This is not humility; this is self-degradation. This is contempt for God's workmanship.

What is sometimes thought to be humility can be inverse pride, as in being "proud of his humility." Some of the Pharisees of Jesus' time had this problem. They affected humility by letting their fasting show in their sad faces. But our Lord said, "they love the place of honor at banquets and the most important seats in the synagogues" (Matthew 23:6).

Christian humility is a virtue, a fruit of faith. The human heart is by nature proud, but the Holy Spirit changed that when He brought us to faith in Christ. With faith He gave humility, that is, being what we are—no more, no less. It fits beautifully with fruit of the Spirit: love, joy, peace, patience, kindness, and all the rest. It helps us to be more Christ-like.

"He humbled Himself and became obedient to death—even death on a cross!" (Philippians 2:8). The humility of Jesus Christ is not only for our example—it is for our redemption. To those who have new life in Christ, it is appropriate to speak of Christ's humility as their example as the apostle did: "Your attitude should be the same as that of Christ Jesus" (Philippians 2:8).

PRAYER SUGGESTION

Pray for the Spirit's grace to become well-dressed with Christian humility.

God Can Do It

You will drink from the brook, and I have ordered the ravens to feed you there. 1 Kings 17:4

A Missouri legend has it that a young boy wandered away from home and became lost in a wooded area for 70 hours. The nighttime temperature sank to ten degrees above zero, but the boy survived because two stray dogs rested beside him to keep him warm. His mother called them "angels from heaven."

Does God use lesser creatures to preserve the lives of people? As a matter of fact, He does so regularly as He provides for our bodily needs through things that grow in nature. God can do it also through special interventions—miracles—as He did for the prophet Elijah. The Lord God commanded the ravens to feed Elijah. Later, in the home of a widow, He provided food and drink by daily replenishing the meager supplies.

"Surely the arm of the LORD is not too short to save" (Isaiah 59:1). Most of us know of times and occasions when it seemed to us that God intervened to keep us from harm. He may have sent total strangers or even angels (Hebrews 13:2) to bring help. Because He has power over the universe, God can also send animals, even stray dogs, to save a life.

A miracle in a special sense occurred when we came to the saving faith in Jesus Christ. The miracle of God's love for an undeserving mankind came when God's own Son became the ransom for us all. Carlton C. Buck said it like this: "I believe in miracles—I've seen a soul set free, Miraculous the change in one redeemed through Calvary."

PRAYER SUGGESTION

Praise the Lord God for His many kindnesses to you, especially for the miracle of bringing you to faith in Jesus Christ.

Retracing One's Steps

The LORD said to him, "Go back the way you came." 1 Kings 19:15

"What are you doing here, Elijah?" (1 Kings 19:9). Elijah had gone into hiding because he was discouraged that people didn't listen to his prophecies and because Queen Jezebel wanted him killed. Then, after a great storm, an earthquake, and a fire, the Lord told him, "Go back the way you came." Elijah still had important work to do.

No one can hide from God. The Lord asks, "Can anyone hide in secret places so that I cannot see him?" (Jeremiah 23:24). Jonah tried it. The prodigal son in Jesus' parable tried it. The Lord finds those who try to escape their divine assignments.

Many people try to run away from God, only to be found by Him and told, "Go back the way you came." No disgrace attends such a return. One does not lose self-respect or the esteem of others to admit the mistake of choosing a wrong destination and the wrong way of getting there. People who, like the son in Jesus' parable, come back to God find His ready acceptance. Those who go into hiding because they are discouraged, as was Elijah, can return to God and to the service into which He called them.

William E. Gladstone, the great English statesman of over a century ago, said, "The problem … is to find out which way God is going and to go that way." Since we cannot expect a cut and dried answer from God, we search His Word and pray for His guidance. All the while we can be certain that Jesus, our Redeemer and Reconciler, is the Way leading us safely and surely to peace with God.

PRAYER SUGGESTION

Ask the Lord Jesus to guide and guard you in your life's journey.

None Is Too Small

[Zacchaeus] wanted to see who Jesus was,
but being a short man he could not. Luke 19:3

In the travels of the fictional Captain Gulliver, he comes upon the strange country of Lilliput. Its people, the Lilliputians, are only six inches tall. Everything in their land is small. For breakfast, Gulliver eats an entire herd of cattle.

Zacchaeus, the tax collector in Jericho, was small but that did not keep him from seeing Jesus or Jesus from seeing him. Zacchaeus invited the Lord to his house then gave proof of his conversion by making generous restitution for his dishonest business practices. Jesus accepted him, saying, "Today salvation has come to this house" (Luke 19:9).

Life's circumstances—height, age, income—are of no significance to Jesus. Because of original sin, we are all spiritual Lilliputians in the sight of God. In Christ, the Mediator, He has compassion on us all. Our Lord is concerned about little people. He accepts and blesses the little children we bring to Him in Holy Baptism. He has a heart for all. In Jericho, He accepted a penitent publican (the Jewish public equated him with "sinners"). On Calvary, the penitent thief was short of personal merit but Jesus promised him a place in paradise. This great truth applies to all: "Believe in the Lord Jesus, and you will be saved" (Acts 16:31).

An impressive scene set in heaven is the great multitude gathered before God's throne and identified as "saints and those who reverence Your name, both small and great" (Revelation 11:18). The church of Christ gathered on earth for worship and His work still consists of the two groups. None is too small to be included.

PRAYER SUGGESTION

Enlarge on the simple prayer: Jesus, You love me dearly—even me.

God Overrules Human Error

You intended to harm me, but God intended it for good to accomplish what is now being done, the saving of many lives. Genesis 50:20

On October 12, 1492, from his flagship *Santa Maria*, Christopher Columbus sighted land. He went ashore on an island in what we now call the Bahamas. Thinking he had reached a part of India, he named the place the West Indies.

Columbus has since been credited (or discredited) with spreading disease to the indigenous people and abusing them. To be sure, Columbus made mistakes. But he was withal a pious man in the context of his times. (He had vesper services held on his ships every evening.)

God has a way of turning human errors so it fulfills His will. This truth clearly emerges from the story of Joseph. His jealous brothers wanted to get rid of him and sold him into slavery, stopping short of murder. God took their evil intents and turned them to good, as Joseph expressed it so well in the verse above. Joseph rose from slavery to leadership. And from his family, particularly the tribe of Judah, the world's Savior was born.

Turning to the New Testament, we see even more clearly how God turned the hatred of Jesus' enemies into the good of mankind, turning the brutal crucifixion into the once-for-all sacrifice of His Son. While God carries out His will, the evildoers are still accountable to Him for their sins.

It would be inconceivable to suppose that God had nothing to do with the discovery of the New World, Columbus's mistakes notwithstanding. During that era of exploration, God was certainly at work, with His good and gracious will prevailing. How thankful we can be for the land Columbus "discovered!"

PRAYER SUGGESTION

Praise the triune God for all His blessings to you in your homeland.

One Lord Jesus Christ

Is Christ divided? 1 Corinthians 1:13

"Divide" means to separate a thing into two parts. We cannot divide Christ's Word from His work. Addition and subtraction don't work either, as John said in Revelation 22:18–19, we should not add to, or take away from, the truth revealed in Christ. Our Lord warned about multiplication, foretelling that many false christs—antichrists—would come into the world. There is only one true Christ.

When Paul asked the fractured Corinthians, "Is Christ divided?" he referred to division in the congregation with some saying they followed Paul or Apollos or Cephas, and the like. This, the apostle maintained, is dividing Christ and effectively destroying the unity of faith in Him. He told the church, "There is one body and one Spirit—just as you were called to one hope when you were called—one Lord, one faith, one Baptism; one God and Father of all" (Ephesians 4:4–6).

Satan has always tried to divide Christ. He raises up false prophets who seek to divide Christ from His cross, as though salvation could be achieved not by His sacrifice but by following His good example: be good, do good, be virtuous, and the like. Another way to divide Christ is to separate Him from His resurrection. If Christ did not rise, then His sacrifice is worthless—we are unredeemed and will remain in our graves forever.

But the Christ we worship and serve is undivided, and so is the holy Christian church, the communion of saints. A remaining task is to bring the visible churches, like the local congregation in Corinth, into line with the unity we have in Christ.

PRAYER SUGGESTION

Tell Christ in your own words that you believe in Him as your one and only Savior.

Our Well-Stocked Wardrobe

"'What shall we wear?'" Matthew 6:31

This question is recorded in Matthew's account of Jesus' Sermon on the Mount. But the first time people worried about what to wear was in the Garden of Eden when Adam and Eve became aware that they were naked. One early English Bible was nicknamed the "Breeches Bible" because it said Adam and Eve had made "breeches" from fig leaves to wear. The King James Version went with "aprons" with a note in the margin about the alternate translation: "things to gird about." We've come a long way.

God has blessed us with ample attire. In his explanation of the First Article of the Apostles' Creed, Martin Luther lists "clothing and shoes, food and drink, house and home," plus many other gifts for our bodily support.

But there is more to the question. If Jesus had not come as our Savior, we would have to ask, "What shall we wear?" with regard to the spiritual clothes we need as we stand before God on the Last Day and every day. Thank God we know His answer to the question, "for He has clothed me in garments of salvation and arrayed me in a robe of righteousness" (Isaiah 61:10).

The Gospel bids us to trust in the atoning merit of Jesus Christ and be clothed in the robes of His righteousness. Paul wrote that he wanted to be found in Christ "not having a righteousness of my own that comes from the law, but that which is through faith in Christ—the righteousness that comes from God and is by faith" (Philippians 3:9).

The question of what we shall wear to be acceptable to God is answered once for all to our great joy and thankfulness.

PRAYER SUGGESTION

Thank God for washing away your sins and, for Jesus' sake, clothing you with His righteousness.

Contentment

If we have food and clothing, we will be content with that.
1 Timothy 6:8

Some people are happy to live a simple life. But more and more often, people demand greater excitement. Simple experiences no longer satisfy them. Adequate food and clothing, basic necessities, are not enough. They want treasures and luxuries, thrills and excitement. A result may be that they are not at peace with themselves or with the people around them. Such discontent shows up in tensions encountered on all levels of life—in the family, in the work place, in the community, even in the church.

The apostle's encouragement in the verse for today is very appropriate: Let's be content with life's basics. If God grants us more, as He often does by giving us good health of body and mind so we can work and learn, to say nothing of windfalls, we have all the more reason to be thankful. We show our gratitude by sharing our surplus with the needy, thereby glorifying our Savior, Jesus Christ. "'Whatever you did for one of the least of these brothers of Mine, you did for Me'" (Matthew 25:40).

How wonderful that the Lord Jesus has met our greatest needs: our salvation, forgiveness, new life, peace with God! We are well supplied with food for our souls, conveyed to us through the means of grace. We have spiritual clothing: the robe of Christ's righteousness imparted by faith.

Truly, as Paul said, "Godliness with contentment is great gain" (1 Timothy 6:6).

PRAYER SUGGESTION

Ask the God of all comfort to grant you contentment even when the sun does not seem to shine in your life.

Rain and Sunshine: Both Real

Sorrowful, yet always rejoicing; poor, yet making many rich; having nothing, and yet possessing everything. 2 Corinthians 6:10

We've all heard the songs. "Put on a happy face." "Let a smile be your umbrella." "Singing in the rain." Easier said than done.

How do we mentally and spiritually overcome the storms in life? To do this, we need something substantive, something beyond pretense and false cheerfulness. Rain is very real and so are our problems. But beyond it, the sun is shining.

In the verse for today, Paul acknowledged the existence of sorrow and at the same time identified the reason for rejoicing: Christ Jesus, who redeemed us and rose victorious over all sorrow and every problem. Alongside the rain we have the very real Son.

Another paradox in Paul's statement is being "poor, yet making many rich." We may have a feeling of utter destitution, yet we have unlimited potential. We have personal assets: the ability to share love and concern, the willingness to befriend others. That is making the sun shine through the rain.

Closely related is the feeling of "having nothing"—no magnetic personality, no gift of oratory, no physical presence to catch the attention of talent scouts. But all the while, we are, as the apostle explained, "possessing everything." It is said, "If you have good health, you just about have everything." There are other possessions not to be overlooked. You have yourself, a family, a place in the community. And as a Christian you have membership in the "communion of saints." To complete the list, you have Jesus Christ.

So, let it rain. You can sing during the storm, not by pretending your trouble doesn't exist but by accepting the truth of your life in Christ.

PRAYER SUGGESTION

Give thanks to Christ for the assurance He brings to your life.

People Come First

"The Sabbath was made for man, not man for the Sabbath."
Mark 2:27

The Old Testament people lived under the law. Besides the *moral* law, the Ten Commandments, there were *political* laws and a multitude of *ceremonial* laws. The latter consisted of religious rules like forbidding work on the Sabbath and seemed to lay heavy burdens on the people.

Still, the well-being of the people was always to be uppermost. The Sabbath law, so Jesus taught, was never intended to prevent works of love or needful action when someone was in need. The law of love always takes precedence.

The Pharisees were inconsistent. They would approve of the owner pulling his ox from a well but objected to Jesus healing the sick on the Sabbath. On one occasion the Pharisees accused Jesus' disciples of working on the Sabbath when they rubbed a few heads of grain and ate the kernels. Jesus reminded them of an exception of the ceremonial law that occurred when David and his fellow refugees were fed with the bread reserved for priests in God's house.

On our Lord's scale of priorities, people come first. The institution of the Sabbath was made for man—to aid him in worship unhindered by weekday work. Never was the believer meant to be a blind slave of the Sabbath.

For us as New Testament people, our freedom is clearly established. Jesus eliminated the ceremonial dos and don'ts. He Himself became our "Sabbath," our Rest (Hebrews 4:11–12), for He fulfilled the whole law of God for us by His obedience, His death on the cross, and His resurrection.

PRAYER SUGGESTION

Offer a prayer of thanks to the Lord Jesus for freeing you from the law so you might serve Him gladly.

The Call to Constancy

"You have neglected the more important matters of the law—justice, mercy and faithfulness. ... You strain out a gnat but swallow a camel." Matthew 23:23–24

The scribes and Pharisees of Jesus' time were inconsistent. In Matthew 23 our Lord cites them as being very thorough in some things, mostly unimportant ones, but they were slack in things that count. For instance, they conscientiously gave a tenth of things grown in the gardens but neglected what Jesus called "important matters": justice, mercy, and faithfulness.

Jesus, by precept and example, encourages constancy in Christian faith and love. In His Sermon on the Mount, He sought to correct religious imbalances, such as this inconsistency: "You have heard that it was said, 'Love your neighbor and hate your enemy.' But I tell you: Love your enemies and pray for those who persecute you" (Matthew 5:43–44). He urged constancy in watchfulness and prayer. He helped us to be consistent by setting this priority: "Seek first His kingdom and His righteousness, and all these things will be given to you as well" (Matthew 6:33).

When we seek God's kingdom first, we will be devoted to what the scribes and Pharisees neglected: justice, mercy, and faithfulness. It keeps us, to use academic terms, from majoring in minors and minoring in majors.

Jesus Himself was fully devoted to the work He came to do for our salvation. He effected justice and righteousness in our behalf when He fulfilled God's law for us and bore the penalty for our disobedience. He was given to faithfulness and mercy when He adhered to His redeeming work until He could say on the cross, "It is finished!" (John 19:30). In Jesus Christ we have perfect constancy.

PRAYER SUGGESTION

Ask for God's strength so you may be constant in your calling.

On the Wings of the Wind

He mounted the cherubim and flew;
He soared on the wings of the wind. Psalm 18:10

Longfellow likened the wind to a musician who uses trees as his instruments: "I hear the wind among the trees Playing the celestial symphonies; I see the branches downward bent, Like keys of some great instrument."

The Bible tells of God using the wind to help His people. When the children of Israel left Egypt, with Pharaoh's charioteers behind and the Red Sea ahead, "the LORD drove the sea back with a strong east wind and turned it into dry land" (Exodus 14:21). Later in the wilderness "a wind went out from the LORD and drove quail in from the sea" (Numbers 11:31).

The Holy Spirit—the creating, life-giving Breath of God—"was hovering over the waters" (Genesis 1:2) when the world was in the making. The psalmist wrote, "By the word of the LORD were the heavens made, their starry host by the breath of His mouth" (Psalm 33:6). In the Hebrew language the same word is used for breath, spirit, and wind.

The Holy Spirit gives life. On Pentecost, the Spirit came to the accompaniment of the sound of a strong wind. He was active through the preaching of St. Peter, giving faith in Christ's forgiveness to thousands in Jerusalem and establishing the Christian church.

The Gospel of Christ's salvation is published throughout the world. Paul and others let the wind drive them as they sailed to many lands as witnesses of God's grace. Today Christ's heralds are more apt to travel by air.

God is at work as He grants us "the wings of the wind" to spread His message.

PRAYER SUGGESTION

Thank God for allowing us the use of the wind to spread Christ's Gospel.

A Wordless Prayer

[Jesus] asked him, "Do you want to get well?" John 5:6

Are elaborate, well-spoken prayers more apt to be answered? Not necessarily. Sincere prayer may consist of many words, a few words, or none at all.

Jesus visited a well-known pool near one of Jerusalem's gates. The place was called Bethesda, literally a house of mercy. From time to time an angel would touch the water, and the first to plunge in afterward would be cured of his affliction. So people with various handicaps such as paralysis or blindness would lie there, waiting to be healed.

Jesus approached a man who had lain beside the pool for 38 years and asked if he wanted to get well. The patient could have said, "Of course I do! Why else do you think I'm here?" But he answered Jesus, who was unknown to him, with respect: "Sir ... I have no one to help me into the pool when the water is stirred. While I am trying to get in, someone else goes down ahead of me" (John 5:7). The man had not spoken words of prayer, but Jesus knew the man's desire. He said, "Get up ... and walk" (John 5:8). Immediately the man got up and walked.

Sincere prayer may consist of many words, a few words, or none at all. "We do not know what we ought to pray for, but the Spirit himself intercedes for us with groans that words cannot express. And He who searches our hearts knows the mind of the Spirit, because the Spirit intercedes for the saints in accordance with God's will" (Romans 8:26–27). Our Lord knows what is in our hearts when in faith we come to Him with words or without.

PRAYER SUGGESTION

Give thanks to the Lord Jesus for being your Physician in body and in soul.

Jesus Comes Our Way

As Jesus and His disciples ... were leaving the city, a blind man, Bartimaeus ... was sitting by the roadside begging. Mark 10:46

Jericho was a beautiful city with lush trees and flowers. The tax collector Zacchaeus made a fortune there. Bartimaeus, however, saw none of that beauty or prosperity. He was blind. Then one day good fortune, greatly eclipsing his misfortune, befell him. Jesus, the promised Messiah and Savior, came his way to give him sight.

Every one of us, at one time or another, experiences some kind of distress. If it isn't a physical disability, it is something else: financial worries, health concerns, career challenges, loneliness, or any number of other challenges. But there is help and hope. We are greatly blessed to have Jesus, Helper and Healer, come our way.

Jesus comes our way, no longer in His physical presence but just as effectively through the Word and Sacraments. Through these means of grace, He conveys all the blessings He gained for us on Calvary's cross—His destination as He traveled along the road from Jericho. Jesus Christ grants us the remission of sins, reconciliation with God, purpose for our life, the certainty of eternal life. He comes our way, whenever the Gospel is brought to us, with consolation and forgiveness.

The Savior, having made us His own, comes our way on the feet of human messengers: friends, family, and fellow Christians in whose hearts the love of God is working. These are His representatives, and through them He imparts spiritual healing. One question remains: How can we be messengers for Christ to people in need?

PRAYER SUGGESTION

Ask the Lord Jesus to make you aware of people who need your help.

Praising God in Our Songs

[The Lord] put a new song in my mouth, a hymn of praise to our God. Psalm 40:3

Victor Herbert, an American composer, made it a practice to write a new song every day. Not all were published, of course, but one of his well-known songs was "Ah! Sweet Mystery of Life."

David and other psalmists drew on life's mysteries for inspiration for their songs. They were also inspired by life's high points and low points. For instance, Psalm 40 was written after David, waiting patiently for the Lord, was delivered from the mire of sin to stand on solid rock. Psalm 137 is a song of sorrow and was written while Israelites were captive in Babylon.

There are occasions when new songs are very much in order, such as the anniversary of a church or happy events in the life of a Christian. Composing new anthems to the glory of God is a way of serving with one's special talents.

Some people are not fond of new songs, preferring the old, familiar ones. At the other end of the scale are those who prefer new things, agreeing with the composer of "I Cannot Sing the Old Songs" because they bring back distressing memories.

Old songs or new, our intention is to sing praises to God. As St. Paul told the Ephesians: "Speak to one another with psalms, hymns and spiritual songs. Sing and make music in your heart to the Lord, always giving thanks to God the Father for everything, in the name of our Lord Jesus Christ" (Ephesians 5:19–20).

God led us out of sin right to Jesus Christ, whose atoning sacrifice gives us much to rejoice and sing about.

PRAYER SUGGESTION

For your prayer quote a hymn verse in praise of Jesus Christ, your Savior.

A Spiritual Harvest

"Unless a kernel of wheat falls to the ground and dies, it remains only a single seed. But if it dies, it produces many seeds." John 12:24

It's amazing. A germinated seed multiplies into many of its kind. It is really a miracle, but because it occurs so regularly we call it a natural process.

Jesus, during His stay in Jerusalem for His last Passover observance, referred to His forthcoming death and burial in the picture of a kernel of wheat becoming a crop. He voiced this brief parable when Philip and Andrew told Him some Greeks wanted to meet Him. These Greeks, representatives of the pagan world, were converts to Judaism. They were among the first fruits of a great harvest of souls in the Gentile world. They had come to Jerusalem for the Passover and expressed their desire to see Jesus.

For Jesus this was a pivotal moment. He said the hour had come for Him to be glorified, to enter the glory of heaven through death. Our Lord had already announced His suffering and dying, telling His disciples that they were going to Jerusalem for these events. His announcement on this occasion was a predicted triumph—the fulfillment of the purpose for which He had come into the world. At stake was a great spiritual harvest. He said, "I, when I am lifted up from the earth, will draw all men to Myself" (John 12:32).

But there could be no harvest unless there had first been a sowing, a planting of the lifeless body of Jesus into the earth. Jesus must die and be buried before there could be fruits of His redemption. His resurrection gave assurance of the sufficiency of His sacrifice. Our Savior is still gathering a harvest, with us as His workers.

PRAYER SUGGESTION

Ask the Holy Spirit to continue to bless the harvest of souls.

Spiritual Growth

Like newborn babies, crave pure spiritual milk, so that by it you may grow up in your salvation. 1 Peter 2:2

A main character in Victor Hugo's novel *The Hunchback of Notre Dame* is a misshapen man named Quasimodo, from the Latin *Quasimodogeniti*. It is the beginning of the introit for the Sunday after Easter. The words in English, taken from St. Peter's first epistle, are the above text: "Like newborn babies. ..."

The people the apostle addressed in his letter were new Christians. Spiritually speaking, they were infants. A good beginning had been made, but newcomers in the faith need to grow.

The apostle clearly explained how spiritual growth comes about. The proper nourishment for beginners is the "pure spiritual milk," the simple Word of God. It teaches that all people are sinners and that Jesus Christ is their only Savior: "It was not with perishable things such as silver or gold that you were redeemed ... but with the precious blood of Christ, a lamb without blemish or defect" (1 Peter 1:18–19). This truth is within the grasp of all, including children, who sing, "Jesus loves me, this I know, For the Bible tells me so." The New Testament teaches that Christians should proceed from milk to meat and potatoes: "Though by this time you ought to be teachers, you need someone to teach you the elementary truths of God's Word all over again. You need milk, not solid food! Anyone who lives on milk, being still an infant, is not acquainted with the teaching about righteousness" (Hebrews 5:12–13).

Our calling is to be Christians who daily grow in the knowledge and faith of Christ.

PRAYER SUGGESTION

Pray that you may daily grow in the grace of our Lord Jesus Christ.

Doing the Church's Business

"It is written, ... My house will be called a house of prayer."
Matthew 21:13

Jesus objected when in the temple courtyard merchants sold animals intended for sacrifice and other concessionaires operated currency exchanges for profit. He objects today when people turn God's house into a marketplace and transact business.

Yet the church is a place of business—the Lord's business. When He was just a boy, Jesus said He was about His "Father's business" when He occupied Himself with God's Word in the temple. When later He called the temple a "house of prayer," He stressed that it was for worship. We do our Father's business in our churches today when we pray, proclaim the Word, administer the Sacraments, bring our offerings, and have fellowship with one another.

To us "church" is more than a building. It is God's people, who believe themselves to be redeemed by Jesus Christ, serve Him on Sundays and weekdays, and profess Him before the world. Our Lord made it the business of the church to "make disciples of all nations, baptizing them in the name of the Father and of the Son and of the Holy Spirit, and teaching them to obey everything I have commanded you" (Matthew 28:19–20).

The church's business is not politics, social reform, or commercialism. It is Gospel preaching and teaching, baptizing, celebrating Holy Communion, joining in prayer and fellowship, ministry and mission. The church building is where God's people gather to receive Him through His means of grace. It is where His children come to and go forth from as they go about God's business.

PRAYER SUGGESTION

Ask the Holy Spirit to help you support the church of Christ as it fulfills its mission.

The Son of God Sleeps

Jesus was in the stern, sleeping on a cushion. Mark 4:38

In early centuries a group known as Docetae (from the Greek *dokein*, to seem) said Jesus only appeared to be human. But that is not how the Gospels describe Him. He was born and He died, and in between He grew up, learned, ate, drank, worked, rested, laughed, and cried. Our reading today reports that He slept.

In the midst of the storm, the disciples thought it was no time to sleep. They woke Him and asked, "Teacher, don't You care if we drown?" (Mark 4:38).

That Jesus slept, however, is meaningful and comforting. It proves that God had assumed a true human nature. He did not pretend to be human, was not an actor who came on stage as somebody else. He was in fact a true human being who fit Himself into our situation. He knows from personal experience what it means to be bone tired, to need rest in the midst of life's storms, to be able to bear only so much physically and emotionally. The writer of the letter to the Hebrews tells us that we have a Savior able to "sympathize with our weaknesses ... one who has been tempted in every way, just as we are—yet was without sin" (Hebrews 4:15).

Jesus does more than sympathize with us, "He took up our infirmities and carried our diseases" (Matthew 8:17). And as true man, He died a true death to free us from sin, Satan, and death. He is also true God. He showed Himself as such when He calmed wind and waves on the Sea of Galilee and on the sea of life.

PRAYER SUGGESTION

Thank the Lord Jesus for understanding the problems of your life and for helping you solve them.

Names Written in the Book of Life

*O LORD, the hope of Israel, all who forsake You will be put to shame.
Those who turn away from You will be written in the dust.*
Jeremiah 17:13

To have one's name written in dust is to stand under God's judgment for one's sins. The first part of the text makes this plain: All who forsake God and His Word "will be put to shame." They have no permanence. On the other hand to have one's misdeeds written in dust implies a promise of the Gospel.

When a woman taken in adultery was brought before Jesus, He bent down to write on the ground with His finger. Giovanni Papini states in his *Life of Christ,* "He chose the sand on which to write expressly that the wind might carry away the words." God's forgiveness of those who look to Christ for salvation is like that. There is no longer a record of their sins, for by faith in the Savior they are declared just. Paul wrote, "Blotting out the handwriting of ordinances that was against us, which was contrary to us, and took it out of the way, nailing it to His cross" (Colossians 2:14 KJV).

Jesus went to the cross so we might have eternal life and have our names written, not in sand or dust, but in granite. When the 72 disciples returned from their mission in great elation because of their power over demons, Jesus told them, "Do not rejoice that the spirits submit to you, but rejoice that your names are written in heaven" (Luke 10:20).

Those who believe in Jesus Christ as their Savior and Lord have been enrolled "in the Lamb's book of life" (Revelation 21:27). They are not only saved, but safe—safe in the hands of Jesus, where no enemy can reach them or delete their names from God's list.

PRAYER SUGGESTION

Thank the Savior Jesus Christ for erasing the record of your sins and for entering your name in the Book of Life.

Sin and Grace

I know that nothing good lives in me, that is, in my sinful nature.
Romans 7:18

The acts of the sinful nature are obvious. Galatians 5:19

At midnight "a gang of youthful good-for-nothings" made their way to a neighbor's pear tree to "shake it down and despoil it ... not as a treat for ourselves but just to throw to the pigs. ... We did so only to be doing something which would be pleasant because it was forbidden." So stated St. Augustine, one of the great church fathers, in his *Confessions.*

This account illustrates the twofold aspects of sin: original and actual. The former is a condition, the latter its enactment. The young Augustine personifies both. Later in his life, Augustine upheld the Bible's teaching on what the human being is by nature and what sins follow from the corrupt condition.

The apostle Paul wrote that nothing good dwells in our inner nature, and his pre-conversion hatred and persecutions of Christians prove it. Paul listed many of the acts that bring evil to outward expression: immorality, drunkenness, orgies, and many more. Not only the crude but also the "refined" sins are included, like selfish ambition, discord, jealousy.

St. Augustine and St. Paul taught what Jesus stressed: "Flesh gives birth to flesh" (John 3:6) and "Out of the heart come evil thoughts, murder, adultery, sexual immorality, theft, false testimony, slander" (Matthew 15:19).

But there is salvation. Jesus, the sinless Son of God, was made to be sin for us that we by faith might be righteous in God's sight. How wonderful is God's forgiving grace: "Where sin increased, grace increased all the more" (Romans 5:20)!

PRAYER SUGGESTION

Express your thankfulness to God for His grace in Christ.

Solid Nourishment

Then Jesus declared, "I am the Bread of life." John 6:35

When Marie Antoinette, queen of France, was told that starving, revolution-minded crowds were demanding bread, she is supposed to have said, "Let them eat cake." She was executed on the guillotine after a long imprisonment. A historian has written that she had her faults but should be remembered also for "her patience, her heroism, her suffering."

Not cake, but bread is called the stuff of life, referring to other foods as well. In fact, when we pray "Give us this day our daily bread," we ask God for "everything that has to do with the support and needs of the body" *(Luther's Small Catechism).*

"Man does not live by bread alone," Jesus said, quoting Deuteronomy 8:3. Moses pointed out that God taught the Israelites a lesson when He gave them manna in the wilderness as an unearned gift. The point is: people depend on God's power as the Provider. He supplies our spiritual provisions, the needed "soul food."

Jesus taught the same lesson when He fed multitudes in uninhabited places. He wanted to give them something beyond bread for the body. People need nourishment of the mind and spirit. Jesus came into the world to secure this. In the discussion following the miraculous feeding, Jesus declared Himself to be the "Bread of life," adding that "he who comes to Me will never go hungry" (John 6:35). The Son of God had become man to procure salvation for all through His death and resurrection. Having come directly from the Father in heaven, He opened the door to eternal life.

The Gospel satisfies the hunger and thirst of the soul.

PRAYER SUGGESTION

Ask the Lord Jesus to satisfy your soul's hunger through the manna of the Gospel.

Temples of the Holy Spirit

Do you not know that your body is a temple of the Holy Spirit, who is in you, whom you have received from God? 1 Corinthians 6:19

In his letter to the church in Ephesus (Revelation 2:1–7), St. John took note of a quasi-Christian sect called the Nicolaitans, which borrowed heavily from Greek philosophy and pagan cults with their fertility rites. How convenient! One could practice sexual immorality under a cloak of religion. The Nicolaitans asserted that the flesh (body), being material, was evil and should be destroyed through exhaustion.

There was a similar problem in the Corinthian church. Some would-be Christians were giving their bodies over to prostitution. Paul encouraged them to "flee from sexual immorality" (1 Corinthians 6:18). He cites a good reason: "Your body is a temple of the Holy Spirit."

Our whole make-up belongs to God. We confess God to be the Maker of heaven and earth, and therefore is also the Creator of each person's body and soul. The whole person is a gift from God. In addition, we belong to God, physically and spiritually, because Christ has redeemed us. The apostle told the Corinthians, "You are not your own; you were bought at a price" (1 Corinthians 6:19–20). Some claim to have the right to do with their bodies as they please: subject it to drugs and drinks that impair health, or practice abortion. How contrary to God's Word!

There is more. Not only do we belong to God because He made us and the Son redeemed us, but also because the Holy Spirit lives in us to enlighten us with His gifts, sanctify us, and keep us in the true faith. What a wonderful Guest to have! How important that we bid Him welcome through holy living!

PRAYER SUGGESTION

Ask the sanctifying Holy Spirit to keep your body healthy and clean.

Sin and Salvation

All have sinned and fall short of the glory of God, and are justified freely by His grace through the redemption that came by Christ Jesus. Romans 3:23–24

The Reformation began on October 31, 1517, when Martin Luther posted his Ninety-Five Theses on the door of the castle church in Wittenberg, Germany. It was long overdue.

Luther's theses reflect the two basic truths of the Law and the Gospel. Thesis 1 quoted Jesus' words calling for repentance, saying that "the whole life of believers should be one of penitence." The Gospel shines through, especially in Thesis 62: "The true treasure of the church is the holy Gospel of the glory and grace of God."

The first truth is Law, the Bible's message of the reality of sin. Through our first parents, Adam and Eve, sin has come down on all of humanity. Sin exacts death as the penalty. The call to repentance goes out because "all have sinned and fall short of the glory of God."

The next truth is Gospel, God's grace extending to all. This grace means free, unearned, and unmerited salvation: the forgiveness of sins, the promise of life eternal, and spiritual newness. Salvation by God's grace comes to us through the merits of Christ, who atoned for the sin of the world. By believing in Him as the risen Lord and Savior we become the beneficiaries of His righteousness and holiness. It is for His sake that God declares us righteous and holy. This is the doctrine of justification. It is the heart of the Gospel, the foundation on which the Christian church stands.

The triad of truths "by grace alone," "for Christ's sake alone," and "through faith alone" has a fourth dimension: *sola Scriptura*. This is to say that the Bible is the only source of what is taught in the church.

PRAYER SUGGESTION

Give thanks to God for restoring the Gospel in its purity and power.

Christians as Saints

Giving thanks to the Father, who has qualified you to share in the inheritance of the saints in the kingdom of light. Colossians 1:12

How would one define a saint? A faithful Christian who has died? Someone who willingly and tirelessly serves others in Jesus' name without thought of compensation? One youngster, thinking of figures in church windows, said "saints are people who let the light shine through." That is a good way of putting it.

Christians, even before they enter the kingdom of light in heaven, are people who let the light of the Gospel shine through in their lives. In all they say and do—and in all the evil things they leave undone—they give evidence of their commitment to God, the Father of lights. They embody the words of Jesus, "You are the light of the world" (Matthew 5:14) and the words of Paul, "You were once darkness, but now you are light in the Lord. Live as children of light (for the fruit of the light consists in all goodness, righteousness and truth)" (Ephesians 5:8–9).

How do people become saints who let the light shine through? It begins when the Holy Spirit enlightens them through the Gospel and Holy Baptism, bringing them to faith in Jesus Christ, God incarnate and their Savior. From the kingdom of darkness they have been transferred into the realm of light, serving their Lord with joy and thankfulness.

To declare Christians as bona fide saints is not to say that they are perfect. They are sinners still because of their continuing spiritual weaknesses. But sin does not rule their lives; Jesus Christ does. For His sake God declares them to be His holy people—saints—serving Him with holy works.

PRAYER SUGGESTION

Pray that God, through His Word, may continue His sanctifying work in you.

Fishing for People

"Come, follow Me," Jesus said, "and I will make you fishers of men."
Mark 1:17

The fish symbol ICHTHYS is an abbreviated confession of faith—shorthand for the Greek *Iesus Christos Theou Hyios Soter:* Jesus Christ, Son of God, Savior.

The fish symbol is particularly fitting because Jesus drew His first disciples from fishermen, from the two sets of brothers: Peter and Andrew and James and John. Further, fish were used in some of His miracles. He multiplied a simple meal of bread and fish into more than enough to feed thousands. He directed Peter to take a coin from a fish's mouth so he could pay taxes. He blessed Peter with a miraculous catch of fish, and after His resurrection He did something similar when He blessed the seven disciples on the Sea of Tiberias with a haul of 153 large fish.

As called and commissioned apostles, Peter and the others went into the world as fishers of people to let down the net of the Gospel. And they were effective. "The disciples went out and preached everywhere, and the Lord worked with them and confirmed His Word by the signs that accompanied it" (Mark 16:20).

It follows, then, that all Christians are fishers of people. We catch people for Christ, who died on a cross and rose from the tomb to save them. This is not to say that we must leave our vocations and become full-time missionaries. We are the Lord's witnesses wherever we are and in whatever we do.

The ICHTHYS symbol is a reminder that Jesus Christ is our Lord and Savior calling us to be fishers of people and "to give an answer to everyone who asks you to give the reason for the hope that you have" (1 Peter 3:15).

PRAYER SUGGESTION

Ask the Holy Spirit to help you be a witness for Christ.

The Clouds—God's Sign Language

*"When you see a cloud rising in the west, immediately you say,
'It's going to rain,' and it does." Luke 12:54*

We can read newspapers and books, but can we read the clouds?

Through the clouds, God conveys messages concerning His power, wisdom, and love. After the Great Flood had subsided, God promised Noah and his family that He would never again send a worldwide deluge. The sign of this covenant was this: "I have set My rainbow in the clouds" (Genesis 9:13). Clouds resplendent with a rainbow also remind us of God's blessing of rain.

Clouds are befitting vehicles for the King who rides in majesty, as the psalmist declared, "He makes the clouds His chariot and rides on the wings of the wind" (Psalm 104:3).

Clouds are connected with the ministry of Jesus. The prophet Daniel said, "In my vision at night I looked, and there before me was one like a son of man, coming with the clouds" (7:13). When Jesus was transfigured in the presence of Peter, James, and John, a bright cloud overshadowed them and a voice from the cloud said, "This is My Son, whom I love" (Matthew 17:5). And when Jesus had fulfilled His redemptive ministry on earth, "He was taken up before their very eyes, and a cloud hid Him from their sight" (Acts 1:9).

When troubles, like dark clouds, descend on us, we are reminded of God's promise to help us. The hymn writer Paul Gerhardt understood the message: "Entrust your days and burdens To God's most holy hand; He cares for you while ruling The sky, the sea, the land, He that in clouds and tempest Finds breakthrough for the sun Will find right pathways for you Till trav'ling days are done."

PRAYER SUGGESTION

Give thanks to God for all His blessings to you through Jesus, His dear Son.

Peter, Reed and Rock

"I tell you the truth," Jesus answered, "this very night, before the rooster crows, you will disown Me three times." Matthew 26:34

Simon Peter answered, "You are the Christ, the Son of the living God." Matthew 16:16

It is hard to be consistent. Albert Einstein, for example, was a genius in physics but failed French.

The apostle Peter was inconsistent in his relationship to Jesus. He was impetuous, restless, and unstable. His worst moment came when he denied knowing Jesus despite his boast: "Even if I have to die with You, I will never disown you" (Mark 14:31).

But Peter was also a rock, firm and solid. When Jesus asked His disciples, after hearing what others thought of Him, "Who do you say I am?" Peter answered, "You are the Christ, the Son of the living God" (Matthew 16:16). On that point Peter never wavered.

Peter was truly *Petros,* a Greek word meaning "rock." He was a rock not because of personal strength but because the faith he confessed was firmly grounded on the *petra,* the stone foundation of Christ's Word. Jesus said to him, "You are Peter (*Petros*), and on this rock (*petra*) I will build My church" (Matthew 16:18).

Peter expressed his conviction and taught about the atoning work of Jesus as the Christ: "You were redeemed … with the precious blood of Christ, a lamb without blemish or defect" (1 Peter 1:19). Like his faith, his love was firm and unwavering after the risen Christ reinstated him in his apostleship. Three times he affirmed his love for the Savior.

How can we become rock-solid in our faith? The Word of God and His means of grace will strengthen our faith in Christ and make us into "a pillar in the temple of My God" (Revelation 3:12).

PRAYER SUGGESTION

Ask the Holy Spirit to give you the strong conviction that Jesus is your Savior and Lord.

The Guest Becomes Host

A woman named Martha opened her home to Him. Luke 10:38

Some guests have ways of becoming unwelcome, perhaps by offending their hosts with bad manners or inconsiderate words and acts. But Jesus was not that kind of a guest, although Martha of Bethany may have had moments of doubt when, as a guest in her home, He told her she was wrong. "You are worried and upset about many things, but only one thing is needed" (Luke 10:41).

Martha's problem lay with her priorities. She was anxious about being a good hostess to their honored guest. But hearing the Word of Christ, as Mary had chosen to do, supersedes all other activities, laudable as they may be. In that home Jesus was the invited guest who became the spiritual host to Mary and to Martha.

Martha meant well. Providing a meal for the Master was an act of faith. Faith works by love when we serve others. The preparation of food and drink are acts of faith performed to the glory of God.

The Word is food for the soul. Nothing is more important than the daily nourishment of the Word of God. Paul told Timothy that he was "nourished on the words of the faith and of the good doctrine which you have followed" (1 Timothy 4:6 RSV). It was through Jesus Christ that God conveyed this truth: He so loved all people that He gave up His Son to be their Savior. When Christ comes into our hearts and homes, He is not only a welcome guest He is also a host who shares this Good News.

When we put God's Word first, everything else we do falls into its rightful place.

PRAYER SUGGESTION

Pray that the Lord Jesus always keeps you mindful of His Word as the greatest need.

An Invitation to Faith

[Jesus] thus revealed His glory, and His disciples put their faith in Him. John 2:11

According to legend, Roman emperor Constantine saw a glowing cross in the sky along with these words: "In This Sign You Will Conquer." After that, Constantine put a cross on his soldiers' shields, won the battle, and became a Christian.

Some people say it would take a miracle to convert them to Christianity. After all, the disciples believed *after* they saw Jesus turn water into wine. Doubtless many others came to belief after they saw Jesus feed multitudes with a few barley loaves and fish. And it is true that Jesus manifested His glory in these miracles.

It is important to realize that Jesus reveals His glory and grace when no apparent miracle accompanies our eating and drinking. We eat and drink what is bought in supermarkets, raised in gardens, or prepared in restaurants. Our own efforts and earnings have provided all this. Or so we think.

However, is not a series of divine acts of love involved? God gives rain and sunshine so crops grow, and He sustains our physical life through these means. God gives wisdom and health so we can work for our daily bread. These daily occurrences speak just as eloquently of divine providence as did Jesus' miracles.

Above all, Jesus Christ revealed His love by coming into our world to live, die, and rise from the grave that we might live. He came to be the Bread of Life and the Living Water. Having manifested His love, He invites us to believe in Him. "Whether you eat or drink or whatever you do, do it all for the glory of God" (1 Corinthians 10:31).

PRAYER SUGGESTION

Tell the heavenly Father that you believe in the grace and glory He revealed in Jesus Christ, His Son.

The Christian's Intercessors

"'Sir,' the man replied, 'leave it alone for one more year.'" Luke 13:8

"He who tends a fig tree will eat its fruit." Proverbs 27:18

Jesus told of a man who was disappointed in his fig tree because it had not born fruit for three years. The owner ordered the tree cut down. But the caretaker of the tree interceded, saying he would tend it for another year. If it still did not bear fruit, the tree would then be removed from the vineyard.

In this parable, Jesus teaches this: God had expected His people to bear the fruits of obedience and faith but such evidences of spiritual life were largely absent. Was it time, then, for the heavenly Father to disown His people? The Son of God, like the tree's caretaker, intervened. He came to this earth to preach that the kingdom of grace and forgiveness was still open to all who repent. Jesus gave His own life as a sacrifice to redeem sinners. Further, He sent out His apostles to spread the news that there still was time to repent and receive eternal life. This parable shows the degree to which Jesus went to extend the era of grace.

Jesus still intervenes for us when we are not fruitful. John wrote, "If anybody does sin, we have One who speaks to the Father in our defense—Jesus Christ, the Righteous One" (1 John 2:1). In addition, the Holy Spirit intervenes for us. Paul wrote, "The Spirit Himself intercedes for us with groans that words cannot express" (Romans 8:26). Both the Son and the Spirit give us prayer support.

"Hear me, for Thy Spirit pleads, Hear, for Jesus intercedes."

PRAYER SUGGESTION

Ask the triune God—Father, Son, and Holy Spirit—to help you become more fruitful in your life.

A Water of Wonders

I baptize you with water. But one more powerful than I will come. ...
He will baptize you with the Holy Spirit and with fire. Luke 3:16

According to an old rhyme, a chemist mistook sulfuric acid for water. Now he is "no more," for "what he thought was H_2O was H_2SO_4."

The water of Holy Baptism has also been misunderstood. For one thing, it does not work like magic, as though a baptized person will be saved even after drifting away from Christ.

Yet the water of Baptism joined to the Word does wonders. It has spiritual power because it is "included in God's command and combined with God's Word" *(Luther's Small Catechism)*. It does miracles in human hearts because the Holy Spirit works through it. It causes a sinner to be born anew, turning him into a saint, that is, one whose sins are taken away because he believes in Christ, the Sin-Bearer. It truly saves, for it is "the washing of rebirth and renewal by the Holy Spirit" (Titus 3:5).

The sacramental water does even more. It makes of baptized, believing persons bearers of the fruit of the Spirit: love, joy, peace, patience, kindness, goodness, faithfulness, gentleness, and self-control. The Christian living as such is "like a tree planted by streams of water, which yields its fruit in season" (Psalm 1:3).

And the church, the communion of saints—your congregation—is an orchard of fruit-bearing trees because the water of Holy Baptism flows through it!

The sacramental water, the visible symbol of Holy Baptism, is not to be mistaken or substituted lest, in a spiritual way, the error of the chemist be repeated.

PRAYER SUGGESTION

Complete this sentence: Lord Jesus, You instituted Holy Baptism so through it I am enabled to _____ .

The Call to Certainty

"Stop doubting and believe." John 20:27

Peter Marshall, a former chaplain of the United States Senate, offered this prayer: "Give us clear vision, that we may know where to stand and what to stand for, because unless we stand for something, we shall fall for anything." Doubt is often responsible for procrastination and other hindrances to confident action. Doubt is to faith as rust is to steel.

The psalmist momentarily doubted God's goodness to him when he "saw the prosperity of the wicked" (Psalm 73:3). And the father of a demon-possessed child confessed his uncertainty: "I do believe, help me overcome my unbelief" (Mark 9:24). Doubt often shakes our confidence when we pray, so Paul advised his readers to "lift up holy hands in prayer, without anger or disputing" (1 Timothy 2:8).

Doubt and outright denial are part of the Easter account. At a mountaintop meeting in Galilee the disciples worshiped the resurrected Christ, "but some doubted" (Matthew 28:17). Thomas was especially afflicted. Weighed down with grief, he said, "Unless I see the nail marks in His hands and put my finger where the nails were, and put my hand into His side, I will not believe it" (John 20:25). To lay down a condition ("unless") is a declaration of unbelief. To predicate belief on a sight test and a touch test is to leave out faith altogether.

The risen Lord changed Thomas's heart by ministering to him. He did more than say, "doubt your doubts." Jesus told Thomas to let go of his doubts completely and to believe. He added—for the sake of all of us—"Blessed are those who have not seen and yet have believed" (John 20:29).

PRAYER SUGGESTION

Pray that the risen Christ may strengthen your faith in Him.

Fulfilling Our Calling

[Jesus] said to Simon, "Put out into deep water, and let down the nets for a catch." Luke 5:4

Martin Luther was born on this date in 1483, earned a Master of Arts degree in 1505, and was ordained an Augustinian priest two years later.

In recent years, more men are "second-career seminarians," that is they enter seminary later in life after having been in the workforce for some time. In a way, they are following the precedent set when Jesus summoned men from secular work to begin a three-year training for the apostleship.

Two sets of brothers—Peter and Andrew and James and John—were fishermen, following in their family's business. Jesus recruited them for a new vocation when He said, "Come, follow Me ... and I will make you fishers of men" (Matthew 4:19). After Christ's ascension and the outpouring of the Holy Spirit 10 days later, the apostles were full-time missionaries. Their calling now was as Christ's witnesses in all the world. They testified that salvation from sin, death, and the devil is found only in the crucified and risen Lord. The Gospel was the net they used to catch people for Christ.

Most of Christ's followers in our time continue in their roles as fishermen, farmers, accountants, salesmen, teachers, software developers, housewives, and so forth. They fulfill their calling through their occupations, serving one another and being Christ's witnesses where they live and work day by day. They are followers of Jesus, serving Him by serving others. And as such, they are doing their part to help build the kingdom of Christ.

PRAYER SUGGESTION

Express your thankfulness to Christ for giving you a place in His kingdom and many opportunities to serve Him.

The God of Peace

He makes wars cease to the ends of the earth. Psalm 46:9

What is the relation of God to the wars we wage? According the psalmist, He makes them stop. He could, of course, intervene directly by destroying the weaponry. But for the most part, God acts through governments. He guides the hearts and minds of the world's rulers so peace prevails. The world's warlords can, for a while at least, resist the will of God and follow their own course. But in the end God's will is done.

It is impossible to imagine what our world would be like if the God of peace abandoned it. Peace in the land and peace between lands is assured if first there is peace with God in the human heart. God sent His Son to earth to bring peace and reconciliation to individuals in their relation to Him.

Estrangement from God and hostility among people exist because of sin. This condition would continue if God had not restored peace. He did more than declare an armistice or cease-fire without resolution to the conflict. He made His Son to be sin for us and to atone for it, thus removing the offenses. The world was reconciled through the death and resurrection of Jesus in our behalf.

Where Christ, the Peacemaker, rules in people's hearts, there are outward expressions of it: peace in the home, peace in the community, and peace between the nations of the world.

Today, Veterans' Day, we honor all men and women who served their country in the armed forces. We thank God for them, for our country. "Blessed are the peacemakers, for they will be called sons of God" (Matthew 5:9).

PRAYER SUGGESTION

Ask for God's guidance to become a peacemaker for Jesus' sake.

Why Christ Came

When the time had fully come, God sent His Son, born of a woman, born under law, to redeem those under law, that we might receive the full rights of sons. Galatians 4:4–5

With the firing of a pistol, the United States government opened a new territory in Oklahoma for settlement. People on horseback and in wagons waited along the starting line for the gunshot that would signal the rush to stake their claims. But some "jumped the gun" and raced off too soon. They were known as "Sooners."

Did Christ come at the right time or was He a sooner? In Gadara Jesus was about to drive demons out of two possessed men. The evil spirits cried out, "What do you want with us, Son of God? ... Have you come here to torture us before the appointed time?" (Matthew 8:29). They, in effect, called Him a sooner.

But, no, the incarnate Son of God did not come too soon. He came at the fullness of the time, at the precise moment appointed by God for His Son to enter our world. Just as He came at the right time, so He came with the right intent. Jesus said, "God did not send His Son into the world to condemn the world, but to save the world" (John 3:17).

In writing to the Galatians, the apostle Paul made it very clear why Christ came. He came as one under the Law to fulfill all its demands with His perfect obedience and to bear the penalty for our disobedience. The outcome is that we are released from bondage to Old Testament law. No longer slaves, we have become the children of God and heirs of eternal life.

PRAYER SUGGESTION

Thank the heavenly Father for including you in all the privileges of being His child in Christ Jesus.

Duel in the Desert

Then Jesus was led by the Spirit into the desert to be tempted by the devil. Matthew 4:1

Duels were usually fought in out-of-the-way places like forests and fields and even islands. It can be said that in the desert, amid the barren, bleak rocks and sand, Satan engaged Jesus in a spiritual duel.

In his temptation the devil appeals to human desires for food and drink, for honor and power. He is an opportunist. With Jesus committing Himself to a 40-day fast, He would be hungry. So the devil said, "If You are the Son of God, tell these stones to become bread" (Matthew 4:3).

Through Moses, God had said that man does not live by bread alone, but, having an immortal soul, he lives by the Word of God (Deuteronomy 8:3). Satan wanted Jesus to deny this truth when he tempted Him with bodily bread. Satan wants disobedience and doubt to occur in matters where God has clearly spoken. The heavenly Father clearly identified Jesus as His Son at His baptism (Matthew 3:17). This is what Satan called into doubt by saying, "If You are the Son of God" (Matthew 4:3).

Jesus, in all respects our Substitute, was subjected to temptations for evil. What Satan did not reckon for was the fact that Jesus was holy and therefore would not succumb. Our Lord held fast to God's Word. That is also how we can defeat the devil when he engages us in spiritual duels.

This was not Jesus' last encounter with His prime opponent. "When the devil had finished all this tempting, he left Him until an opportune time" (Luke 4:13). The final showdown came in the encounter on the cross. We thank God that Jesus triumphed totally then too.

PRAYER SUGGESTION

Ask God to grant you steadfastness when Satan comes to tempt you.

Falsehood and Truth Personified

"When [the devil] lies, he speaks his native language, for he is a liar and the father of lies. ... Yet because I tell the truth, you do not believe Me!" John 8:44–45

A manufacturer was accused of Satanism because its trademark shows 13 stars and a moon with a human face, said to be satanic symbols. The company explained: the stars symbolize the 13 colonies and the moon with a face was a popular design in the 1800s when the trademark was adopted.

Things are not always what they seem. Sometimes lies are implied by taking words out of context. Jesus was accused of blasphemy when He said He would destroy the temple (Matthew 26:61). In fact, Jesus was referring to the temple of His body, which would rise again on the third day.

The master liar is Satan. He spreads falsehoods in many ways. When he tempted Jesus in the desert, he showed Him "all the kingdoms of the world and their splendor" (Matthew 4:8). Satan added a lie when he said he would give it all to Him if He fell down and worshiped Him. Satan is falsehood personified. St. Paul warned the Corinthians about "false apostles, deceitful workmen, masquerading as apostles of Christ. And no wonder, for Satan himself masquerades as an angel of light" (2 Corinthians 11:13–14).

In contrast, Jesus not only proclaims the truth, He personified it: "I am the Way the Truth and the Life. No one comes to the Father except through Me" (John 14:6). Jesus spoke the truth, lived the truth, and died for the truth—the truth that He opened the way to heaven for us by making full restitution for our sins and making us God's children and heirs of eternal life.

PRAYER SUGGESTION

Pledge your loyalty to Jesus Christ, who is the Truth.

God's Eye Is on Us

"Don't be afraid; you are worth more than many sparrows." Luke 12:7

How do troubles affect you? Do you feel "cumbered with a load of care"? Do you feel as though you carry the weight of the world on your shoulders? The psalmist said he felt like "a bird alone on a roof" (Psalm 102:7).

The poet speaks of God having His "eye on the sparrow," and that is true. Jesus declares, "Are not two sparrows sold for a penny? Yet not one of them will fall to the ground apart from the will of your Father" (Matthew 10:29). The lesson to be drawn pertains to our reliance on the providence of God. If His care extends to sparrows that have little value, then certainly His children have total coverage.

Paul and Barnabas told a crowd in Lystra, "[God] has shown kindness by giving you rain from heaven and crops in their seasons, ... and fills your hearts with joy" (Acts 14:17). God provides through the laws of nature and by giving us the ability to work. If someone were to say he is not worthy of a place in God's house, too sinful to have a share in God's forgiving love in Christ, the psalmist would reply, "Even the sparrow has found a home, ... a place near Your altar, O Lord Almighty" (84:3).

We are under the umbrella of God's grace. All people are sinners, but Jesus Christ deemed them worth dying for so they might have forgiveness, peace, eternal life. The Holy Spirit has sanctified the believers, making their bodies His temple. Yes, in a total sense, God's eye is on His people.

PRAYER SUGGESTION

Give thanks to God for bodily blessings and for His saving grace in Christ Jesus.

Women who Serve

These women were helping to support them out of their own means.
Luke 8:3

There were practical matters to attend to. Jesus, the disciples, and others who followed them needed food and accommodations. How did they meet expenses? We know they had a treasury over which Judas Iscariot presided. When Jesus rested at Jacob's well, the disciples were in the village buying food. When the apostles were on preaching and healing missions, they received room and board from willing hosts.

At times, Jesus and His group were in Jerusalem for religious festivals. Where did they stay and what arrangements did they make for meals? On occasion Jesus was a guest in the home of Martha, Mary, and Lazarus in nearby Bethany. But what about the others?

Undoubtedly attending to the practical side of Jesus' ministry were the pious women mentioned in the reading for today: Mary Magdalene, Joanna, Susanna, and "many others," as Luke added. And certainly among them was Salome, the mother of James and John and wife of Zebedee. They were women of means and economic know-how. These women likely assisted Jesus in the care of the sick and in other aspects of His ministry.

Our Lord did not appoint women as apostles but He certainly welcomed—and created opportunities for—their services. They were the last to leave His cross on Good Friday and the first at His empty tomb on Easter morning. In the ministry of Jesus to us, and in our ministry to Him as Christians, no one is excluded. As Paul clearly stated, "You are all one in Christ Jesus" (Galatians 3:28).

PRAYER SUGGESTION

Thank the Lord Jesus for giving you a place in His kingdom with opportunities to serve Him.

Jesus, Our Benefactor and Friend

"Greater love has no one than this, that he lay down his life for his friends." John 15:13

The hymn of simple faith, "What a Friend We Have in Jesus," is loved by many. President Eisenhower called it his favorite. And when Chiang Kai-shek of Taiwan passed away in 1975, a brass band played it in the funeral procession.

We can claim Jesus as a Friend because He first befriended us. He laid down His life for His friends—and for His enemies as well. "God demonstrates His own love for us in this: While we were still sinners, Christ died for us. Since we have now been justified by His blood, how much more shall we be saved from God's wrath through Him! For if, when we were God's enemies, we were reconciled to Him through the death of His Son, how much more, having been reconciled, shall we be saved through His life!" (Romans 5:8–10). And another: "Christ died for our sins once for all, the righteous for the unrighteous, to bring you to God" (1 Peter 3:18).

The love and honor Jesus imparts to us prompts and enables us to exclaim in return: What a Friend we have in Jesus! He bore all our sins and will likewise help us endure our sorrows. We are privileged to call Him our Friend, love Him, serve Him and confidently take everything to Him in prayer.

Jesus Himself explains our willing action when we regard Him as our Friend: We will do His will and carry out His command—We will love one another. He adds, "Then the Father will give you whatever you ask in My name" (John 15:16).

PRAYER SUGGESTION

Tell the Lord Jesus in your own words why you regard Him your Friend.

One Person Can Make the Difference

"I am the only one left." 1 Kings 19:10

You've heard it said that one person can make a difference. In Israel during Elijah's time, the majority of people had turned to idolatry, although some 7,000 Israelites chose not to worship Baal. Elijah remained true to the faith and he prevailed.

Daniel did not give in to pressure, even the threat of death. He stood strong in his faith and he was preserved (Daniel 6).

Many years later, the apostle Paul was in a similar situation: "everyone in the province of Asia has deserted me" (2 Timothy 1:15). Yet this one man, in life and in death, remained steadfast in the faith he confessed and in the Gospel of Christ's redemption he proclaimed. It made all the difference in the world.

Elijah's words, "I am the only one left," are not a declaration of defeat; they are more than a complaint. They express his continuing loyalty to the Lord despite extremely adverse circumstances. Satan could not win the battle so long as one faithful prophet remained on the scene.

Through one steadfast witness God can turn things around. He can make it clear that amid human frailty He can manifest His strength. What God did in the past through faithful Elijah, through Daniel who dared to stand alone, through the courageous ministry of Paul, He can do today when one person stands up for the truth of God's Word. President Andrew Jackson said, "One man with courage makes a majority." This is also true also in Christ's church.

PRAYER SUGGESTION

Ask the Lord to give you the courage and strength to confess your faith, even if you are the only one to do so.

If the Moon Could Speak

Praise Him, sun and moon, praise Him, all you shining stars.
Psalm 148:3

In a way, the moon is an advertisement as it turns our attention to the eternal Creator. Along with God's other works in nature, it underscores the wisdom, forethought, power, and love of its Maker. If it could speak, it would tell us to praise God.

In our time we have seen men walking on the surface of the moon. It took great technical skill to put them there, but scientists can do no more than investigate what is there. How much greater is the wisdom of God, who made the moon in the first place and gave it its function.

"The moon marks off the seasons" (Psalm 104:19). Marking the seasons was important in the Old Testament when much of life was exercised according to nature's calendars. In one passage the Lord said, "On the first day of the seventh month, you shall have a day of rest, a sacred assembly commemorated with trumpet blasts" (Leviticus 23:24).

The setting of Old Testament holy days and festivals in keeping with the moon's schedule reminds us of St. Paul's words to the early Christians, "Do not let anyone judge you ... with regard to a religious festival, a New Moon celebration or a Sabbath Day. These are a shadow of the things that were to come; the reality, however, is found in Christ" (Colossians 2:16–17). Now that Christ has come and fulfilled His work of redeeming us from sin, we worship God in spirit and in truth and are no longer bound to sacrifices, types, and shadows of things to come.

PRAYER SUGGESTION

Praise God for His marvelous works, especially for granting you salvation in Christ.

Rediscovering What Was Forgotten

"The Counselor, the Holy Spirit, whom the Father will send in My name, will teach you all things and will remind you of everything I have said to you." John 14:26

Fashions often go in cycles. Old dress modes are revived and offered as new. This may have prompted the fashion designer to say to Marie Antoinette, the queen during the French Revolution, "There is nothing new except what is forgotten."

It is human to forget and then to rediscover. Jesus knew that the minds and memories of His disciples were often like a sieve. Their inability to retain what He taught is evident from the gospel accounts. For example, Jesus had clearly declared that His kingdom was not political but spiritual, that it consisted in the forgiveness of sins, thanks to the giving of His life as the sinners' ransom. Yet at the time of His ascension the disciples were still asking, "Lord, are You at this time going to restore the kingdom to Israel?" (Acts 1:6). Another instance, no people were more surprised at Jesus' resurrection than the disciples. They had forgotten His promise that He would rise on the third day.

Christ had a remedy for the apostles' forgetfulness: He sent the Holy Spirit to renew His teaching with life, power, and spiritual fire. The effect on the apostles was new insight into divine revelation. On the basis of remembered truths the Spirit would correct misconceptions, teach, guide, enlighten, and energize.

How are our memories? We have forgotten many things our instructors once taught us. But thanks be to God we have a higher Instructor, the Holy Spirit, who through the Word we read and study brings things back. In some instances our new insights may seem like a fresh revelation of truths.

PRAYER SUGGESTION

Pray that the Holy Spirit may bring you the word and work of Christ.

Surprises

"Make every effort to enter through the narrow door." Luke 13:24

Some have found Jesus' words in today's verse surprising. They expected Him, as one who recruited people for discipleship, to lower the bar and make Christianity easy. Should He not stand at the entrance of His kingdom and say, "Come right in and be comfortable. No great effort is required of you to be a Christian." Some would expect Jesus, the Lord of love, to say, "Come to Me anytime—whenever you feel like it. My door is always open."

But the Savior does not say He is always at our beck and call, as though it makes no difference whether we come to Him today, tomorrow, or any other day. Those who spurn His grace, assuming they can come to Him on their own terms and in their own time, will hear Him say, "I don't know you."

A third surprise is that the ones to be seated at the table of Christ's grace are not necessarily the "logical" ones—those who take their salvation for granted because of their long-standing membership in the visible church. If they lack faith and love, they will be on the outside looking in while strangers will be welcomed because they believed in Jesus as their Savior.

If what Jesus said in this portion of Luke's Gospel seems harsh, we should bear in mind that He is speaking to hard-hearted people. When we read on in Scripture, we will find that the Lord's words of warning take nothing away from His promise of salvation to those who look to Him for salvation. To them He says, "Come to Me, all you who are weary and burdened, and I will give you rest" (Matthew 11:28).

PRAYER SUGGESTION

Tell the Lord Jesus that you are coming to Him in faith, for He is your Savior.

God, Our Highest Good

Give thanks to Him and praise His name. For the LORD is good and His love endures forever. Psalm 100:4–5

As Christians we are thankful to God at all times. We receive His blessings every day: food, clothing, shelter. God grants us gifts for good citizenship and government to maintain order. Beyond civic considerations, God grants spiritual blessings, notably His acceptance of us as His children and heirs of eternal life.

The greatest basis for our thankfulness is God's giving of Himself to us. He is our Highest Good, the Fount and Source of all goodness, past, present, and future.

First, God for Jesus' sake grants us *pardon for the past*. We need not worry about our past sins. What is past is not only past, it is also forgiven. In true repentance, we can lay all our sins on Jesus, the Sin-Bearer, who carried them all to the cross and left them there.

Second, God is good because He imparts *power for the present*. God's power is mediated and perfected in us through the Gospel, enabling us to meet the spiritual challenges of today. Scripture assures us that we are kept by the power of God through faith unto salvation. God's power makes solid rocks of those who by nature are like reeds shaken by the wind.

Third, God is our Highest Good because of His *promise for the future*. Through Jesus Christ, His Son, God promises to be with us always, "to the very end of the age" (Matthew 28:20). God's promise of forgiveness and His sustaining grace, mediated through His Word and Sacraments, are "for you and your children" (Acts 2:39), as Peter declared in his Pentecost sermon.

Here we have three good reasons to be thankful to God, our Highest Good.

PRAYER SUGGESTION

Give thanks to God for all His gifts, especially for the gift of His Son.

Gratitude for God's Grace

Although they knew God, they neither glorified Him as God nor gave thanks to Him. ... Therefore God gave them over in the sinful desires of their hearts. Romans 1:21, 24

People throughout the world erect statues to show gratitude to their heroes. For example, in Sarajevo, Bosnia, a statue of Gavrilo Princip was erected for what he did June 28, 1914, when he assassinated Archduke Francis Ferdinand of Austria-Hungary and his wife, an act that launched World War I.

To go a step farther, people show their gratitude to false gods by erecting temples and graven images in their honor. Paul dwells on the terrible price of commitment to idols. He wrote that the heathen, despite their knowledge of God, "exchanged the glory of the immortal God for images made to look like mortal man and birds and animals and reptiles" (Romans 1:23). In divine judgment God gave them over to folly and sexual immorality. Abandonment by God is the worst form of punishment. When the knowledge of God moves out, the depravity of human nature moves in.

The Holy Scriptures were written for our learning. They teach us, who know the true God, to give Him thanks for all His blessings, especially for the revelation of His truth and grace in His Son, whom He raised from the dead as our Savior. This good news is revealed in the Gospel, which Jesus wants preached everywhere and which the apostle called "the power of God for the salvation of everyone who believes" (Romans 1:16).

Unbelief, plus ingratitude, has its terrible price—rejection by God—but faith in and through the Gospel brings the blessings of God's grace: forgiveness, peace, and eternal life.

PRAYER SUGGESTION

Give thanks to God for all His benefits to you, especially for the gift of His Son as your Savior.

The Lesson of a Fig Tree

Now learn this lesson from the fig tree: As soon as its twigs get tender and its leaves come out, you know that summer is near. Matthew 24:32

At the beginning of the Old Testament, Adam and Eve make coverings for their nakedness from fig leaves (Genesis 3:7). As the New Testament opens, we find Jesus referring to fig trees when He recruits disciples. When Nathanael was introduced to Jesus, he was not a total stranger, for the Lord said, "I saw you while you were still under the fig tree before Philip called you" (John 1:48).

Jesus taught many things about the kingdom of God. On occasion He used fig trees as illustrations. In the text for today, for example, Jesus said that a fig tree announces the nearing of summer by budding twigs and leaves. In the same way, said Jesus, there are signs that announce His Second Coming in glory.

At another time Jesus spoke of an orchard owner who wanted a fig tree cut down because for three years it had borne no fruit. But the servant pleaded for the tree, wanting it to have another chance to prove its worth. The lesson is that Jesus in heaven intercedes for erring people. The Father extends the time of grace to sinners, hoping that they will repent and believe in Christ as their Savior.

On a fig tree the fruit appears before the leaves; if a tree has foliage but no figs, it is a good sign it is barren. Important truths about salvation parallel this. People cannot plead foliage when figs are missing. They cannot cover sinfulness with patched-together attire, as Adam and Eve tried to do. They can stand before a holy God only when they are dressed in the robe of righteousness. That robe is theirs by faith in Christ's merit and mediation.

PRAYER SUGGESTION

Ask the Lord Jesus to grant you stronger faith so you may be clothed with His righteousness.

Thankfulness—a Surprise?

Jesus asked, "Were not all ten cleansed? Where are the other nine?"
Luke 17:17

Sometimes a person's thank-you comes as a surprise. An old joke goes, "A man gave a woman his seat on a bus. She fainted. When she came to, she thanked him, and he fainted."

We might be surprised that of the 10 lepers Jesus healed, only one returned to thank Him. That grateful one was a Samaritan, a member of a deprived race. "Where are the other nine?" Jesus asked. In the excitement of their healing they may have hurried home to families and friends, quite forgetful of Jesus, their Benefactor.

Ingratitude, at its various levels, is a common human failing. We ourselves must plead guilty of it. It is easy to take things for granted, not realizing that all blessings flow from God—food, clothing, home, and the like. It is God who provides all our possessions by giving us health and strength to work. The prophet Isaiah voices the Lord's complaint at Israel's thoughtlessness: "The ox knows his master, the donkey his owner's manger, but Israel does not know, My people do not understand" (Isaiah 1:3).

Thanksgiving pleases God and lifts up our own hearts and minds. With thanksgiving goes praise to God in recognition of His goodness. This awareness moves our hearts, adding joy to our gratitude.

We have so much to be thankful for, especially God's giving of His Son, Jesus Christ. St. Paul said it well: "In Him we have redemption through His blood, the forgiveness of sins, in accordance with the riches of God's grace that He lavished on us with all wisdom and understanding" (Ephesians 1:7–8). We have good reason to sing, "Come, you faithful people, come."

PRAYER SUGGESTION

Count your blessings; then thank God for them.

Reason to Celebrate

"There is rejoicing in the presence of the angels of God over one sinner who repents." Luke 15:10

Some years ago, after 26 lives were lost in a mine explosion in southeast Kentucky, safety measures were taken, causing the price of coal to rise. But this was taken in stride. One man said, "If it saves one man's life, it is well worth it."

Jesus, at various times, stressed the worth of a human being. In Luke 15 He tells three parables about the recovery of lost people through repentance. He describes the joy of finding a lost sheep, a lost coin, and a lost son. There were great celebrations in each case.

To celebrate means to rejoice over an event—a birthday, a wedding, a victory, some good fortune. The repentance of one human being touches off joyful celebrations among the angels in heaven. Of course, they rejoice also over the others who remain true to their Savior. They are happy over their faithfulness, spiritual growth, continuance in the flock to which the Good Shepherd ministers. But there is also joy—exceedingly great joy—over one sinner who returns to Christ.

This great joy is touched off because a confessed sinner has become a declared saint. That one person—his soul, his life—is worth more than all the material wealth of the world. It means the reinstatement of a person for whose redemption Jesus Christ shed His precious blood.

If a sinner's repentance causes great joy in heaven, we on earth can rejoice too, and work all the more at bringing straying sheep back into Christ's fold.

PRAYER SUGGESTION

Ask the Lord to bring a straying sinner to your attention so you may pray for him and show your Christian concern and love.

A Humility That Exalts

"Everyone who exalts himself will be humbled, and he who humbles himself will be exalted." Luke 14:11

A country tale has it that a squire boasted that he walked with his head high because he wanted to stand tall before the Lord. His neighbor, a simple farmer, said that in a wheat field the stalks that stand tall are the ones with empty heads.

A guest in the home of a Pharisee, Jesus noted how the guests sought places of honor for themselves. "When you are invited, take the lowest place, so that when your host comes, he will say to you, 'Friend, move up to a better place.' Then you will be honored in the presence of all your fellow guests" (Luke 14:10).

A comparable situation in our time would be an official dinner for government leaders where guests are seated by rank. It would be folly and infringement on protocol for someone to occupy a high place by his own choice. He would run the risk of being demoted and lose face with the assembly.

Our Lord's concern is not table manners but the virtue underlying good behavior: humility. Pride displayed among people is often a symptom of pride before God. In great arrogance a Pharisee prayed, "God, I thank You that I am not like other men. ... I fast twice a week and give a tenth of all I get" (Luke 18:11–12).

Before God none can be declared righteous on the basis of good works or character. We are acceptable to God only if we are stripped of our own righteousness and are by faith adorned with the merit purchased with Christ's blood. Trust in Jesus Christ makes for true humility—the kind that exalts, the kind that enables us to stand before God.

PRAYER SUGGESTION

Ask the Lord Jesus to keep you from both false pride and false humility by enabling you to follow His example.

God: Majestic and Merciful

[God] rides on the heavens to help you and on the clouds in His majesty. Deuteronomy 33:26

The sky often appears to be a firmament, a dome over the earth green with grass and bedecked with colorful flowers, shrubs, and trees. Everywhere we see evidences of the Creator's sense of beauty.

The might and majesty of God come to our rescue, as Moses declared, "There is no one like the God of Jeshurun [poetic term for the nation of Israel] who rides on the heavens to help you. ... The eternal God is your refuge" (Deuteronomy 33:26–27).

People who live in wide, open spaces have skills uncultivated by city dwellers, such as the art of "reading the sky." They see messages there about the weather. In the day they can tell the approximate time by looking at the sun; at night they can determine their whereabouts by looking at the polestar.

What spiritual "read out" is available to us from the sky above? The blue reminds us of the faithfulness of God, whose "words are trustworthy and true" (Revelation 21:5). The heavens declare to all, "The Word of the LORD is right and true; He is faithful in all He does" (Psalm 33:4).

It is especially in Jesus Christ, God's Son and our Savior, that all divine promises find their yes and amen. Through faith in Him, all our sins are taken away; the guilt is erased; the fear of death is removed. And over us is stretched the blue, sunlit sky of peace with God in Christ, our Advent King. We sing, "The cloudless Sun of joy He is, Who brings us pure delight and bliss, We praise Thee, Spirit, now, Our Comforter art Thou."

PRAYER SUGGESTION

Thank God for revealing His mercy in Christ, our Savior.

The Priceless Pearl

"The kingdom of heaven is like a merchant looking for fine pearls."
Matthew 13:45

God moves in various ways to perform His wonders. Sun, moon, and stars are "the work of Your fingers" (Psalm 8:3). But the pearls God does not fashion directly; He does it through oysters. More mysteriously still, He does it through an irritant—a grain of sand the oyster coats with a secretion that hardens into a pearl. This is almost a parable: God sometimes sends us irritants that turn into blessings.

In *The Pearl,* John Steinbeck wrote about a pearl diver, very poor, who found a large pearl, truly "the Pearl of the World." The man thought his poverty would turn into riches, but it brought him and his family only misery. In the end he threw the treasure back into the sea. Earthly wealth does not guarantee happiness.

The merchant in Jesus' parable likewise sought "fine pearls." One day he found one of great value. He converted all his assets into ready cash so he could buy this perfect pearl. In His parable Jesus teaches that the kingdom of heaven, with all its spiritual treasures— amazing grace, forgiveness, peace with God, the promise of eternal life—is like such a pearl. It is more precious than anything else we may acquire, including the promise of wealth in the pearl found by Steinbeck's diver. Remarkably, it is not acquired by any kind of a purchasing price but only by faith in the redeeming merit of Jesus Christ.

The pearl of salvation is a treasure to be retained at all costs, for nothing can compare with it, nothing can replace it. "Jesus, You are mine forever; Never suffer me to stray, Let me in my weakness never Cast my priceless pearl away."

PRAYER SUGGESTION

In your prayer, repeat in your own words what the poet said above.

The Rock of Our Salvation

Lead me to the rock that is higher than I. For You have been my refuge. Psalm 61:2–3

Bible lands are full of rocks and stones, boulders and pebbles. Consequently we find many references to them in Scripture. Rocks that are higher than people offer shade and protection against the burning desert sun. They are a shield against sandstorms. They are a fortress against the foe. God, "our refuge and strength" (Psalm 46:1) is like a sheltering rock.

Sometimes rocks represent solid footing. We need God's help when we are caught in a slippery mire or in quicksand. The believer is confident that God "will hide me in the shelter of His tabernacle and set me high upon a rock" (Psalm 27:5). Again, this testimony of the psalmist: "He lifted me out of the slimy pit, out of the mud and mire; He set my feet on a rock and gave me a firm place to stand" (Psalm 40:2).

In a very specific sense, Jesus Christ is the Rock of our salvation, the chief Cornerstone of His church. God's New Testament people are "built on the foundation of the apostles and prophets, with Christ Jesus Himself as the chief cornerstone" (Ephesians 2:20).

Christ became the rock foundation of the church when He gave His life as a sacrifice for the world's sin and, in demonstration of His victory, rose from the dead. Now the church's one foundation, much higher than any foundation man could lay, is none other than Christ, her Lord. Now all Christians wandering through the desert of this world have a Rock, higher than they, to guide and guard them. They have Jesus Christ as Lord and Savior who comes to us in His Word.

PRAYER SUGGESTION

As a closing prayer read the hymn "Rock of Ages."

The Tree of Life

"Behold, I am coming soon! ... Blessed are those who wash their robes, that they may have the right to the tree of life and may go through the gates into the city." Revelation 22:12, 14

The age-old testimony of the murmuring pines and the hemlocks of Nova Scotia and California's giant sequoias is this: "The hand that made us is divine." Trees join the rest of the universe in declaring the glory of God.

Trees enter the Bible accounts of man's sin and God's grace. In Revelation John refers to the tree of life in the heavenly paradise, references to the Garden of Eden where the tree of life stood. There was also the tree of death—the tree of the knowledge of good and evil. Tempted by Satan, Adam and Eve ate of this tree's fruit, and by this act of disobedience the world fell into sin and death.

But the Bible tells another tree story. "On the tree of the cross You gave salvation to mankind that, whence death arose, thence life also might rise again and that he who by a tree once overcame [Satan] likewise by a tree might be overcome, through Jesus Christ our Lord."

In Palestine a tree yielded wood from which a rough cross was formed. On it our beloved Savior fashioned our eternal salvation. Those who believe that Christ's shed blood cleanses them from all sin have access to the tree of life in heavenly Jerusalem.

"Behold, I am coming soon!" Jesus' coming marks the opening of the gates to heavenly Jerusalem where the tree of eternal life stands. The coming of Jesus to be our Savior, His continual coming through the Gospel and the Sacraments, and His Second Coming are the great themes of the Advent season.

PRAYER SUGGESTION

Ask the Holy Spirit to make you a tree that bears much fruit of the Spirit.

Signs of Christ's Coming

"Tell us," [the disciples] said, ... "What will be the sign of Your coming and of the end of the age?" Matthew 24:3

Many events are preceded by signs. Severe weather, for example, is often forecast and preceded by warnings.

The coming of Christ on the Last Day for the judgment of all mankind and the joyful homecoming of Christians likewise has preceding signs. The disciples wanted to know what these signs were, so Jesus explained them. We note that the signs foretell the destruction of Jerusalem and its temple, and the end of the world. We note also, since Christ has not yet come, that the signs are still in effect.

One sign is the coming of more false prophets and false "christs" claiming to be the "saviors" of a deeply perplexed people. The Savior bids us to look around us—our world is not one of peace but of warfare as nations rise against nations. As is always the case, wars bring about famines, pestilences, the uprooting of populations, and the loosening of social and moral foundations.

Signs will appear also in God's created world—signs of sun, moon, and stars, earthquakes, the "roaring and tossing of the sea" (Luke 21:25). As for people, they will be perplexed, fearful, confused, and prone to magnify trivia and to neglect important truths of life.

In the end, said Jesus, "the sign of the Son of Man will appear in the sky" (Matthew 24:30). This is the important event itself as our Lord comes in glory to gather the elect and take them with Him to heaven. He will come again for the consummation of our salvation, as St. Paul wrote, "He who began a good work in you will carry it on to completion until the day of Christ Jesus" (Philippians 1:6).

PRAYER SUGGESTION

Ask Jesus to fill you with joy at the prospect of His return.

Advent Witnesses

In the past God spoke to our forefathers through the prophets at many times and in various ways. Hebrews 1:1

Two witnesses of the advent of the Messiah were Isaac and John the Baptist. They had several things in common. Both were born of aged parents. God clearly foretold the birth of each. To Abraham God had promised a son who would continue his line from which the Savior would come. To Zechariah God's angel said, "Your wife Elizabeth will bear you a son, and you are to give him the name John" (Luke 1:13).

Above all, both Isaac and John stood close to the coming Christ. God speaking through them is renewing the promise of the woman's Seed. One of the "various ways" God spoke in Old Testament times was through types. Isaac prefigured Christ in that he was led to a mount to be sacrificed, carrying the wood on which he was to be offered. Jesus was taken to another mount, carrying the wooden cross on which He was offered. Isaac was spared. But Abraham believed that "God could raise the dead, and *figuratively* speaking, he did receive Isaac back from death" (Hebrews 11:19). God's Son *literally* came back from the dead.

John the Baptist witnessed to Christ in precise words: "Look, the Lamb of God, who takes away the sin of the world!" (John 1:24). John urged multitudes to repent, believe, and be baptized. Jesus said of him: "Among those born of women there is no one greater than John" (Luke 7:28). Jesus certified him as the foretold messenger who was to prepare the way for the coming Messiah.

God speaks to us still through Isaac and John. And "in these last days He has spoken to us by His Son" (Hebrews 1:2).

PRAYER SUGGESTION

Tell God you are taking to heart what His spokesmen have said concerning Jesus, your Savior.

David and Jesus

The crowds that went ahead of Him and those that followed shouted, "Hosanna to the Son of David!" Matthew 21:9

David and Jesus have much in common. Both were born in Bethlehem. Both Mary and Joseph "belonged to the house and line of David" (Luke 2:4). Jesus, on His mother's side, was a descendant of a mortal king.

David had been a great king. Under him the 12 tribes were united. He was called "the man exalted by the Most High, the man anointed by the God of Jacob, Israel's singer of songs" (2 Samuel 23:1). God spoke through him as the foremost psalmist, especially as he prophesied of the coming Messiah.

A descendant of King David, Jesus was often called the "Son of David," a Messianic title. On one occasion, after Jesus had healed a demon-possessed man, the people asked tentatively, "Could this be the Son of David?" (Matthew 12:23). Toward the end of Jesus' ministry it was no longer a question but a fact in the minds of many. At our Lord's entry into Jerusalem, the multitude sang "Hosanna to the Son of David." Some hoped that Jesus, like King David, would establish a political kingdom.

Of course, Jesus was not only David's Son but also his Lord. Jesus brought this out in an exchange with the Pharisees: in the opening words of Psalm 110, David called Him his Lord.

Jesus, the Son of David, was divine—God's Son—while King David was human. Despite the similarities, the difference was great. Peter testified to this in his Pentecost sermon. He referred to David's tomb, then still present in Jerusalem. But Jesus left no tomb. When He had completed His work on earth, He rose triumphantly from the tomb. "Hosanna to the Son of David!"

PRAYER SUGGESTION

Praise the Son of David for His advent into our midst.

Two Thankful Mothers

Hannah prayed and said: "My heart rejoices in the Lord."
1 Samuel 2:1

Mary said: "My soul glorifies the Lord." Luke 1:46

Hannah and Mary were different in their ages, marital status, the times and places of their lives, and the sons they bore. Hannah rejoiced over Samuel, a prophet in a time when "the Word of the LORD was rare" (1 Samuel 3:1). Active in public affairs, her son anointed kings. Mary's Son was the great Prophet, the Word Incarnate, and King of kings.

Hannah and Mary also had much in common. Their faith shone through in their words, deeds, and prayers of thanksgiving. Hannah's doxology followed her petition for a son. Mary was taken completely by surprise when the angel Gabriel announced her motherhood of God's Son. She composed her Magnificat ("My soul doth magnify the Lord") in response.

The prayers of both reflect faith in the might and mercy of God. "There is no Rock like our God" (1 Samuel 2:2), said Hannah. Mary glorified God not only for His grace to her but to all His people. She said, "He has helped His servant Israel, remembering to be merciful" (Luke 1:54).

God did indeed demonstrate His great mercy in the advent and activity of Jesus Christ, His Son, who was born of the Virgin Mary. As for Hannah's son, identified as "Samuel and the prophets" (Hebrews 11:32), he witnessed to the coming Messiah, "Beginning with Moses and all the Prophets, He explained to them what was said in all the Scriptures concerning Himself" (Luke 24:27).

We are thankful for Hannah and Mary and model their faith.

PRAYER SUGGESTION

Give praise to God for redeeming His people through His Son.

Man-God and God-Man?

In those days Caesar Augustus issued a decree that a census should be taken of the entire Roman world. Luke 2:1

From them [people of Israel] is traced the human ancestry of Christ, who is God over all, forever praised. Amen. Romans 9:5

Augustus was the Roman emperor when Jesus was born. It was by his decree that Joseph and Mary went to Bethlehem for the census. Augustus was the first in a line of rulers given to mounting arrogance and absolute power. Self-declared to be divine, Augustus and those after him were men-gods who died in due time.

The psalmist warned, "Do not put your trust in princes, in mortal men, who cannot save. … Blessed is he whose help is the God of Jacob, whose hope is in the LORD his God" (Psalm 146:3–5). Truly blessed are all who find their refuge and strength in Jesus Christ, true God and true man. He was born in Bethlehem in order to take the place of sinners as their Savior—as the Second Adam to regain what the first Adam had lost. To be the Lamb, it was necessary for Him to be a true man.

But our Lord is also true God, "God over all" (Romans 9:5). The gospel of John supports this: "The Word was with God, and the Word was God" (1:1). And later in the same chapter: "The Word became flesh and made His dwelling among us" (verse 14).

The incarnation of the Son of God to be our Savior is what Advent and Christmas are all about. Truly, "God sent His Son, born of a woman, born under law, to redeem those under law, that we might receive the full rights of sons" (Galatians 4:4–5). The Roman emperors, their claim to divinity notwithstanding, are long gone. But Jesus Christ, the God-Man, is "the same yesterday and today and forever" (Hebrews 13:8).

PRAYER SUGGESTION

Ask the Lord Jesus to make His advent into your heart and home with His blessings.

The Desert in Bloom

The desert and the parched land will be glad; the wilderness will rejoice and blossom. Like the crocus, it will burst into bloom.
Isaiah 35:1–2

During the Israelites' 40-year journey to the Promised Land, God made it clear that Aaron was His duly appointed high priest. So He directed Moses to put 12 rods (or branches) into the sanctuary, with Aaron's name on the rod of Levi. The next day Aaron's rod "had budded, blossomed and produced almonds" (Numbers 17:8). It showed that Aaron was the high priest, foreshadowing the great High Priest who was to come, Jesus Christ.

It was not from the tribe of Levi and the house of Aaron, but from the tribe of Judah and the house of Jesse that the Messiah came. It was prophesied, "A shoot will come up from the stump of Jesse; from his roots a Branch will bear fruit" (Isaiah 11:1).

Jesus was indeed a fruitful Branch bearing much fruit and nourishing the spiritual desert that sinful mankind had become. Jesus, in His time, did everything the Messiah was prophesied to do. When the followers of John the Baptist asked if He was the one who was to come, Jesus answered, "The blind receive sight, the lame walk, those who have leprosy are cured, the deaf hear, the dead are raised, and the good news is preached to the poor" (Matthew 11:5). Jesus truly proclaimed Himself as the Messiah.

"In Him we have redemption through His blood, the forgiveness of sins, in accordance with the riches of God's grace" (Ephesians 1:7). We can sing: "Lo, how a rose is growing, A bloom of finest grace; The prophets had foretold it; A branch of Jesse's race Would bear one perfect flow'r Here in the cold of winter And darkest midnight hour."

PRAYER SUGGESTION

Ask the Savior to make you fruitful in all good works.

From Heaven He Came

This is the name by which He will be called:
The LORD Our Righteousness. Jeremiah 23:6

When in 1969 Neil Armstrong stepped on the moon, he said, "One small step for a man, one giant leap for mankind." It was indeed a giant leap for mankind when the Son of God came to earth. He brought what the human race needed the most: redemption from the guilt of sin and from death as the penalty. Through faith in Him we have forgiveness and can stand before God robed in His righteousness.

The purpose of Christ's coming is built into the names He bears. The Christmas angel called Him Savior and Christ the Lord. To Joseph the Lord's angel said, "You are to give Him the name Jesus, because He will save His people from their sins" (Matthew 1:21). Isaiah said His name is Immanuel, which means "God with us" (Matthew 1:23). In another passage he called Him the Prince of Peace, because through faith in Him we have peace with God (Isaiah 9:6).

But no name the prophets ascribed to the Savior is more meaningful than the one Jeremiah gave Him: the Lord Our Righteousness. His righteousness is ours by faith in Him, as St. Paul explained, "God made Him who had no sin to be sin for us, so that in Him we might become the righteousness of God" (2 Corinthians 5:21).

The astronaut who first stepped on the moon could be no savior. But Jesus is different. He came to an earth full of sinners and for all who believe in Him He is what the name Jesus means: the Savior. For them He is the Lord, their Righteousness.

PRAYER SUGGESTION

Ask the Holy Spirit to increase your faith in Christ, your Righteousness.

Evening, a Time of Healing

That evening after sunset the people brought to Jesus all the sick and demon-possessed. Mark 1:32

Peace is God's gift at eventide. Often He wraps it up in beautiful sunset colors that are a delight to the eyes. The sun's afterglow is a time of healing. It was that in a literal sense for people mentioned in the verse for today.

Sundown can be a time of healing for us too. Evening is a time of striking balances, of "evening" things off. It is a time for peace-making, for reconciliation. As Paul advised, "Do not let the sun go down while you are still angry" (Ephesians 4:26).

The setting sun bids us cease from our labors. It reminds us of Jesus' words: "As long as it is day, we must do the work of Him who sent Me. Night is coming, when no one can work" (John 9:4). The night comes to give us rest, allowing us to thank God for His many blessings throughout the day. "May my prayer be set before You like incense; may the lifting up of my hands be like the evening sacrifice" (Psalm 141:2).

Evening is a time of fellowship with our family in the presence of our Savior and risen Lord. "Stay with us," the Emmaus disciples urged the Stranger, "for it is nearly evening; the day is almost over" (Luke 24:29). The peace with God that Jesus earned with His death and sealed with His resurrection is His gift to us at all times, especially at eventide.

PRAYER SUGGESTION

Ask Jesus to grant you His presence day and night.

Rough Water, Abundant Water

You give them drink from Your river of delights. For with You is the fountain of life. Psalm 36:8–9

A Christian's life can be compared to a river in that it contains the water of trouble but also the water of divine grace. A river may flow along evenly and peacefully for a while. Then, as its water descends to lower levels, it begins to churn. Whitecaps form and currents roil as it cascades over rocks, hurrying to its destination. In due time the waters arrive home, the sea.

Paul and Barnabas, missionaries, told the members of young churches in Asia Minor: "We must go through many hardships to enter the kingdom of God" (Acts 14:22). They said this to encourage the converts to "remain true to the faith" (Acts 14:22).

But the rough water of affliction yields to the abundant water of God's sustaining grace. The psalmist compared it to a river flowing from God, the fountain of life. Jesus Christ is with us at all times, even when the turbulent water of adversity threatens to roll over us. "From the fullness of His grace," wrote John, "we have all received one blessing after another" (John 1:16). Jesus Christ came from the Father, as the message of Advent strongly emphasizes, not empty-handed but "full of grace and truth" (John 1:14). And we draw comfort from Paul's words to the Romans: "Where sin increased, grace increased all the more" (Romans 5:20).

Our Savior provides us with the water of life through His sustaining Word. He comforts us. Even now we hear His invitation: "The Spirit and the bride say, 'Come!' And let Him who hears say, 'Come!' Whoever is thirsty, let him come; and whoever wishes, let him take the free gift of the water of life" (Revelation 22:17).

PRAYER SUGGESTION

Thank God for refreshing you daily with the living water of His Word.

Advent Adventures

Speak to one another with psalms, hymns and spiritual songs. Sing and make music in your heart to the Lord, always giving thanks to God the Father for everything, in the name of our Lord Jesus Christ. Ephesians 5:19–20

Advent and adventure are related words. Advent means approach or arrival, and as a proper noun it refers to Christ's coming in a threefold sense: His birth in Bethlehem, His continual coming through the Word and Sacraments, and His Second Coming at the end of time. The word "adventure" suggests that something exciting is about to take place. Both words are appropriate to use during the four weeks preceding Christmas, a time for spiritual adventures.

What adventures? Giving gifts is one. God is pleased if our gift giving is done out of love, especially when we share our excess with those less fortunate.

Advent adventures continue in the home with family members gathered. Time spent talking with one another, such as in devotions or informal faith talk, is important. Lighting candles in an Advent wreath is an ideal time to grow in faith together.

Advent adventures can include singing Christmas carols and playing musical instruments, giving thanks to God for sending His Son to redeem us and make us members of His family and heirs of salvation.

These spiritual adventures are also enacted in the larger family that is Christ's church. They consist in attending Advent services and inviting friends to accompany us. All aspects of the Advent season are part of the spiritual adventure. "The Advent of our God Shall be our theme for prayer; Come, let us meet Him on the road And place for Him prepare."

PRAYER SUGGESTION

Give thanks to God for every gift, especially for the gift of His Son.

The Messiah, Born in Bethlehem

You, Bethlehem Ephrathah, though you are small among the clans of Judah, out of you will come for Me one who will be ruler over Israel. Micah 5:2

In 1868 Phillips Brooks wrote "O Little Town of Bethlehem" for a Sunday school Christmas festival. Three years before, he had stood on the Judean hills and viewed the Bethlehem below. His impressions stayed with him and were expressed in the song.

Brooks called Bethlehem "little," which is also how the prophet Micah described it—"small among the clans of Judah." Although small, Bethlehem would not only yield David as king of all Israel but, above all, the Messiah.

Jesus, born in Bethlehem, is truly the Messiah of whom Micah prophesied. All statements of fact converge on Him. A shepherd? Indeed, for Jesus said, "I am the Good Shepherd" (John 10:11). His birthplace? When the Wise Men inquired where the Messiah was to be born, the biblical scholars answered, "In Bethlehem in Judea" (Matthew 2:5), citing Micah's prophecy to support their statement. Led by a star, the Magi went to Bethlehem where they found Jesus. Peace with God through Him? Micah said, "He will be their peace" (Micah 5:5), and Isaiah called Him the Prince of Peace (Isaiah 9:6). Paul wrote: "He came and preached peace to you" (Ephesians 2:17). The peace He proclaimed was our reconciliation with God which He effected, as the apostle stated, "through the cross" (Ephesians 2:16).

The name Bethlehem means "house of bread." It is the birthplace of Jesus, who is Himself the Bread of Life. All who in faith receive Him as their Savior are nourished with spiritual food to sustain them.

PRAYER SUGGESTION

Thank the heavenly Father for sending His Son to be your Savior and spiritual Provider.

Christ, the Bridge to Heaven

There is one God and one Mediator between God and men, the man Christ Jesus. 1 Timothy 2:5

The rainbow could easily remind us of a bridge to another world, to heaven itself.

The thought is not farfetched. The writer of the book *Ecclesiasticus* wrote: "Look upon the rainbow, and praise Him who made it, exceedingly beautiful in its brightness. It encircles the heaven with its glorious arc; the hands of the Most High have stretched it out." And giving us a glimpse into heaven, John wrote that he beheld God on His throne encircled by a "rainbow, resembling an emerald" (Revelation 4:3).

The true bridge to heaven—"the Mediator between God and men"—is Jesus Christ. He became this when He "gave Himself as a ransom for all men" (1 Timothy 2:6). Our Lord Himself declared that His purpose was "to serve and to give His life as a ransom for many" (Matthew 20:28). In response, Christ's church invites Him, in the words of an Advent hymn, to "Come, You precious Ransom, come."

Because Jesus is the bridge—the radiant rainbow—connecting earth with heaven, we have what is both an assignment and a privilege, as Jesus says, "You will be My witnesses" (Acts 1:8). A witness is also a messenger. We are little rainbows, witnesses and ambassadors for Christ, telling the world: "God so loved the world that He gave His one and only Son, that whoever believes in Him shall not perish but have eternal life" (John 3:16). We hear our Savior say, "My Father's home of light, My rainbow-circled throne, I left for earthly night, For wanderings sad and lone, I left it all for thee; Hast thou left aught for Me?"

PRAYER SUGGESTION

Ask God for help to tell others that Christ of the cross is the crossing to heaven.

Cradle, Cross, Crown

Let us fix our eyes on Jesus, ... who for the joy set before Him endured the cross, scorning its shame, and sat down at the right hand of the throne of God. Hebrews 12:2

Olympia was a plain in ancient Greece where athletic contests were held every four years. They were considered important enough to stop whatever battles were being fought at the time—a rare instance of a peaceful activity superseding warfare.

The apostle Paul was acquainted with the Olympics. He knew that participants underwent vigorous training and put forth consummate effort during the race. They did it for crowns or chaplets of leaves that soon faded. The apostle drew lessons from these games: living a Christian life requires training and great effort, not in order to be saved but as a response to salvation.

The writer of Hebrews stressed perseverance as another essential. To have staying power in the race of faith, it is necessary to "throw off everything that hinders and the sin that so easily entangles" (Hebrews 12:1). To persevere, we need encouragement and inspiration. For the Hebrews writer, that great model was not a Greek athlete but the Lord Jesus.

Jesus had a most important race to run. Simeon declared, "This Child is destined to cause the falling and rising of many in Israel" (Luke 2:34). And to Mary, he said, "A sword will pierce your own soul too" (Luke 2:35). But the cross was not the end. Jesus, having fulfilled His work as the Redeemer, was "crowned with glory and honor because He suffered death" (Hebrews 2:9).

The faith the Holy Spirit works in us through the Gospel enables us to follow in Christ's footsteps as we run the race set before us.

PRAYER SUGGESTION

Pray that the Lord Jesus may inspire and strengthen you in the race of faith.

Spiritual Moisture

Does the rain have a father? Who fathers the drops of dew? Job 38:28

God works through nature to give us tokens of His providence and love. All that emerges from the heart and hand of God, especially His Word, comes to us in purity, as Moses intoned, "Let my teaching fall like rain and my words descend like dew, like showers on new grass, like abundant rain on tender plants" (Deuteronomy 32:2).

Together with rain and snow, dew helps make the land fruitful. "The seed will grow well, the vine will yield its fruit, the ground will produce its crops, and the heavens will drop their dew" (Zechariah 8:12). The book of Isaiah is more explicit in comparing rain and snow with the Word of God: "As the rain and the snow come down from heaven, and do not return to it without watering the earth and making it bud and flourish ... so is My Word that goes out from My mouth: it will not return to Me empty, but will accomplish what I desire and achieve the purpose for which I sent it" (Isaiah 55:10–11).

As a rule, God does not pour out His Word on us with as much force as He did on Pentecost. More often God speaks to us, as He did to Elijah, in "a gentle whisper" (1 Kings 19:12). Spiritual moisture comes not as a gully-washer but as dewdrops.

God's purpose is fulfilled in the sending of His Son, Jesus Christ, who is in a true sense the Water of life, the Dew from heaven for a spiritually parched world. God's Son did not come as a ravaging flood; He came as a small child, as a dewdrop. Indeed, "Every morning mercies new Fall as fresh as morning dew."

PRAYER SUGGESTION

Give thanks to God for sending us His Son as the Living Water.

Little Ones Included

A voice came from the throne, saying: "Praise our God, all you His servants, you who fear Him, both small and great!" Revelation 19:5

People visiting the historic Jefferson Barracks National Cemetery at St. Louis note that death claims persons of all ages when they see the grave of the two-year-old son of Zebulon Pike, an army officer and explorer, namesake of Pike's Peak.

In His dispensation of grace, God embraces the young as well as the old. They are a part of the "all nations" (Matthew 28:19) whom Jesus wanted His apostles to teach and baptize. Children receive the love of God in Christ. Peter stated that they are to be included in the church's ministration, for the promise of salvation, he said, "is for you and your children" (Acts 2:39). They are sinners and need forgiveness, which is theirs through Baptism.

How pleased is our Lord when parents bring little ones to church so their voices blend with the praise of God. Jesus was pleased when children sang "Hosanna to the Son of David" (Matthew 21:15). The temple authorities were indignant and wanted them restrained. But Jesus said, "Have you never read, 'From the lips of children and infants You have ordained praise?'" (Matthew 21:16).

John gave us a glimpse into heaven, reporting on the great Hallelujah chorus before God's throne, saying that all of God's servants should praise God, "both small and great."

The joys and delights of the Christmas season give us a foretaste of heaven, with the children joining and leading us in the singing of praise to Jesus Christ, the divine infant in Bethlehem's stable. "When children's voices raise the song, Hosanna to the heavenly King! Let heaven, with earth, the strain prolong, Hosanna! Let the angels sing."

PRAYER SUGGESTION

Join the children in praising God for the gift of His Son.

God Cares for Us

"Look at the birds of the air; they do not sow or reap or store away in barns, and yet your heavenly Father feeds them." Matthew 6:26

Jesus said we can learn from God's lesser creatures, the birds. In His Sermon on the Mount, He told those inclined to worry to consider that God will attend them in their needs of body and soul, for does He not provide for the birds? At another time Jesus wanted His hearers to draw the proper conclusion for themselves from the fact that no lowly sparrow falls to the ground without the will of the heavenly Father. He adds, "You are worth more than many sparrows" (Matthew 10:31).

Birds can be our examples and even our teachers when it comes to finding our way through life. God has endowed them with remarkable instincts. They are skilled aviators and navigators with a sure sense of direction during their transcontinental migrations. Does God do any less for us? In his poem "To a Water Fowl," William Cullen Bryant draws this lesson from the flight of fowls: "He who from zone to zone, Guides through the boundless sky thy certain flight, In the long way that I must tread alone, Will lead my steps aright."

When a teacher volunteered to follow Jesus, our Lord said to him, "Foxes have holes and birds of the air have nests, but the Son of Man has no place to lay His head" (Matthew 8:20). The birth of the Son of God amid deep poverty gives us an inkling of the love of God that exceeds our comprehension. We are the recipients of "the grace of our Lord Jesus Christ, that though He was rich, yet for your sakes He became poor, so that you through His poverty might become rich" (2 Corinthians 8:9).

PRAYER SUGGESTION

Thank God for His care of you through Jesus Christ, His Son.

Jesus Christ, Our Star of Hope

A Star will come out of Jacob; a Scepter will rise out of Israel.
Numbers 24:17

King Balak of the Moabites was not happy that the migrating children of Israel were camping on the borders of his land. To stop them, he engaged Balaam, a free-lance pagan diviner, to put a curse on them. Instead, Balaam spoke a blessing on the people, predicting that the Messiah would come from their midst to the discomfort of pagan nations. This remark from an unexpected source is similar to what the unbelieving Caiaphas, the high priest, said when he prophesied, "not on his own," that Jesus would die for the good of God's people (John 18:14).

Balaam called the coming Savior a star. A star gives off light. From its fixed position in the sky, the polestar, for example, gives guidance to night travelers. This is what Jesus does. He enlightens us with the truth of God's Word about the salvation of sinners through His atoning sacrifice. He guides us on the road to eternal life with our heavenly Father. Jesus Himself is the one and only Way. In His role as Guide, Jesus is like the star of Bethlehem that led the Wise Men to the Savior. As the book of Revelation declares, Jesus is "the Root and the Offspring of David, and the bright Morning Star" (Revelation 22:16).

When we adorn our Christmas tree with a star, we are using a symbol of Him who in a most reverent sense is the star of our salvation.

PRAYER SUGGESTION

Pray that Jesus, your Lord and Savior, may shine as a bright star in your life.

The Apostles, Trustworthy Witnesses

We did not follow cleverly invented stories when we told you about the power and coming of our Lord Jesus Christ, but we were eyewitnesses of His majesty. 2 Peter 1:16

People become legendary as their accomplishments are magnified. For example, the Swiss patriot and expert archer William Tell was credited with many legendary feats, such as shooting an apple from his son's head with bow and arrow.

Is Jesus of Nazareth the bearer of overblown stories? Is the account of His virgin birth true? Did an angel appear from heaven to announce His birth to the shepherds? Did a choir of angels really sing the anthem of God's glory and peace on earth? Or were these accounts added to embellish Christ's nativity?

False accusations were made even in the apostolic age, and Peter addressed such claims. He stressed that he and the other disciples were eyewitnesses of what Jesus did and said. John agreed: They saw, they heard, they touched (1 John 1:1). Peter, James, and John were present when Jesus raised Jairus's daughter from the dead. The same three saw Jesus transfigured on a mount, where they beheld His glory and heard God's acknowledgement of Jesus as His Son. They were with their Lord in Gethsemane where they saw His great agony. All the apostles and many others were eyewitnesses of His resurrection appearances.

If the claims of the apostles had brought them fame and fortune, one might suspect they would support the "cleverly invented stories." But their preaching Christ's Gospel brought persecution, hatred, and death. How thankful we are that the apostles faithfully and truthfully testified "about the power and coming of our Lord Jesus Christ," who saves His people from their sins.

PRAYER SUGGESTION

Express your gratitude to God for sending His Son for your salvation.

Honoring Mary as a Wife

An angel of the Lord appeared to him in a dream and said, "Joseph son of David, do not be afraid to take Mary home as your wife, because what is conceived in her is from the Holy Spirit." Matthew 1:20

Some husbands go to considerable expense to honor their wives. For example, Shah Jahan, a mogul ruler in Agra, India, built his deceased wife a mausoleum known as the Taj Mahal.

Joseph, a carpenter in Nazareth, honored his wife, but not with a splendid structure. Joseph honored her by serving as a pious husband, protector, provider, and foster father of God's Son.

Usually we concentrate on Mary, a young virgin, as the *mother* of our Lord whom God selected to give birth to His Son at the fullness of the time. This Son, born under the Law, as Paul told the Galatians, was "to redeem those under law, that we might receive the full rights of sons" (Galatians 4:5). But we also do well to honor her in her role as Joseph's *wife*.

The first to do this was Joseph himself. He believed the Lord's angel, who told him Mary's child was conceived by the Holy Spirit, and he took Mary as his wife. The angel added that the unborn child was the Messiah, Immanuel, to be called Jesus, "because He will save His people from their sins" (Matthew 1:21). Joseph attended Mary at Bethlehem, led the way during the flight to Egypt, and served her and Jesus during their residence in Nazareth. Not much is known of Joseph beyond that.

It is easy to imagine how Mary took care of the baby Jesus in Bethlehem's stable and later as He grew up in Nazareth. She was also a good wife, good and kind to her lawful husband. We join Joseph in honoring Mary as a wife.

PRAYER SUGGESTION

Give thanks to God for the good examples set by Joseph and Mary.

Christ, Born of a Virgin

"How will this be," Mary asked the angel, "since I am a virgin?"
Luke 1:34

In the Apostles' Creed we confess that Jesus Christ, the Son of God, was "born of the virgin Mary." The creeds and confessions of the church set forth only what the Holy Scriptures teach. So it is with the Savior's birth of a virgin. Luke records Mary's own testimony in response to the angel Gabriel's announcement that "the Son of the Most High" (Luke 1:32) would be born of her.

The virgin birth of the Messiah had been foretold long before. Matthew quoted one such prophecy (that of Isaiah) and pronounced it fulfilled by Jesus' virgin birth: "All this took place to fulfill what the Lord had said through the prophet: 'The virgin will be with child and will give birth to a son, and they will call Him Immanuel—which means God with us'" (Matthew 1:23).

Sometimes it is asked whether Mary had other biological children. The Bible doesn't answer the question, but we read that the people of Nazareth referred to "His brothers James, Joseph, Simon, and Judas" and to "His sisters with us" (Matthew 13:55–56). The Bible sometimes uses a term like "brother" in a wider sense. For example, Abraham on one occasion called himself and Lot brothers, when in fact they were uncle and nephew. Another point to remember is that while on the cross Jesus put Mary into the heart and hands of the disciple John, not to the aforementioned brothers or sisters.

Whether Joseph and Mary had children after Jesus was born takes nothing away from the Savior's birth of the virgin. We can joyfully sing: "Crown Him the Virgin's Son, The God incarnate born."

PRAYER SUGGESTION

Give thanks to the heavenly Father for sending Jesus, His virgin-born Son, to be our Redeemer.

When to Make Haste

[The shepherds] hurried off and found Mary and Joseph, and the baby, who was lying in the manger. Luke 2:16

The Latin saying *festina lente* means to make haste slowly. There are times when we must not act rashly. Jesus cited the error of a man who left a tower unfinished because he had not anticipated the cost. He wanted His apostles prepared for their mission; He didn't want them to rush in unprepared but to await the outpouring of the Holy Spirit.

We all need to avoid reckless responses. "Everyone should be quick to listen, slow to speak, and slow to become angry" (James 1:19). But when is it time to make haste?

The shepherds set a good example. After they had heard the angel's announcement, they did not dally. They hastened to Bethlehem to worship the Christ Child. They were convinced they had found the promised Messiah, who would save His people from their sins.

Another great event calling for immediate response was Jesus' resurrection. The angel told the women at the empty tomb to go quickly and tell His disciples that He had risen from the dead. They rushed to do this because they believed.

When is it time to make haste? Surely when God confronts us in His Word. Agrippa is reported to have said, "Do you think that in such a short time you can persuade me to be a Christian?" (Acts 26:28). But today is the time. St. Paul said, "Now is the time of God's favor, now is the day of salvation" (2 Corinthians 6:2).

In spirit, we all hurry to the stable in Bethlehem to worship Christ, our Savior.

PRAYER SUGGESTION

Give thanks to God for giving you the opportunity to express your faith in Jesus, His Son.

Mary's Memories

Mary treasured up all these things and pondered them in her heart.
Luke 2:19

We can be certain that Mary rejoiced at the birth of Jesus, her Son and her God. She saw fulfilled what she had anticipated in her Magnificat: "My soul glorifies the Lord and my spirit rejoices in God my Savior" (Luke 1:47).

Now that Christ was born, Mary had a wonderful remembrance to cherish and ponder. But sorrowful times were ahead. The terrible day would come when she would stand at the foot of the cross to watch Him die. But faith sustained her. She had the memory of Jesus' birth, when angels from heaven worshiped Him.

We learn from Mary to treasure our Christian experiences, pondering the truths we learn from God's Word. Fond, faith-strengthening remembrances will sustain us in dark days. It helps us when we recall the joy of Christmas, when we celebrate the birth of our Savior, God's great gift to us. To mind will come joyful carols and hymns, holiday greetings, and gifts given out of love. We can think back on worship services and the message: "Today in the town of David a Savior has been born to you; He is Christ the Lord" (Luke 2:11).

Add the many other events in our lifetime that we treasure, and remember: the glorious resurrection of our Savior; our relation to the risen Lord, begun in Baptism and strengthened at the Holy Table. Our hearts are strengthened by the rite of confirmation and family marriages and birthday celebrations, each marked by God's promise in Christ. These are memories that bless because they are based on God's great acts in Christ Jesus for our salvation.

PRAYER SUGGESTION

Ask God to fill your heart with joy at the remembrance of Christ's birth.

Joseph's Joy

[Jesus] was the son, so it was thought, of Joseph. Luke 3:23

Mary had her joyful memories, and Joseph his memorable joys—the joys that accompany the duties of fatherhood.

Although not Jesus' father, Joseph had ample reason for joy because God had revealed to him that Jesus would save the world from their sins—including Joseph. The assurance of salvation in Christ causes joy.

Joseph played his God-appointed role well, and this comes out in the post-Nativity events. He saw to it that the ceremonial temple rites for mother and son were duly observed. He served as provider and protector of the holy family during the flight to Egypt and later in Nazareth. A carpenter—an honest and honorable vocation for a descendent of King David—he taught his skills to Jesus, who worked as a carpenter before His public ministry. Joseph's devoted service to his family was complete.

In the historical accounts of the four gospels Joseph fades from sight as the focus on Jesus increases. The last mention of him occurs in John's account of the heated discussion following our Lord's feeding of the 5,000. Jesus had said that He was the true Manna, the Bread come down from heaven. The people replied, "Is this not Jesus, the son of Joseph, whose father and mother we know? How can He now say, 'I came down from heaven'?" (John 6:42).

Joseph is a role model not only for natural fathers but also, and especially, for foster fathers, stepfathers, and guardians of children.

As we join the shepherds in our faith-journey to Bethlehem, we thank the heavenly Father for Jesus Christ, His Son, and also for Joseph, His foster father.

PRAYER SUGGESTION

Ask the Lord to enable all parents to follow the example of Joseph and Mary.

The Original Christmas Carol

"Glory to God in the highest, and on earth peace to men on whom His favor rests." Luke 2:14

Under the impact of commercialism, the Christmas switch is from "deck the *halls*" to "deck the *malls*."

An early Christmas carol, sung by the angels, praised God for the Messiah's birth. The heavenly herald announced, "Today in the town of David a Savior has been born to you; He is Christ the Lord" (Luke 2:11). This message was emphasized by Paul, "When the time had fully come, God sent His Son, born of a woman, born under law, to redeem those under law, that we might receive the full rights of sons" (Galatians 4:4–5).

The first Christmas carol was stated in the Old Testament when the Lord God announced to Adam and Eve that the woman's offspring would crush Satan's power. Another carol speaks of the Star to emerge from Jacob. Another foretold that Christ would be born in Bethlehem.

These original Christmas carols are followed by expressions of what Christ's birth means to us now. We can say and sing that God's Son became poor so He might enrich us spiritually with forgiveness, peace with God, and the promise of eternal life. He became a servant in our behalf, inciting us to serve Him gladly by befriending the needy. We echo the carol when we, like the shepherds, spread the good news of the Savior's birth.

There is yet another to be sung in heaven: "Worthy is the Lamb, who was slain, to receive power and wealth and wisdom and strength and honor and glory and praise!" (Revelation 5:12).

It is Christmas Day, a time to sing all the songs of salvation.

PRAYER SUGGESTION

Praise God for the birth of His Son for the salvation of all.

The Journey to Bethlehem

The shepherds said to one another, "Let's go to Bethlehem and see this thing that has happened, which the Lord has told us about." Luke 2:15

People still go to Bethlehem. Every year thousands of pilgrims go there to worship in Manger Square outside the Church of the Nativity. Bethlehem is called a "little town" in a Christmas song, and it is described by the prophet Micah as "small among the clans of Judah" (Micah 5:2). Nowadays it is a city of some 50,000 inhabitants.

The first pilgrims to worship Christ in Bethlehem were the shepherds. It was more than curiosity that brought the shepherds to the manger. It was faith, for they knew the angel's message was the Word of the Lord and they expressed their faith in their worship of the Christ Child. Upon leaving the stable they became heralds of Christ's incarnation when they "spread the word" (Luke 2:17) of the Nativity. They became missionaries, all the while honoring God in their vocation as shepherds.

We may not be among the pilgrims who nowadays journey to Bethlehem to worship in Manger Square, but we make this journey of faith in spirit. It is for us an act of faith to celebrate Christ's birth in our homes and churches. We believe that the promised Savior came in the person of Jesus. He came to be our Savior from everything that separated us from God and heaven. Jesus came into the world to liberate us *from* the grip of sin and the fear of death. And He set us free *for* something: to sing His praise with glad voices, to serve Him with willing hearts and hands, and to spread the word as did the shepherds.

PRAYER SUGGESTION

Give thanks to God for the gift of His Son for our salvation.

The Gospel Gets Told

"This gospel of the kingdom will be preached in the whole world as a testimony to all nations, and then the end will come." Matthew 24:14

At Christmas time the Gospel of the Savior's birth is formally proclaimed from church pulpits. In our schools and homes children sing familiar carols, all announcing that "Christ the Savior is born."

But there is another way for the Gospel to be told. In our increasingly secularized, religiously illiterate society, many people do not grasp the concepts of redemption and reconciliation underlying the Christmas story. One bridge to people of simple perception is the popular "Gospel" music. This is a distinctive form of music drawing from life's daily experiences and told in familiar, everyday language. Recently heard at Christmastime were such spirituals or "Gospel" songs as "Go, Tell It on the Mountain" and "Rise up, Shepherds, and Follow."

God wants the Gospel told throughout the world. The shepherds at Bethlehem and aged Simeon and Anna spread the Word among their acquaintances in Jerusalem. After our Lord's ascension the apostles and many converts proclaimed the Gospel on a wider scale. They preached and taught that Jesus, God in the flesh, gave His life as a ransom for sinners and then rose victorious over sin, death, and the devil. They did their work well.

There is still a mission field for us. We witness in person and we make use of the "information highway" and other media. We keep the rally going by teaching God's Word in formal classes in theological seminaries and lessons in Sunday school. And we can get the message across in down-to-earth "Gospel" songs.

PRAYER SUGGESTION

Ask the Holy Spirit to help you find ways and means of telling the Gospel.

Christ Prevailed

[Joseph] got up, took the Child and His mother ... and left for Egypt.
Matthew 2:14

Evildoers often try to destroy what God has wrought, especially His church. In Charlotte, North Carolina, after a church building was set on fire, the pastor had this word for the arsonist: "You destroyed a building, but you did not destroy the church." The real church is God's people, the communion of saints.

Christ's enemies can do little to destroy the church as Christ's body with Christ as its head. King Herod found this out. He could kill the male children in and about Bethlehem, making them the first martyrs for Christ. But the Savior Himself escaped.

Some 30 years later the enemies did lay hands on Jesus and nailed Him to a cross. They thought they had put an end to Him and His kingdom. Even the prime instigator, the devil, undoubtedly thought so. But the celebration was premature. The foe had not reckoned with the Resurrection. Christ's victory was complete, "Since Christ was raised from the dead, He cannot die again; death no longer has mastery over Him. The death He died, He died to sin once for all, but the life He lives, He lives to God" (Romans 6:9–10).

Christ is the Resurrection and the Life. He is the indestructible Head of the church. King Herod could kill the young children, known as the "holy innocents," and Roman emperors could persecute Christians. But Christ prevailed.

PRAYER SUGGESTION

Thank the living Christ for preserving His church and for making you a member of it.

Our Holiday Celebrations

Whether you eat or drink or whatever you do, do it all for the glory of God. 1 Corinthians 10:31

It is quite proper to have food and drink at festive occasions. The festivals kept by the Israelites, including wedding celebrations, were marked by eating and drinking. Unleavened bread, herbs, and wine were on the table when Jesus celebrated the Passover with His disciples. At the wedding in Cana He turned water into wine for the enjoyment of the guests. Early Christians ate and drank when they came together for agape (love) feasts. St. Paul approved of such get-togethers, provided the participants did not give offense to the weak in faith. When there is this concern and moderation is observed, Christians, always thankful for the gift of God's Son at Christmas time and for His blessings through the year, are eating and drinking for the glory of God.

In recent years much emphasis has been given to the vice of drunken driving on streets and highways. Thousands lose their lives or are maimed for life because of intoxicated motorists. Alcohol abused in this way is not for Christians. Paul told Timothy that God "richly provides us with everything for our enjoyment" (1 Timothy 6:17). But God does not provide it for abuse.

In Bethlehem Christ was born to be our Savior. He died for our sins and rose again from the dead. As God He crowns the years with His blessings. These are sufficient reasons for holiday celebrations—joyful but moderate.

PRAYER SUGGESTION

Give thanks to God for the gift of His Son as you observe the holiday festivals.

Looking Ahead

Forgetting what is behind ... I press on toward the goal to win the prize for which God has called me heavenward in Christ Jesus. Philippians 3:13–14

We have all made mistakes in the year about to close. Some of them were original, some repetitions of people's errors recorded in the Bible. Case studies can be found among Christ's disciples. Judas preferred silver to the Savior. Peter grossly overestimated his loyalty to Jesus. Thomas declared his disbelief in His resurrection. All the disciples were at times quarrelsome as they jockeyed for positions of leadership. And Paul—how could he forget all his errors as a Pharisee?

We ourselves, if we are candid, can recount our errors of this year. Whatever our mistakes, including those the psalmist called "hidden faults" (Psalm 19:12), we confess them before God. For the sake of Jesus, who atoned for all our sins, God forgives them. He clears them from His records. He casts them behind Him. The prophet Micah declared that God "will tread our sins underfoot and hurl all our iniquities into the depths of the sea" (Micah 7:19).

We too, for Jesus' sake, can forget what is behind and "throw off everything that hinders" so we can complete the race of faith. We fix "our eyes on Jesus, the Author and Perfecter of our faith," who finished His course with joy for our salvation (Hebrews 12:1–2).

In the meantime, before the year ends, we have the opportunity, as Paul advised, to "straighten out what was left unfinished" (Titus 1:5).

PRAYER SUGGESTION

Ask God to forgive you, for Jesus' sake, all your failing during the year.

Jesus: Beginning, Middle, End

"I am the Alpha and the Omega, the First and the Last, the Beginning and the End." Revelation 22:13

T. S. Eliot, the English poet and playwright, thought of life as ongoing exploration. And what is the end of our exploring? It will be "to arrive where we started."

We cannot avoid beginnings and endings. Our earthly life had a beginning and will have an end. Our undertakings start then stop. So it is with our measurements of time. The year begins and it ends.

Caught in the vicissitudes of time, we need a timeless anchor, and we have one in Jesus Christ, risen from the dead and now ruling at the right hand of God in heaven. He is eternal, unchanging, as is the Father with whom He is one. He is "the same yesterday and today and forever" (Hebrews 13:8).

Calling Himself Alpha and Omega, the beginning and ending of the Greek alphabet, He is also everything in between. He is complete in that He is the center of the Gospel of our redemption. How all-encompassing is His grace, His love for all sinners! Jesus Christ is the Beginning, Middle, and End—the total content of our faith.

Paraphrasing Eliot and applying his words to time, the end of the year was inherent in its very beginning, for clocks and calendars do not stop. However, the end opens the door to a new beginning, to a new year. Before we begin the New Year, we thank God for His goodness to us in the past—for food and drink, and especially for His saving Word. It is the bread of life; it is "the free gift of the water of life" (Revelation 22:17). "Amen. Come, Lord Jesus."

PRAYER SUGGESTION

Let yours be a prayer of thanksgiving to God for His grace in Christ Jesus.

Devotions for Special Festivals and Occasions

A Time of Spiritual Revival

Lift up your heads, O you gates ... that the King of glory may come in
Psalm 24:7

The psalmist asked, "Wilt thou not revive us again: that thy people may rejoice in thee?" (85:6 KJV). To *revive* means, "to make to live again, or to have new life."

Revival is usually associated with mass meetings marked by spirited preaching and singing. It does not seem to suit the Advent season. Advent does not call for a lot of outward clamor, excitement, and activism. The spiritual quickening it intends stems from introspection, repentance, renewal of faith, and prayer. During Advent, the church returns to the acknowledgement of sin, renewed faith in the grace of God bringing salvation in Jesus Christ, and advancement in Christian maturity. It is for this that prayerful, reflective, and prophecy-centered Advent services are held in the busy, pre-Christmas weeks.

Seed sown into the ground sprouts quietly and out of the sower's sight. But what a miracle of revival takes place when, in the words of William Jennings Bryan, it "takes off its jacket and goes to work"! Seeds germinate; new plants emerge; the stalks give promise of a harvest. So the seed of God's Word revives faith and hope in the coming Messiah. Christians grow in the newness of life during Advent.

The Advent message is one of spiritual revival. It awakens us from the sleep of sin to greet the Bridegroom who is near. It tells Christians, if they are to be properly dressed for the day of salvation, to "put on the Lord Jesus Christ"—the same Son of God who was incarnate by the Holy Ghost of the Virgin Mary and was made man.

PRAYER SUGGESTION

Ask God to revive you again, to stir you up.

Staying Awake

The hour has come for you to wake up from your slumber, because our salvation is nearer now than when we first believed. Romans 13:11

One of the problems facing Charles A. Lindbergh as he flew across the Atlantic Ocean in 1927 was staying awake. The flight was long and lonely; so it is easy to understand that he could fall asleep.

St. Paul's readers in Rome confronted the problem of falling asleep spiritually. In fact, some of the converts, in Rome and in other places, had succumbed to the slumber of the soul. No longer awake and alert, they could easily become the prey of Satan. For those so recently come out of paganism, the temptation would be great to forsake the saving faith in Christ and return to the old forms of immorality.

The apostle advances a good reason for staying awake: Our salvation is nearer now than when we first believed. Salvation from sin is ours by faith in Jesus Christ, who gained it for us by His death on the cross and conveyed it to us through the means of grace. All the promises of a full and free salvation are in effect, except the one that the Savior will return in glory to take us to heaven on the Last Day. We are closer to this forthcoming event now than when we first came to faith. What a great event to anticipate! We don't want to be asleep in sin when Christ comes, but to be fully awake to receive Him.

The Advent message speaks to us about Christ's coming in Bethlehem to be our Savior. The apostle urges us to be spiritually awake to celebrate His birthday and to receive Him in faith.

PRAYER SUGGESTION

Ask God to grant you an alert faith so you may receive the coming Savior with joy.

Beauty for Ashes

The LORD has anointed me ... to bestow on them a crown of beauty instead of ashes, the oil of gladness instead of mourning, and a garment of praise instead of a spirit of despair. Isaiah 61:1, 3

Ashes are not a pretty sight. They represent the leftovers of a ruinous fire. Imagine what the ancient city of Rome looked like in A.D. 64 after a fire burned for nine days and nights!

Ashes, in both a literal and figurative sense, can come into the lives of God's people. Imagine the misery of Job as he sat in ashes wearing sackcloth! Among the Israelites ashes signified mourning over some great loss or the threat of God's judgment because of sin. People were to show sorrow for their disobedience by wearing ashes.

God shows mercy to those who in faith turned to Him in their distress. He provides for their salvation through the sin-atoning suffering and death of Jesus Christ, His Son, as observed especially during Lent beginning with Ash Wednesday. Through Isaiah God declared that Christ, the Anointed One, would make an exchange for those who repented. The ashes of mourning He would replace with "a crown of beauty." He would bestow "the oil of gladness" to those who mourned.

Most of all, Christ was to present a beauteous garment to those in despair. This is the robe of His righteousness imparted to those who come to Him, trusting in Him to lift them out of despair into hope and joy.

On Ash Wednesday we are reminded that Jesus Christ denied Himself to the utmost—suffered death on a cross—that He might grant us the beauty of forgiveness for the ashes of sin.

PRAYER SUGGESTION

Thank the Lord Jesus for turning your despair into hope and joy.

Again the Lenten Journey

Jesus took the Twelve aside and told them, "We are going up to Jerusalem, and everything that is written by the prophets about the Son of Man will be fulfilled." Luke 18:31

The journeys Jesus took as a boy with Mary and Joseph for the Passover festival in Jerusalem were undoubtedly delightful. But this was not the case with the journey He announced to the Twelve in today's text. There would be no smooth road to follow. At the end of the trip no shining city would await them. Instead it was Jerusalem, on what the hymn writer called a "green hill" outside the city wall, where Jesus Himself would be crucified.

All that Jesus had predicted, on the basis of prophetic writings, was fulfilled. He was handed over to the Gentiles—to Pontius Pilate and the Roman troops—to a humiliating and agonizing death. What was coming was not pleasant. Yet His love prompted Jesus to proceed with the journey. He knew there was no other way for a world of sinners to be saved. With His death He would pay the price for their redemption.

In spirit we travel with Jesus to learn anew the great price He paid for our salvation. It will be a 40-day journey. In doing this, we will realize that divine grace is not cheap but that we were bought with a high price. The Lenten journey we are about to make is no picnic. No, it calls us to repentance. Our love for the Savior prompts us to say: "Jesus, lead the way! We will follow."

PRAYER SUGGESTION

Tell Jesus you will follow Him to serve Him and with Him rise to life eternal.

Jesus Is Present

Is not the cup of thanksgiving for which we give thanks a participation in the blood of Christ? And is not the bread that we break a participation in the body of Christ? 1 Corinthians 10:16

Mark was going to Sunday school for the first time. His grandfather encouraged him by saying he would hear stories about Jesus. When Mark came home, he was asked how he liked it. He said, "Oh, it was all right. But Jesus wasn't there."

It is a sad commentary on some church-sponsored affairs. Many say Jesus is not in the Lord's Supper. They say they receive bread and wine, but not His true body and blood.

As we celebrate Holy Communion, which our Lord instituted on Maundy Thursday, we commemorate His death. He said we should do so in remembrance of Him. But we do more than observe a memorial meal. We celebrate a solemn Sacrament in which Jesus imparts His true body and true blood, the body given for us on the cross and the blood shed for us. These are conveyed when we eat the consecrated bread and drink the consecrated wine. Our eating and drinking in the Sacrament make us participants of our Lord's body and blood.

It is a comfort to know as we gather at the Lord's Table that Jesus is there. His promise is: "Surely I am with you always, to the very end of the age" (Matthew 28:20). And "where two or three come together in My name, there am I with them" (Matthew 18:20). In addition, we have His very specific promise that He is with us in a very special way when we attend Holy Communion.

"Come forward then with faithful hearts sincere, And take the pledges of salvation here. O Lord, our hearts with grateful thanks endow As in this feast of love You bless us now."

PRAYER SUGGESTION

Ask the Holy Spirit to prepare your heart for receiving the Lord's body and blood.

High Priest and Lamb

[Christ] sacrificed for their sins once for all when He offered Himself.
Hebrews 7:27

On Good Friday Christians express sorrow. They are downcast because their sins made the death of Jesus Christ necessary. They sing, "My burden in Thy Passion, Lord, Thou hast borne for me, For it was my transgression Which brought this woe on Thee."

But sorrow is not the overruling feeling in a Christian's heart. St. Paul said Christ's followers are "sorrowful, yet always rejoicing" (2 Corinthians 6:10). While we sorrow over the death of Jesus, we have hope and joy in our hearts, indeed not a joy that shouts hosannas and hallelujahs but one that is mixed with gratitude that Christ sacrificed Himself for our sins, once for all. Human priests in the Old Testament had to make sacrifices every day, but for our heavenly High Priest this was not necessary, and for us it is now not necessary to observe Good Friday every day.

The Good Friday event, the death of Christ, is viewed in Holy Writ from two points of view. It presents Christ in the dual role of the sacrificing priest and of the offering that He brought. The Hebrews epistle gives strong emphasis to Christ as our high priest. Other Scriptures add to that by speaking of Christ as the sacrificial lamb. John the Baptist called Jesus the Lamb of God, and St. Paul, writing to the Corinthians, declared, "Christ, our Passover Lamb, has been sacrificed [for us]" (1 Corinthians 5:7).

Both truths make Good Friday a day of hope and gratitude to God, for Christ has taken away our sins. Do Christians observe Good Friday every day? Indeed they do, but always in context of our Lord's redemption and resurrection.

PRAYER SUGGESTION

Tell the Savior that you are sorry that your sins caused His death, but thankful that it brought you life.

The Easter Breakthrough

God raised [Jesus] from the dead, freeing Him from the agony of death, because it was impossible for death to keep its hold on Him. Acts 2:24

The fear of death torments many people. While Pablo Picasso was having lunch with a guest in his home, a bird in a cage dropped dead. His wife, without his knowledge, replaced the bird with a living one so he wouldn't know that death had entered his home.

The devil, of course, plays a prominent part in promoting the fear of death. The epistle to the Hebrews states, "Since the children have flesh and blood, [Christ] too shared in their humanity so that by His death He might destroy him who holds the power of death— that is, the devil—and free those who all their lives were held in slavery by their fear of death" (2:14–15).

The resurrection of Jesus clearly demonstrated His conquest of death. Death seemed to have won out when His lifeless body was laid into a tomb. He was enclosed in a sealed grave, with a guard posted to watch it. But Christ could not be contained. He effected a breakthrough, not only in that He was freed from the grave but from the prison of death. God raised His Son from the grave and from everything associated with death—the agony and the tyranny caused by the sins of mankind.

Our Lord's resurrection signals our freedom from sin and death. The prophet Isaiah had said of the Messiah that He would come "to free captives from prison and to release from the dungeon those who sit in darkness" (Isaiah 42:7). This promise was brought to glorious fulfillment on Easter morning when Jesus rose from the dead.

PRAYER SUGGESTION

Give thanks to God for raising His Son to set you free from the fear of death.

The Holy Spirit Converts

Those who accepted [Peter's] message were baptized, and about three thousand were added to their number that day. Acts 2:41

On Pentecost Day the Holy Spirit was poured out on Christ's disciples, who began to preach to the multitudes. Peter especially set forth the meaning of Christ's crucifixion and resurrection, calling on people to repent and be baptized for the forgiveness of their sins. Three thousand were moved by the Holy Spirit to respond.

The Holy Spirit and the Gospel through which He comes into our hearts have lost none of their power. They are still the divine dynamo and power line. If God so desires, He can, as a hymn line has it, convert "a nation in a day." Most generally, however, the Spirit leads people to Christ one by one. That is how things went as in later times the apostles went on their missionary journeys. In Philippi, Paul gained two people: Lydia and the jailor. In Athens, the converts were Dionysius of the Athenian court, a woman named Damaris, and "a number of others." After Pentecost there seems to have been no mass conversions. The Holy Spirit caused the church to grow by one at a time.

So it is today. Individuals come to their Savior one at a time, not by their own reason or strength but by the Spirit's power through the Gospel. It was Pentecost on a personal scale when Saul was converted. In more modern times, Fulton Oursley stated that "after 25 years of contented agnosticism," he visited the Holy Land, became a Christian, and wrote the best-seller *The Greatest Story Ever Told*. It is a miniature Pentecost, an event celebrated by the angels of heaven, when the Holy Spirit leads a person to repentance and the saving faith in Christ.

PRAYER SUGGESTION

Pray that the Holy Spirit may continue to bless you with His gifts, especially the gift of faith.

Christ's Heavenly Homecoming

He who descended is the very one who ascended higher than all the heavens. Ephesians 4:10

Out of critical times, especially celebrations, songs emerge. The end of war is such a time. As one song marked the homecoming of a local young man: "The laurel wreath is ready now To place upon his loyal brow."

Great must have been the celebration in heaven when the Son of God returned to His Father's house. The one who ascended had previously descended to earth. He had come to impart gifts to people—the gifts of salvation, forgiveness, peace with God. It was not easy for Him to give these gifts. He had to go through a terrible war against Satan, an encounter that cost Him His life.

But Christ's death was not the end. The heavenly Father raised Him from the dead and seated Him in heaven as clear proof of His victory. Our Lord emerged from the deadly conflict as the obvious victor, the indisputable Lord of all.

Before Jesus ascended into heaven, He gave more gifts to Christendom: apostles, prophets, evangelists, pastors and teachers. These persons were appointed by Him to carry on the work of proclaiming the Gospel in all the world. Before the apostles went out to teach and baptize all nations, He sent the Holy Spirit as counselor and chief witness on Pentecost Day.

Forty days after His resurrection, Christ ascended into heaven in triumph. We can well imagine the "welcome home" celebration He received. Now seated at the right hand of God, He continues to govern His church and all its members with grace and truth.

PRAYER SUGGESTION

Thank the ascended Lord for continuing to bless you through His Word and Spirit.

Scripture Index

Matthew 3:13–17	April 27, May 25
Matthew 4:1–11	November 13
Matthew 4:18–22	April 18, August 1
Matthew 6:5–15	July 22
Matthew 6:19–25	June 4
Matthew 6:25–34	October 14, December 17
Matthew 7:7–12	February 25
Matthew 7:24–29	March 11, March 24
Matthew 8:18–22	January 26, April 20
Matthew 11:25–29	May 18
Matthew 12:13–21	October 5
Matthew 12:38–45	June 26
Matthew 13:31–35	March 31
Matthew 13:44–46	November 29
Matthew 15:21–28	January 5, August 22
Matthew 16:13–20	November 4
Matthew 18:1–9	June 14
Matthew 18:21–35	May 28
Matthew 18:23–35	August 19
Matthew 19:1–12	February 11
Matthew 21:1–11	December 4
Matthew 21:12–17	June 21, October 25
Matthew 22:34–40	May 29, August 12
Matthew 23:23–32	October 18
Matthew 23:29–39	January 19
Matthew 24:1–14	December 2, December 27
Matthew 24:15–25	June 7
Matthew 24:30–35	November 24
Matthew 24:36–51	August 29
Matthew 25:1–13	January 16
Matthew 25:31–46	August 15
Matthew 26:6–16	March 14
Matthew 26:31–35	November 4
Matthew 27:1–10	April 13
Matthew 27:62–64; 28:11–13	January 18
Matthew 28:16–20	July 5, July 17

MARK

Mark 1:9–15	February 27
Mark 1:14–20	March 21, November 2
Mark 1:21:28	July 8
Mark 1:29–34	December 9
Mark 1:40–45	July 29
Mark 2:1–12	July 25
Mark 2:23–28	October 17
Mark 4:26–29	September 25
Mark 4:35–41	October 26
Mark 6:1–6	September 28
Mark 6:7–13	August 8
Mark 6:30–46	February 14
Mark 8:34–38	September 23
Mark 9:33–37	October 3
Mark 10:13–16	April 30
Mark 10:46–52	October 21
Mark 11:20–25	July 23
Mark 12:28–34	April 22
Mark 16:14–20	March 25

LUKE

Luke 1:26–38	December 21
Luke 1:46–56	December 5, December 23
Luke 1:67–80	February 18
Luke 2:1–14	December 25
Luke 2:1–20	December 26
Luke 2:15–20	December 22
Luke 2:21–23	December 24
Luke 3:15–17, 21–22	November 8
Luke 4:14–19	January 12
Luke 4:20–44	July 27
Luke 5:1–11	August 26, November 10
Luke 6:17–22	March 23
Luke 7:1–10	January 8
Luke 7:16–50	February 29
Luke 8:1–3	November 16
Luke 8:22–25	October 4
Luke 8:40–56	September 5
Luke 9:46–49	May 23
Luke 10:38–42	November 5
Luke 11:1–13	May 14
Luke 11:14–28	March 7
Luke 12:1–7	November 15
Luke 12:21–34	April 22
Luke 12:22–31	August 13
Luke 12:22–34	August 18
Luke 12:54–59	November 3
Luke 13:1–9	July 15
Luke 13:6–9	November 7
Luke 13:22–32	November 21
Luke 14:1–11	November 27
Luke 14:25–34	March 6
Luke 15:1–10	February 23, November 26
Luke 15:9–16	November 17
Luke 15:11–32	July 18
Luke 16:1–9	September 1
Luke 16:19–31	July 24
Luke 17:11–19	July 19, November 25
Luke 17:28–37	February 28
Luke 18:1–8	September 14

Luke 18:9–14 — February 9
Luke 18:10–14 — January 3
Luke 18:18–27 — May 3
Luke 18:31–34 — April 5, Lent
Luke 19:1–10 — October 11
Luke 19:28–38 — January 28, March 22
Luke 19:41–44 — May 20
Luke 20:27–40 — June 24
Luke 22:28–38 — June 19
Luke 24:36–53 — February 12

JOHN

John 1:1–13 — March 10
John 1:1–14 — August 2, October 1
John 1:43–51 — June 30
John 2:1–11 — June 25, November 6
John 3:16–21 — September 17
John 3:22–36 — February 10
John 5:1–15 — October 20
John 5:16–23 — May 24
John 5:16–30 — September 6
John 5:31–47 — June 18, August 21
John 6:35–40 — October 29
John 8:31–41 — May 22
John 8:42–47 — November 14
John 9:1–12 — January 2, June 20
John 9:35–41 — June 22
John 10:11–18 — June 9
John 11:45–57 — March 28
John 12:20–36 — October 23
John 13:12–17 — September 24
John 13:31–38 — July 20
John 14:1–7 — August 10
John 14:1–14 — September 3, September 30
John 14:15–31 — November 20
John 14:23–29 — May 7
John 15:1–8 — September 11, October 6
John 15:9–17 — October 7
John 16:5–16 — May 15
John 19:16–27 — March 1
John 19:25–27 — March 30
John 20:10–18 — April 7
John 20:24–31 — November 9

ACTS

Acts 1:12–26 — April 19
Acts 2:1–13 — May 2
Acts 2:22–28 — Easter Sunday
Acts 2:36–41 — Pentecost
Acts 2:44–45; 4:32 — February 2
Acts 4:13–20 — April 2

Acts 9:1–19 — January 23
Acts 14:8–20 — February 1
Acts 16:25–35 — September 7
Acts 21:1–9 — July 14

ROMANS

Romans 1:16–32 — March 9
Romans 1:18–25 — November 23
Romans 3:21–26 — February 16, October 31
Romans 3:21–31 — March 2, July 6
Romans 6:1–10 — April 21
Romans 6:1–14 — June 3
Romans 6:15–23 — March 8
Romans 8:12–17 — January 29, August 28
Romans 8:28–36 — February 6
Romans 8:28–39 — August 11
Romans 9:1–5 — December 6
Romans 10:1–4 — May 16
Romans 12:1–8 — June 11, July 11, August 16
Romans 13:1–7 — August 31
Romans 13:8–14 — September 19
Romans 13:11–14 — Advent
Romans 15:1–4 — February 21

1 CORINTHIANS

1 Corinthians 1:10–17 — October 13
1 Corinthians 1:18–31 — March 3
1 Corinthians 1:26–31 — February 19
1 Corinthians 4:1–5 — January 20
1 Corinthians 6:12–20 — May 8, October 30
1 Corinthians 10:14–17 — Maundy Thursday
1 Corinthians 10:23–33 — December 29
1 Corinthians 12:4–11 — February 3
1 Corinthians 13:1–13 — May 27, July 9
1 Corinthians 15:20–28 — April 14

2 CORINTHIANS

2 Corinthians 1:3–11 — June 15
2 Corinthians 3:7–18 — July 3
2 Corinthians 5:1–5 — June 13
2 Corinthians 5:11–21 — January 24
2 Corinthians 6:3–13 — October 16
2 Corinthians 12:1–10 — September 20

GALATIANS

Galatians 1:18–24 — May 12
Galatians 3:6–18 — January 9
Galatians 3:10–22 — January 27
Galatians 4:1–7 — November 12
Galatians 5:16–26 — October 28
Galatians 6:1–10 — July 7
Galatians 6:11–18 — July 26

EPHESIANS

Ephesians 1:15–23	August 7
Ephesians 2:1–14	May 21
Ephesians 2:8–9	April 15, September 16
Ephesians 2:11–22	January 25, May 9, July 13
Ephesians 3:14–21	February 7, March 13, June 2, August 17
Ephesians 4:7–16	Ascension
Ephesians 4:17–28	February 13
Ephesians 4:25–32	March 16
Ephesians 5:15–21	December 11
Ephesians 6:10–20	August 27

PHILIPPIANS

Philippians 1:1–11	February 8
Philippians 1:3–11	May 30
Philippians 2:5–11	February 4, March 17, August 20
Philippians 3:1–11	January 11, June 6
Philippians 3:12–21	December 30
Philippians 4:1–9	April 12

COLOSSIANS

Colossians 1:5–13	November 1
Colossians 2:6–15	October 27
Colossians 3:5–17	March 18
Colossians 3:12–17	July 10

1 THESSALONIANS

1 Thessalonians 2:13–16	September 2

1 TIMOTHY

1 Timothy 1:3–7	June 16
1 Timothy 2:1–7	December 13
1 Timothy 2:1–8	September 16
1 Timothy 4:11–16	February 17
1 Timothy 6:3–10	January 17
1 Timothy 6:6–10	October 15

2 TIMOTHY

2 Timothy 1:3–7	August 30
2 Timothy 1:8–12	September 8

TITUS

Titus 3:3–8	March 27, April 26

HEBREWS

Hebrews 1:1–4	December 3
Hebrews 1:1–14	May 6
Hebrews 2:5–13	January 21
Hebrews 3:1–6	August 24
Hebrews 4:9–13	June 17
Hebrews 4:12–13	August 4
Hebrews 5:7–14	March 5
Hebrews 7:23–29	Good Friday
Hebrews 9:11–14	April 25
Hebrews 12:1–3	December 14
Hebrews 12:1–13	August 3
Hebrews 13:1–6	September 10

JAMES

James 1:2–8; 5:7–11	February 5
James 5:7–12	September 26
James 5:13–20	March 20

1 PETER

1 Peter 1:13–25	April 1
1 Peter 2:1–3	October 24
1 Peter 2:13–25	August 23
1 Peter 3:8–22	June 8
1 Peter 3:13–22	October 2
1 Peter 4:7–11	January 31
1 Peter 5:6–11	January 15
1 Peter 8:1–11	October 8

2 PETER

2 Peter 1:12–16	December 19

1 JOHN

1 John 1:5–10	January 4
1 John 2:1–6	August 9
1 John 2:1–14	May 5
1 John 3:1–10	May 10
1 John 3:10	June 10
1 John 3:7–10	January 14
1 John 4:1–6	August 25

2 JOHN

2 John 7–11	May 19

REVELATION

Revelation 3:7–13	January 13
Revelation 5:1–5	April 23
Revelation 12:7–12	September 22
Revelation 19:1–10	December 16
Revelation 22:1–6	February 24, August 5
Revelation 22:7–21	June 27, December 1, December 31